Business to Business Marketing

Business to Business Marketing

Caster Sumner

WILLFORD **P**RESS
www.willfordpress.com

Published by Willford Press,
118-35 Queens Blvd., Suite 400,
Forest Hills, NY 11375, USA

ISBN: 978-1-68285-731-1

Cataloging-in-Publication Data

Business to business marketing / Caster Sumner.
    p. cm.
Includes bibliographical references and index.
ISBN 978-1-68285-731-1
1. Industrial marketing. 2. Marketing. 3. Business. I. Sumner, Caster.
HF5415.1263 .B87 2019
658.8--dc23

For information on all Willford Press publications
visit our website at www.willfordpress.com

Contents

Preface

Business marketing refers to any marketing practice performed by an individual or an organization. When one business makes a commercial transaction with another, it is known as business to business or B2B. In this transaction, both the parties have comparable negotiating power. However, large companies can have advantages over smaller companies in terms of commercial and information resources. The principal models in B2B marketing are vertical B2B model and horizontal B2B model. This book is a valuable compilation of topics, ranging from the basic to the most complex theories and principles in business to business marketing. It outlines the problems and applications of business to business marketing in detail. This book is meant for students who are looking for an elaborate reference text in this field.

To facilitate a deeper understanding of the contents of this book a short introduction of every chapter is written below:

Chapter 1- Business-to-business is the arrangement in which one business makes a commercial transaction with another business. It is generally adopted when a business sources materials for their production process, requires the service of another business for operational reasons or re-sells products produced by another.

Chapter 2- There is a difference in the marketing strategies when it is approached from a business-to-business or a business-to-consumer context. This chapter has been carefully written to provide an easy understanding of the varied B2B marketing strategies and discusses in depth about B2B branding, pricing, promotion, effective communication, market analysis, etc.

Chapter 3- An understanding of B2B marketing requires an understanding of pricing strategies and pricing mistakes that a business can make in B2B commerce. This chapter has been written so as to give a detailed explanation of the different aspects of B2B pricing and discusses the central concepts of market risk, market price, clean price, price ceiling, price floor and dirty price.

Chapter 4- The aim of this chapter is to provide a basic understanding of the different facets of B2B sales and distribution. It includes topics such as solution selling, selective distribution, exclusive distribution, inclusive distribution, push strategy, pull strategy, etc. for an extensive understanding.

Chapter 5- When products and services are sold between businesses via a sales portal through the Internet, such commerce is called B2B e-commerce. This chapter discusses in detail the important aspects of e-commerce and its significance in the context of the modern economy as well as current e-commerce trends, business models and mobile commerce.

Finally, I would like to thank the entire team involved in the inception of this book for their valuable time and contribution. This book would not have been possible without their efforts. I would also like to thank my friends and family for their constant support.

Caster Sumner

An Introduction to Business Marketing

Business-to-business is the arrangement in which one business makes a commercial transaction with another business. It is generally adopted when a business sources materials for their production process, requires the service of another business for operational reasons or re-sells products produced by another.

Business-to-Business (B2B) Marketing

B2B (business-to-business) marketing is marketing of products to businesses or other organizations for use in production of goods, for use in general business operations (such as office supplies), or for resale to other consumers, such as a wholesaler selling to a retailer.

Key Aspects of B2B Marketing

Larger Sale Prices

Unlike business-to-consumer (B2C) marketing, when marketing within a business-to-business environments you must take into account the purchase prices for these accounts are typically much greater than you will find elsewhere. These higher purchase prices may tend to lead to fewer sales but each at a higher individual price. When working with larger sale prices involves a nurturing process for more is at stake. This nurturing process is the focus of the next key.

Longer Sales Process

With higher prices comes more hesitation. This hesitation directly leads to a longer sales process. Each account must be carefully nurtured and lead along this sales process through to a successful sale. This sales process involves multiple points of contact, meetings, and can occur over weeks, or even months. When many business-to-consumer transactions occur within minutes, hours, or at the longest, days; this stands distinctly different.

Partnerships and Brand Loyalty

B2C marketing and sales typically lead to a small purchase and possibly no ongoing interaction or relationship. However, B2B marketing is one where the longer sales process and the high price lead to a relationship between the businesses. These are not frivolous decisions made without thought or care. These relationships continue long past the initial purchase and involve ongoing communication and discussion. This leads to a very strong brand loyalty from the purchasing business.

Committee Purchases

B2B this purchasing decision is typically handled by a committee, or group of key players. These individuals each have a unique role and purpose and represent a different interest of the purchasing business. This committee is part of the reason why the B2B sales cycle is longer and more elaborate. The purchase-by-committee aspect also implies a lead nurturing process must engage across a variety of departments and goals.

Now that we have examined the definition of B2B marketing and a few of the key aspects of this specific type of marketing we must now turn our attention to ways in which you can successfully implement this knowledge into a specific marketing campaign. You may find several of these suggestions can be used effectively in many types of marketing. B2B marketing does indeed overlap with other formats and the suggestions shared here can be used in other marketing efforts as well.

Implementing Successful B2B Marketing

When creating your marketing strategy for business-to-business these are a few areas you should pay special attention to. Again you may be experienced in these already from your other marketing campaigns but special attention should be paid when working within a B2B environment.

Content Creation

Just as with every other type of marketing today you need to focus heavily on content creation. It's almost wearisome to hear the same tired catchphrase used time and again, but content truly is king. Creating fresh, shareable, informative content is a cornerstone of every good marketing strategy. B2B marketing is no different. You saw the statistic earlier which showed the number of B2B marketers who were using content creation as a marketing strategy. Here another statistic in case you just aren't completely sold that content marketing is here for the long term. 78% of CMOs think custom content is the future of marketing.

This percentage is impressive. But how do businesses use content marketing in their B2B strategies? There are nine top goals used to measure the effectiveness of their content marketing. These are shown in the chart below.

Notice, interestingly enough that sales actually comes in at the bottom of the list. B2B marketers define 8 other goals as more important than the actual sale. This underscores the importance of the many different aspects of B2B marketing beyond simply landing a sale. This also clearly demonstrates how B2B is different and has different key aspects.

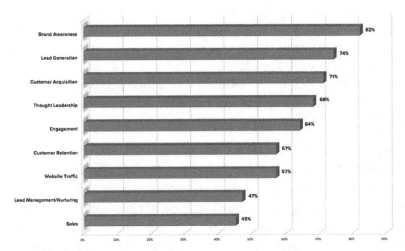

So if content creation is important in the B2B marketing strategies, we should explore how to successfully implement this within your campaign. First, you will need to follow the basics of creating a marketing campaign, just as you would for any other campaign. This involves, identifying your target audience, determining your keywords and then organizing your content. There's also this excellent guide to help you with this entire process; it's a thorough article so be prepared to learn when you are ready to begin reading.

Creating your content is the first major part of a successful B2B campaign. Writing this content should always remain focused on the goals we've outlined above. Don't try to turn every post into a simple call-to-action purchase page. With this type of marketing you are looking more to build your brand awareness, generate the beginning of a long-term relationship, and engage your potential customers. Truly, you want to nurture them along a sales process; not jump directly into a purchasing situation.

Social Media

The second aspect of a strong B2B marketer's strategy involves the rather obvious social media aspect. Every business must use social media within their marketing campaign and B2B is certainly no different. Social networks are the modern version of radio or television outlets found in old marketing. But more than just a platform for broadcasting a message as yesterday's technology allowed, today social media allows for brand engagement between the buyer and the seller. And businesses focused on marketing to other businesses must take advantage of this medium as well.

Campaign Construction

Understanding the unique way that B2B marketing involves a much longer sales process, a more focused relationship, and a strong brand loyalty will affect how you structure your marketing campaigns. When you begin your campaign construction you must take time into account. This means don't schedule your beginning to ending campaign workflow to last a single week. Don't even construct your campaign on a two week schedule. B2B marketing campaigns should be structured over a minimum of 4 weeks. You can have branches of your campaign that end sooner should you have an interested lead ready to move forward faster but your primary campaign should unfold over a much longer time period than a traditional B2C campaign. 88% of B2B companies plan on implementing marketing automation in their organizations by the start of the 2017-2018 financial year.

This massive focus by B2B marketers demonstrates the priority that marketing automation holds within their organization. Marketing automation platforms are ideal for creating a very long automated drip flow campaign. These campaigns are useful not only for identifying new leads over a longer period of time but also quite good at maintaining relationships with existing customers. When you recognize the importance of brand loyalty to B2B marketing and the power of an ongoing relationship you create campaigns that also target your existing customer base. This is one way in which you can get ahead with your B2B marketing. Because marketing automation is still a very fast-growing technology many B2B have not yet tapped fully into the potential of their marketing automation software.

Also, B2B marketers that use marketing automation have seen incredibly high improvements in their lead generation percentages: "Businesses using marketing automation to nurture prospects see a 451% increase in qualified leads". It seems hard to believe that such a high percentage increase is possible but it's been proven time and again. Since B2B is focused on providing a brand loyalty and long term relationship, marketing automation is the perfect tool for this. This basic infographic will show you how to structure a beginner drip flow campaign quickly.

Campaign construction does not have to be done only in marketing automation software. While many statistics prove the tremendous value of using these platforms you can still create your campaigns in a variety of ways and using a number of tools. The important part to remember is B2B marketing takes time and your campaigns should be structured to offer a strong, nurturing lead process over a longer period of time than B2C.

Partnerships

B2B marketing is more about building partnerships than it is about making a quick sale. B2B marketers must be looking for and encouraging brand loyalty and long-term partnerships. This can be done using a marketing automation tool as mentioned above. This software can be used for marketing to new leads as well as continuing to build your relationship with existing customers. Different campaigns, different outcomes, but the same software. Building partnerships with B2B marketing is important for several reasons:

Trust

We recognize that B2B sales generate a much higher price per sale than other industries. With these larger purchases the ability to trust the business you're working with is important. You must be able to have faith that the quality of the product or service will meet your standards and that the company will stand behind their product and ensure your success. This is a trust-based relationship, and for good reason. Once that trust is established the partnership can continue for many years to come.

Support

B2B marketing must focus on providing more than merely a product or service for sale. B2B must focus on providing a sense of security to the purchaser. Building a strong brand loyalty often means going the extra mile in supporting your existing customers. Doing the unexpected and looking for ways to improve the relationship. This is a very pro-active position and does require a dedication of time as well as a priority placed on listening.

The best way to be pro-active in providing support and service is by first listening to the needs of the customer. Listening not just on direct engagements (phone call or support ticket) but also listening on social media where the customer may not even direct the message to you. This pro-active approach to support is fundamental to building brand loyalty.

Quality

If your B2B marketing is not backed by quality products, engaging support, and a fundamental assurance of reliability then you will not be able to build a lasting partnership. However, when businesses sense that you place quality as a priority this will become quickly evident and will encourage brand loyalty.

Loyalty Test

One of the best ways to get a quick feel on how your B2B clients are feeling about your partnership is through the use of a one-question Net Promoter Score (NPS). You're probably quite familiar with this strategy already but in case you're not. The NPS is a single one question form that helps to determine your customer loyalty metric which can be used to gauge a company's customer relationships.

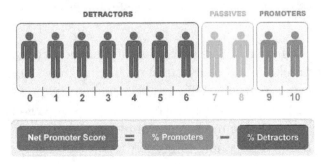

Implementing something like a loyalty metric or test helps to ensure that you stay on target and on point with your marketing. You want to make sure you are building those relationships and partnerships and establishing a customer base that will be loyally devoted to your brand.

Purchases

The purchase process in B2B is vastly different from other marketing verticals. So perhaps a good place to begin is by looking at some sample purchase cycles as they specifically relate to B2B.

And in this process they are significantly farther along this process before they ever reach out to you. This means your content, your social media impact and your campaign funnels must all be organized fully to assist and help this process that occurs before you ever come into direct contact with your leads. B2B customers are 65-90% of the way through the purchase decision process before they contact your firm.

While this purchase process may seem tricky and at times convoluted, the case can be made that in B2B marketing you have the best possible situation for using marketing automation and other tools to perform tasks, organize campaigns, and nurture potential leads with little to no personal time spent until they reach a qualified lead status. Of course there's nothing wrong with early personal contact, but when time is your most valuable resource and your limiting factor you need to be smart in your approach. And as we've shared before (power of personal) – automated marketing can still be personal marketing.

Once you have nurtured your B2B leads into customers you should never neglect the potential for future purchases. As everyone in marketing knows, it is far easier to keep a customer than to gain a new one. This means focusing not on a single purchase but on the lifetime potential purchases from each customer. Your B2B marketing campaign must consider the lifetime value of each customer and what it will require to build a strong partnership, brand loyalty, and ultimately repeat purchases.

B2B Marketing vs. B2C Marketing

B2C vs B2B marketing

	B2C 'low involvement'	B2B 'high involvement'
Target market	Larger	Smaller, niche
Purchaser(s)	Single	Multiple
Buying process	Single step	Multiple step
Sales cycle	Shorter	Longer
Sales driver	Recognition and repetition	Relationship and detailed information

Business-to-Business (B2B) and Business-to-Consumer (B2C) marketers aim to capture the attention of two distinct audiences. And while there are many similarities between the types of marketing in general, driving prospects from each channel requires different communication approaches, especially on social media:

1. Marketers can use industry jargon to excellent effect on B2B platforms, but on B2C, the voice must be at least relatable to the majority of consumers — meaning fewer buzzwords and (usually) simpler language.

2. Drivers matter, the B2B audience is seeking efficiency and expertise, while the consumer audience is more likely to be seeking deals and entertainment. Accordingly, the B2B purchase process tends to be rationally and logically driven, while consumer choices are typically emotionally triggered (whether by hunger, desire, status or cost).

3. B2B clientele want to be educated and provided with expertise. They often want to look like the workplace rock stars or heroes thanks to their excellent decisions. B2C customers just want to enjoy themselves, be happy with their purchase and have it adequately fulfill the needs.

4. Highly detailed content is required for B2B marketing. It's an audience that expects to be catered to by a sales and marketing team. On the other hand, B2C social media activities simply need to meet the basic needs of being useful, humorous and shareable, which admittedly, can be just as complicated.

5. Lengthy content tends to work for B2B since a brand or business has to prove its expertise and give its target audience a reason to buy in. Consum-

ers tend to prefer something short and snappy, especially for lower-priced B2C products.

6. A B2C consumer following your brand isn't necessarily looking to build a close relationship with it. Inversely, the B2B crowd wants information and the ability to build a close relationship with brands.

7. B2B marketers have a much longer chain of command to deal with since procurement, accounting and their superiors often need to approve purchases. On the other hand, an individual typically makes their own speedy B2C purchase choices — possibly with the slight influence of others via recommendations or suggestions.

8. The B2B buying cycle is often much longer than the B2C decision process. Therefore, it requires much more nurturing and close attention. B2C buys tend to satisfy immediate needs, while B2B decisions are meant to complete long-term goals.

9. A contract for a B2B purchase tends to last months or even years, making it a much more significant decision. On the contrary, the total B2C cycle can be as short as a few minutes depending on the product.

10. The two types of marketers have distinctive problems, often, the largest problem that B2B marketers have is a lack of content and time to create it. This differs from B2C marketers who would rather have a bigger advertising budget and other ways to spread the word about their products. Naturally, this has a significant effect on tactical executions.

B2B Selling Process

Steps to build a Business to Business Sales process are mentioned below:

Understanding Customer Demands

The first step in building a sales process is to understand the demands of customers. A customer demand is comprised of two elements:

1. The customer's *need or desire* for a product or service.

2. The customer's *ability to pay* for a product or service.

Verifying both elements of customer demand accomplishes the first two steps in building a sales process. By talking to potential customers, a company can find out what they really need and whether they have the ability to pay. Their ability to pay depends on their budget, of course, but it is also affected by the timeframe within which they could sign off on a deal. It is not inappropriate to ask a potential customer if they have the budget, who would sign off on the deal, and in what timeframe a deal could be closed. These questions allow a company to prioritize potential customers and identify those most willing and likely to buy the company's offering. It is worth knowing which customers have the need, but not the ability to pay, but the initial focus will be on those customers that have both elements of demand.

Developing a Solution

Once the customer's demands are understood, the next two steps in the process are to develop a solution that will meet these demands and then propose it to the customer. In some cases, these steps may be reversed so that the proposal is made to the customer before the solution is developed. In other cases, it may be preferable to present a proposal based on an incomplete solution that will be refined based on feedback from the customers.

Proposing the solution requires input from the potential customer. This step verifies that the proposed solution fits the customer's requirements. Also, it reconfirms that they have the ability to pay for it. If they cannot reconfirm this, then it is better to move on to a customer that can. By focusing on a customer that has the ability to pay for the solution, the probability of a successful deal increases.

Evaluating the Solution with the Customer

The next step is to evaluate the solution with the customer. If the customer is enthusiastic and initiates contact without prompting, this is a good sign. If constant hounding is required to get a technical or business response to a solution, the sale is likely going nowhere.

Assuming the proposal meets the customer's needs and the price point matches the customer's value point, then this step in the sales process should be limited to a few small areas of refinement. The key is to act decisively on customer feedback. Changes should be implemented (or dismissed with explanation) as quickly as possible to close this step. One effective strategy to close the step is for the supplier company to agree to a set of product changes, but in return, the customer agrees to buy the solution "as is," with or without a discount. This guarantees the sale early in the process, gets the customer using the solution as soon as possible, and provides the opportunity for further feedback and updates in the next version of the solution.

Typically, this is one of the steps where there is a high risk of the customer withdrawing their interest. The main reasons for losing the customer at this step in the process are:

1. Misleading information was provided by one of the parties.

2. The customer no longer sees the fit between the solution and their needs.

3. The supplying company is not able to introduce the required changes to the solution in a timely or cost-effective manner.

Negotiation and Contracts

If the previous steps in the sales process have been completed successfully, there is typically not a lot left to negotiate. The key points to focus on in the negotiation process are:

1. Outstanding product features to be implemented;

2. Release date;

3. Selling price, including volume discounts;

4. Warranties or maintenance costs.

The goal of the negotiation step is to resolve all of the *business* issues, not the legal issues, which are covered in the contract step. Introducing legal departments too early will stall the negotiation and jeopardize the sales process. The negotiation team should include the signing authority, a finance representative, and a business line manager.

Once agreement has been reached, the negotiation step is formally closed by issuing a letter of intent outlining all of the business issues. This letter is then forwarded to the legal team and becomes the main content of a formal contract.

Note that sales can be lost even in the contract phase, for example if a legal department finds an issue relating to intellectual property. The contract step in the process does not necessarily represent a won sale and it might initiate a further round of negotiations or even a lost sale.

Deals Lost Along the Way

Failing to pass any step in the process means the sale is lost. If the customer does come back at some point in the future, then the sales process should start again from the beginning because the conditions of the sale are likely to have changed. Although losing a sale is undesirable, it is critical to learn from the loss. If the potential sale was in response to a request for proposal (RFP), an official debrief can be requested, especially if the RFP was issued by a government organization. In any case, it is important to follow up with the customer and find out why they did not purchase the solution. From this feedback, the supplier can determine what changes to the solution or process could be made so that the sale will be won if the opportunity presents itself again.

Closing a Deal

This step is a milestone rather than a specific task. When the contract is signed by both parties, this marks the end of the sales process and the beginning of a customer relationship management process. Hopefully, it is also the beginning of a long-term relationship. The supplier should work hard to keep the new customer, since it typically costs 10 times more to attract a new customer than to sell to an existing one.

Building a Sales Funnel

The sales process represents the natural evolution of a deal and it is straightforward to follow one deal through the process. In reality, many deals may be in progress at the same time and at different steps. A sales funnel is a way to track potential customers through the sales process. It helps assess the health and balance of projected sales by providing information on the following:

- The progress of each customer through the sales process;

- The value of the opportunity associated with a customer;

- How long customers are taking to move down the funnel;

- How many customers are at each step;

- Projected revenue forecasts for cash flow statements.

The funnel metaphor for a sales process is based on the gradual narrowing of potential deals into actual deals. Figure shows a graphical representation of the properties of a sales funnel. As customers progress from one step in the sales process to another, some potential deals fall through, but the company's confidence in the remaining deals increases.

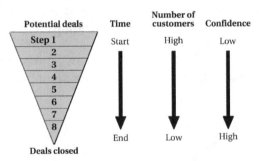

Properties of a Sales Funnel

The first step in setting up a sales funnel is to assign a probability to each step in the sales process. Typically, this is the estimated probability of a customer at that stage in the process, ultimately reaching the final step in the process. In other words, it is the likelihood that a customer at a given stage will eventually buy the solution. Using the sales process steps outlined earlier, hypothetical probabilities can be assigned to each step of the sales process, as follows:

1. Establish that the customer need or desire exists (5%);

2. Establish that the customer has ability to pay for a solution (10%);

3. Develop solution (30%);

4. Propose solution (60%);

5. Evaluate solution (65%);

6. Negotiate deal (70%);

7. Create contracts (90%);

8. Close deal (100%).

Another approach would be to assign a probability of the customer moving to the next step in the process. The calculations are different in this case, but the overall effect is the same.

The next step is to take a potential customer, insert them in the process, and assign a contract value to the opportunity. In this way, a spreadsheet representation of the funnel is built. This spreadsheet is used to track the flow of customers through the sales process. Relevant information about individual deals or the entire sales process can then be extracted.

To illustrate this process, figure below shows a hypothetical spreadsheet for a company's sales funnel. Note that they are proposing a solution to Generic Ltd. This deal is currently at the proposal step in the sales process, which has a 60% probability of leading to a closed deal, at which point it would be worth $100,000. Each deal will either close or not, but the probabilities of closing can be used to calculate a weighted value for each potential deal. This provides a reasonable estimate of what actual value is likely to come from the group of deals as a whole. In the case of this particular deal, the weighted value is $60,000 ($100,000 x 60%). The analysis is extended by including an estimated closing date.

The final step is to add the credit terms, which gives a projection of cash in the bank. Unfortunately, this exercise sometimes can become demoralizing because it is human nature to overestimate:

*   The probability of getting a sale,

*   The sale amount,

*   When the sale is going to close.

However, when coupled with honest estimates, these calculations truly show when the "rubber hits the road."

Company	Opportunity name	Funnel stage	Stage probability	Contract value	Funnel value	Est Close Date	Days to close
		Totals/Average	52%	$390,000	$202,000	02-Jan-11	127
Generic Ltd	Product A	Propose Solution	60%	$100,000	$60,000	05-Jan-11	130
Alpha Co	Product A and B	Initial Communication	10%	$50,000	$5,000	15-Apr-11	230
Beta Co	Product B	Fact Finding	25%	$40,000	$10,000	01-Dec-10	95
Gamma Corp	Product A	Develop Solution	40%	$30,000	$12,000	16-Dec-10	110
ABC Ltd	Product C	Propose Solution	60%	$50,000	$30,000	15-Dec-10	109
DEF Inc	Product A, B and C	Solution Evaluation	75%	$30,000	$22,500	24-Nov-10	88
Kappa Ltd	Product C	Negotiation	85%	$40,000	$34,000	04-Nov-10	68
Bob Co	Product C	Contract	95%	$10,000	$9,500	30-Sep-10	33
Lambda Ltd	Product A	Propose Solution	60%	$30,000	$18,000	05-Jan-11	130
Epsilon Inc	Product B	Initial Communication	10%	$10,000	$1,000	01-Jun-11	277

A Hypothetical Spreadsheet Representation of a Company's Sales Funnel

Business-to-Government (B2G) Marketing

In marketing, "B2G" stands for business-to-government. Unlike most marketing endeavors, which target end consumers or other businesses, business-to-government marketing deals with the tricky world of public policy and administration. However, the ultimate business objective is the same: making money by securing clients.

Government Markets

Government markets include federal, state and local governments. Like any other organizations, government markets have needs they must pay businesses to fulfill. Some government projects are limited to large companies that have sufficient resources for the task. Buyers for military agencies, for example, often negotiate with just a few defense contractors. But at all levels of government, there are projects small business owners can bid on. A city government's building, for example, might need repainting, or a state government might have plans to develop a small after-school recreation center. Such projects are well within the capabilities of local small businesses.

Red Tape

Government officials are accountable to the public, so they must follow strict rules for contracting with businesses. Marketing the business to a government entity thus involves learning complex procedures, which often vary by region and level of government. This red tape dissuades many businesses from pursuing government customers, according to the book "Marketing," by William M. Pride and O.C. Ferrell.

Research

If you want to market the business to a government entity, start by learning the bidding and negotiation procedures of the particular organization you want to approach. These procedures are usually available to the public. Some government entities even issue comprehensive guidelines to help businesses learn the ropes. The U.S. Government Printing Office, for example, publishes documents outlining the buying procedures of various government agencies.

Qualification

For smaller projects, typically a business first must apply to become a qualified bidder. If approved, the business then can bid against competitors as projects are announced. In other words, marketing successfully to governments often involves two hurdles: First, you must demonstrate to government buyers that the company meets the minimal qualifications for the job. Second, you must choose a bid amount for the job that is competitive but also ensures you will make a profit.

Strategy

Once you are familiar with the procedures, analyze the likely competitors. For instance, see which companies won previous projects and get a sense of how they performed. If there are some obvious weaknesses-high budget overruns, for example, or missed deadlines-demonstrate how the company is a better choice, perhaps by focusing on the history of meeting the clients' budgetary and time expectations. In other words, even if the process of securing a government contract requires mountains of red tape, the fundamental message should be the same as it would be in any other marketing endeavor: that the company provides more value than its competitors.

Business-to-Business (B2B) Model

B2B means business-to-business. A business is B2B if it sells its product or service to other businesses rather than to individual consumers. B2B differ from B2C because their approach to marketing and selling their products are necessarily very different. B2C generally sell millions of units at small prices and often via an intermediary (through a channel). B2B often sell a few units at high prices and usually directly to the customer organization.

Vertical = an industry. The term is used when thinking of the industry as a market. A vertical is not necessarily a small market. Some verticals contain many potential customers. Others contain only a few, but the companies in that industry are enormous and capable of consuming very large amounts of a product or service. Most verticals are self-organized, meaning they have industry trade organizations and have defined shared conventions around how they perform their business, the language they use to describe their business, and how they prefer to be sold to.

Key Factors to Make B2B Vertical Marketplace a Success

Be the First Mover

Being the first in a market vastly improves chances of success. Alibaba was able to build a B2B generalist marketplace because it was a first mover in its space and, like Amazon, now protects its business through sheer scale. Today, the business has an untouchable supply chain, which billions have been invested into. Even B2B generalist marketplace competitors all have similar resources (Amazon Business, eBay Business) but cannot keep up with the scale and volume of Alibaba. Being first allowed them to solidify their foothold in the space and build out the appropriate technology and supply chain to be successful. You will be surprised to know that there are still a lot of areas that have not been tapped in B2B vertical marketplaces.

Provide SAAS Tooling to One Side

Providing necessary software tooling to attract one side of the marketplace is becoming more and more a key to success. Examples include Construct Connect, which provides RFP management solutions for construction sites and leverages that data to build a marketplace to go after the manufacturer to construction management industry. Companies do not want to build out their own suite of services and benefit from a solution that provides multiple solutions as part of the marketplace service package. Simplicity is essential in a marketplace. Platforms that provide these tools improve stickiness and allow companies and customers to focus on selling and buying resources.

Eliminate Key Offline Brokers

Removing a massive offline broker, if one exists (e.g. CH Robinson in the freight industry, Vizient in the healthcare industry) is another important strategy. There are massive economic advantages for both sides to removing a major barrier and providing a technology enabled solution. As Bill Gurley notes, marketplaces can reduce unnecessary costs, increase efficiency, and improve the situation for both buyers and sellers. Brokers benefit from information asymmetries and require a tax for their services. As marketplaces improve transparency and provide a supply chain management solution, the need for a broker is removed.

Improve the Overall Buying Process

Simplifying some element of a tough or complex buying process can also be key to success. For example, local construction auctions (IronPlanet), overseas quality assurance testing (Upwork), or office supply purchasing across suppliers (Coupa) are all solving the buyer challenge and simplifying the process for that side of the marketplace. Prior to these marketplaces being created there was an extensive amount of friction in the procurement and sales process. Marketplaces reduce this friction by increasing clarity for both sides and allowing customers to choose the best service for their business.

Vertical within a Vertical Creates Incredible Power

Focusing on a highly specific area of an industry vertical (e.g. E&P in the Oil & Gas space) can create serious advantages from a pricing and competition standpoint. In most of these sub-verticals, you have supply that is exceptionally fragmented or localized. Ultimately, they can win with the proposition that aggregation will drive down prices substantially. In addition, the ease of access will lock in demand. Looking at what small and large examples like Makers Row, Joor, Architizer, and Expedi are doing are good lessons. In markets with this high fragmentation, buyers need real help connecting to sellers and there is less loyalty to specific suppliers combined with the fact that users want transparency.

It is important to scale a platform, but it is even more important to provide incentives for them to remain on the platform. As noted above, these are key factors to B2B vertical marketplace success that will ultimately increase user engagement, outside of building the tech. By executing on these key factors to B2B vertical marketplace success, teams can provide clear value and build the next multi-billion dollar B2B vertical marketplace.

A horizontal market means the customers are in multiple industries. Many people seem to think that a horizontal market is necessarily larger than a vertical one but this does not necessarily follow. A product which is essential to every company in one vertical may in fact have a larger market than a horizontal product which is only a nice-to-have convenience.

	Vertical Hub	Horizontal Hub
Content and relationships	Industry-sector specific	Specializes in products and services that are not used directly in finished products Includes products and services that are often referred to as Maintenance, Repair, and Operating (MRO) inputs
Source	Includes manufacturing inputs such as raw materials, components, or sub-assemblies for manufacturers within a specific industry sector	Includes human resources or capital equipment
Critical success factors	Existing non-eBusiness vertical supply chain is inefficient, but it can be made efficient through the introduction of catalogs and advanced search techniques	Offers vast depth of content and expertise that has a great breadth of demand
Sub-classified	Can be sub-classified into Catalog hubs and Exchange hubs	Are not sub-classified

References

- What-is-the-definition-of-vertical-specific-B2B-and-how-does-it-relate-to-a-company-that-has-a-product-to-sell-and-how-it-would-help-in-defining-and-locating-their-target-market: quora.com, Retrieved 31 March 2018

- E-business-architecture/module3/vertical-horizontal-b2b-hubs: seomining.com, Retrieved 18 July 2018

- 5-key-factors-to-b2b-vertical-marketplace-success: bowerycap.com, Retrieved 21 May 2018

- Differences-b2c-b2b-marketing: hubspot.com, Retrieved 28 April 2018

- Understanding-b2b-marketing: mautic.org, Retrieved 11 April 2018

Understanding Business-to-Business (B2B) Marketing Strategies

There is a difference in the marketing strategies when it is approached from a business-to-business or a business-to-consumer context. This chapter has been carefully written to provide an easy understanding of the varied B2B marketing strategies and discusses in depth about B2B branding, pricing, promotion, effective communication, market analysis, etc.

B2B Marketing Strategies

A strong B2B marketing strategy is one of the fundamental ingredients for success in today's highly crowded global marketplace. With digital content and properties capturing an increasingly larger share of B2B decision-makers' attention, it's critical for the brand to develop a B2B marketing strategy that addresses both traditional and emerging promotional opportunities.

But creating a B2B marketing strategy is easier said than done. Walker Sands specializes in helping growing firms design and execute a B2B marketing strategy that engages key audiences and significantly improves the brand's credibility with prospective buyers. In our experience, there are several components that nearly every successful B2B marketing strategy has in common.

Developing an Effective B2B Marketing Strategy

When developing a B2B marketing strategy, it's important to understand that there is no such thing as a "one-size-fits-all" approach. Marketing plans and tactics that are effective for one brand may not pack the same punch for the next—sometimes even if the two companies are direct competitors.

Instead, the B2B marketing strategy needs to be tailored to the organizations unique goals as well as the needs of the company's that comprise the customer base. With that in mind, here are a few elements that you will need to address as you create a B2B marketing strategy for the brand:

- Brand Messaging: You can't broadcast the brand message to the world until you know it yourself—that's just common sense. So for many B2B firms, the first step toward developing a B2B marketing strategy is to identify and clarify key messages based on brand priorities and the needs of the customers. After you have identified the most important brand messages, you can begin to develop strategies to align them with various audiences and distribute them via various online and offline channels.

- Competitive Analysis: Simply duplicating the competitors' strategies won't cut it. However, it is valuable to understand which marketing tactics and strategies are connecting with customers in the industry. By gaining insight into the most effective initiatives in the corner of the marketplace, you can significantly improve the impact of the organization's B2B marketing strategy.

- Digital Strategy: Most B2B companies leverage a variety of digital tactics (e.g. company website, PPC campaigns, etc.); But to achieve digital advantage, B2B firms need to move from a tactical, siloed approach to a strategic approach—developing a coordinated digital strategy that dovetails with organization's comprehensive B2B marketing strategy.

- Measurement and Analysis: Constant improvement should be a hallmark of the B2B marketing strategy. Measurement and analytics provide visibility to marketing performance and highlight critical gaps in the marketing program, enabling you to more accurately align the B2B marketing strategy with industry benchmarks and the demands of the marketplace.

Marketing Tactics that will Boost B2B Strategy

- Deliver Big on Your Promises

This tactic can be summed up in two words avoid clickbait. We have all experienced the bitter disappointment of clicking on a link that promises big and fails to deliver. This might get you clicks, but in the long run it damages your relationship with your audience.

You might not have out-and-out clickbait on your site, but no B2B business strategies should use messaging that raises false expectations or makes exaggerated claims.

Be upfront and honest in all of your content, and avoid hype. If the title of a blog is "10 Mind-Blowing Ways to Increase Your Business Profit," your audience will want to read fresh, new content not mediocre, predictable, and run-of-the-mill content.

- Integrated Channels

No doubt many effective channels comprise your strategy and generate leads. These channels include:

- o Content marketing;

- o Email marketing;

- o Social media marketing;

- o Search engine optimization;

- o Paid ads;

- o Webinars/Events.

As powerful as these strategies are alone, they work best if integrated. Here's a common example: You enjoy a blog post so much that you click the CTA on the post to subcribe to the blog's newsletter.

Look for ways to guide your audience to your other channels, which ultimately strengthens their relationship with your brand. For example, you might encourage your blog's audience to interact with you on social media. Or use paid ads on social media to direct people to your blog. You might even use a webinar or live events to highlight primo content on your blog or email newsletters.

Such integration fuels powerful interactions between your audience and your brand. This makes it an ideal marketing strategy for B2B businesses.

- • Advocacy Programs

Your customers are your largest resource and for many companies, this resource has yet to be tapped. Take your happy customers and encourage them to take your business relationship public.

This goes beyond testimonials or case studies, where you showcase your customer's feedback with your followers. This gets your brand in front of a wider audience as your customers share their positive experience, their audiences see that and it plants a positive seed in their mind about your brand.

Create a system that rewards participants with opportunities and benefits. Search out and engage with prospective advocates on social media. When someone puts your brand in a positive light, reach out to thank him or her for the gesture. Even such a simple gesture will make your brand seem more human and real to your audience.

You can take this one step further by rewarding individuals who advocate for your brand. This could be through resharing their content on social media, or offering an additional benefit, such as a freebie for fans or followers or early access to a new product or service. When people see that you appreciate such advocacy, they will be more likely to think of you in the future.

Don't forget about your employees. They can be a powerful force within your marketing tactics. Employees who sing the praises of their brand are few and far between, which makes their voices stand out.

- Interact with Your Online Community

Where online do your customer's conversations take place? LinkedIn groups? Quora? Facebook? Dsicover where your customers are asking questions, or talking about industry matters. Once you learn where they are, get involved. Begin by determining which issues your customers care about. When you are able to add meaningfully to the conversation, do so.

You can take this a step further by creating your own online forum where customers can share feedback and opinions all with a comfortable level of anonymity. This creates a trusted database of information that potential customers can tap into before making a purchase decision.

Many companies have successfully set up such online communities, and are reaping the rewards. If a business has its plateform, it can:

- Have more control and flexibility of how it interacts with its audience;
- Own it;
- Have more unique design options;
- Have more extensive analytics;
- Won't have to compete for its audience's attention;
- Use Facebook live.

Since, Facebook rolled out its new Live streaming feature in 2016, it has had amazing results. For instance, one study found that Facebook users comment 10 times more on Live videos than on regular posts. In another study, 80% of audience prefer live video over blog posts.

So how can you use Facebook Live effectively to engage your audience? Consider using Live video to stream:

- Interviews with members of your team;
- Interviews with industry influencers;
- FAQ about products or services;
- Live industry events;
- Webinars;
- Educational, how-to style tutorials;

When going live, keep your tone relaxed and conversational. Keep a few notes with you about how you want to steer the conversation, but don't be tied to them. Just let the conversation flow naturally.

Most of all, get creative, and imagine more new and special ways to utilize this fun and engaging tool. This is one of the top B2B marketing tactics that is not going anywhere, so now is the time to jump on board and join the era of live streaming.

- Mobile Marketing

One study showed that on average people consume 69% of their media on smartphones. Error. Hyperlink reference not valid.highlighted that mobile devices are expected to drive 80% of future global internet usage.

These statistics show that mobile marketing has become a must-have marketing strategy for B2B businesses. Busy CEOs and other decision makers digest their content on their smartphones or tablets while they're on the go.

Many erroneously assume that their website and content are automatically mobile-friendly. While it is true that many websites are "ready" for mobile, there is still a lot to do to ensure that your content is fully optimized for mobile.

As part of your mobile strategy, ask yourself these questions:

- Is my content easy to see on mobile devices?
- Are all links and buttons easy to tap?
- If there are pop-ups, will my audience easily be able to exit to view my content?
- Is visual content, such as ingrographics and videos, easy to read or view?

- Interactive Newsletters

Email marketing is one of the best B2B strategies for businesses -- 41% of companies still send out newsletters. In fact, 86% of professionals prefer to use email when communicating about business, and three quarters of companies agree that email offers "excellent" to "good" ROI. Many companies are taking this one step further, however, with interactive newsletters.

Your next interactive newsletter could include:

- Video downloads;
- Surveys;
- Feedback requests;

- o Contests;

- o Links to in-depth content on your website;

- o White paper downloads.

- Customer User Groups

Ever wish you could get inside the head of your B2B buyers? You can! Arrange customer user groups and events to get to know your customers. Learn more about your customers, their B2B business challenges and product needs. Your groups could include hands-on demos or feedback discussions to encourage open conversation.

These groups are two-way streets. While it gives you the opportunity to learn more about your customers, your customers will have a chance to learn more about your company. It fosters a positive relationship where both sides get to know and see each other in action.

- Personal Branding

Personal branding has become one of the most important marketing B2B strategies available today. Previously, executives focused more on branding their companies. However, buyers have begun to look more at the faces and voices behind the company logo.

Your personal brand is how the public perceives you. It is a culmination of your reputation, industry expertise, and personality.

There are a number of ways to define, and even refine, your brand. For starters, showcase your industry expertise through your blog posts and social media. Look for opportunities outside of your company, such as speaking engagements at industry events. Individualize your style and delivery according to your personality.

- Cross-sell or Up-sell

What do these terms mean? Cross-selling is when you offer more products complementary to the one your customer just bought. Up-selling is when you offer your customer a chance to upgrade a product.

When your customers purchase a product, it shouldn't be the end of the line. Think about it, they have already done their research, and decided on your brand. Why not show them a compatible product or an upgrade that may help them with a similar challenge or fit their needs even more? By doing so, your customers realize the array of options within your company. It also shows how well you understand their needs.

- Referral Program

Encourage happy customers to spread the word about your brand and when that word-of-mouth turns into a completed sale, reward the customers who put it into motion.

Let your customers know the benefits of spreading the word to their fellow business owners about your products or services. That could be a discount on a future purchase or something else that shows your appreciation and motivates a customer. We cannot emphasize this enough word of mouth is the leading way to reach potential B2B buyers.

- Influencer Marketing

Sure, influencer marketing has been in vogue for a few years, but recent changes have led to a more mature marketing strategy B2B businesses can rally behind.

For starters, we see more tools designed to find and utilize influencers to their maximum potential. Tools like Traackr and Buzzsumo help marketers to find industry influencer who fit their brand, develop a solid strategy, and measure the results. Other tools include:

- o Klout;
- o Kred;
- o Webfluential;
- o Revfluence;
- o Keyhole.

Another development in the field of influencer marketing is the rise of micro-influencers. These are individuals with between 1,000 and 50,000 followers who have the power to shape opinions and motivate purchase decisions.

Why would marketers want to use micro-influencers? Sure they have a smaller audience, but that's not a bad thing. In reality, these micro-influencers usually connect more meaningfully with their audience and it's more likely their messages will be heard and acted on.

- Case Studies and Testimonials

B2B buyers are inundated on a daily basis with advertisements and marketing pandemonium. How can you break through this noise and earn the trust of B2B buyers in your industry? One very effective way: Customer testimonials.

The unbiased voice of other buyers can make all the difference. Studies show that 53% of B2B buyers rely on peer recommendations before they make any purchase decisions. You can use customer testimonials in a number of ways to get the attention of buyers. For instance, use this valuable material.

- o On your website

- o   As snippets on social media images

- o   In marketing materials that you send out to your leads

- o   In a blog post

- o   In a Slideshare

- o   In a video (with your customer front and center)

- o   In your email marketing campaign.

- Personalization

Personalization started out as a mainly B2C tactic, but has quickly grown to be one of the most important business to business marketing strategies available today. Through the years it has become more sophisticated. For many, the first thing that comes to mind when they hear "personalization" is their name in the header of a marketing email. But this small, software-automated example is just scraping the surface.

Let's start with a fresh definition. Personalization is the action of taking data about your audience, and using it to make your content (whether it's blogs, emails, infographics, etc.) more useful and pertinent.

This could mean using demographic data, such as age, gender, and career of your audience to create more engaging content. For instance, if the majority of your audience includes executive males in their late 40s., you could use this data to compile blog posts to fit their needs and concerns.

Or say you notice that the majority of your website traffic is from blog posts about social media. You will want to create content that's more focused on that subject, such as an in-depth eBook or video.

- Niche Targeting

Some companies aim to be more general in their messaging, believing it will resonate with more people. This method, however, often produces a "meh" response. But the more specific a message is to your niche, the more engagement it will generate -- and the more it will truly resonate with your niche audience.

It really pays to segment your audience into specific buyer personas. Drill down to the specific niche you want to reach. Then create messages focused on each segment. Your audience will be more responsive to such messages and ultimately more loyal to you.

Key Points to Remember

- Case studies and testimonials are a key way to break through the constant noise of advertisements, and reach B2B buyers.

- Make your email newsletters more interactive to engage with your prospects.

- Use customer advocate and referral programs to reward those who sing your brand's praises to others.

- Get as specific as possible when you segment your audience, in order to create a message that resonates with individual buyers.

Market Analysis

A market analysis is a quantitative and qualitative assessment of a market. It looks into the size of the market both in volume and in value, the various customer segments and buying patterns, the competition, and the economic environment in terms of barriers to entry and regulation.

Market segmentation is a marketing term referring to the aggregating of prospective buyers into groups or segments with common needs and who respond similarly to a marketing action. Market segmentation enables companies to target different categories of consumers who perceive the full value of certain products and services differently from one another.

Companies can generally use three criteria to identify different market segments: homogeneity, or common needs within a segment; distinction, or being unique from other groups; and reaction, or a similar response to the market. For example, an athletic footwear company might have market segments for basketball players and long-distance runners. As distinct groups, basketball players and long-distance runners respond to very different advertisements.

Market segmentation is an extension of market research that seeks to identify targeted groups of consumers to tailor products and branding in a way that is attractive to the group. The objective of market segmentation is to minimize risk by determining which products have the best chances for gaining a share of a target market and determining the best way to deliver the products to the market. This allows the company to increase its overall efficiency by focusing its limited resources on efforts that produce the best return on investment.

Companies can segment markets several ways: geographically by region or area; demographically by age, gender, family size, income or life cycle; psychographically by social class, lifestyle or personality; or behaviorally by benefit, uses or response. The objective is to enable the company to differentiate its products or message according to the common dimensions of the market segment.

You can see examples of market segmentation in the products, marketing and advertising that people use every day. Auto manufacturers thrive on their ability to identify market segments correctly, and create products and advertising campaigns that appeal to those segments. Cereal producers market actively to three or four market segments at a time, pushing their traditional brands that appeal to older consumers and their healthy brands to health-conscious consumers while building brand loyalty among the youngest consumers by tying their products to popular movie themes.

A sports shoe manufacturer might define several market segments that include elite athletes, frequent gym-goers, fashion-conscious women and middle-aged men who want quality and comfort in their shoes. In all cases, the manufacturer's marketing intelligence about each segment enables it to develop and advertise products with high appeal more efficiently than trying to appeal to the broader masses.

Dimensions of Market Analysis

David A. Aaker outlined the following dimensions of a market analysis:

Market size (current and future)

- Market trends
- Market growth rate
- Market profitability
- Industry cost structure
- Distribution channels
- Key success factors
- Key success details.

Market analysis strives to determine the attractiveness of a market, currently and in the future. Organizations evaluate future attractiveness of a market by understanding evolving opportunities, and threats as they relate to that organization's own strengths and weaknesses.

Organizations use these findings to guide the investment decisions they make to advance their success. The findings of a market analysis may motivate an organization to change various aspects of its investment strategy. Affected areas may include inventory levels, a work force expansion/contraction, facility expansion, purchases of capital equipment, and promotional activities.

Elements

Market Size

The market size is defined through the market volume and the market potential. The market volume exhibits the totality of all realized sales volume of a special market.

The volume is therefore dependent on the quantity of consumers and their ordinary demand. Furthermore, the market volume is either measured in quantities or qualities. The quantities can be given in technical terms, like GW for power capacities, or in numbers of items. Qualitative measuring mostly uses the sales turnover as an indicator. That means that the market price and the quantity are taken into account. Besides the market volume, the market potential is of equal importance. It defines the upper limit of the total demand and takes potential clients into consideration. Although the market potential is rather fictitious, it offers good values of orientation. The relation of market volume to market potential provides information about the chances of market growth. The following are examples of information sources for determining market size:

- Government data;

- Trade association data;

- Financial data from major players;

- Customer surveys.

Market Trends

Market trends are the upward or downward movement of a market, during a period of time. The market size is more difficult to estimate if one is starting with something completely new. In this case, you will have to derive the figures from the number of potential customers, or customer segments.

Besides information about the target market, one also needs information about one's competitors, customers, products, etc. Lastly, you need to measure marketing effectiveness. A few techniques are:

- Customer analysis;

- Choice modelling;

- Competitor analysis;

- Risk analysis;

- Product research;

- Advertising the research;

- Marketing mix modeling;

- Simulated Test Marketing.

Changes in the market are important because they often are the source of new opportunities and threats. Moreover, they have the potential to dramatically affect the market size.

Examples include changes in economic, social, regulatory, legal, and political conditions and in available technology, price sensitivity, demand for variety, and level of emphasis on service and support.

Market Growth Rate

A simple means of forecasting the market growth rate is to extrapolate historical data into the future. While this method may provide a first-order estimate, it does not predict important turning points. A better method is to study market trends and sales growth in complementary products. Such drivers serve as leading indicators that are more accurate than simply extrapolating historical data.

Important inflection points in the market growth rate sometimes can be predicted by constructing a product diffusion curve. The shape of the curve can be estimated by studying the characteristics of the adoption rate of a similar product in the past.

Ultimately, many markets mature and decline. Some leading indicators of a market's decline include market saturation, the emergence of substitute products, and/or the absence of growth drivers.

Market Opportunity

A market opportunity product or a service, based on either one technology or several, fulfills the need(s) of a (preferably increasing) market better than the competition and better than substitution-technologies within the given environmental frame (e.g. society, politics, legislation, etc.).

Market Profitability

While different organizations in a market will have different levels of profitability, they are all similar to different market conditions. Michael Porter devised a useful framework for evaluating the attractiveness of an industry or market. This framework, known as Porter five forces analysis, identifies five factors that influence the market profitability:

- Buyer power;
- Supplier power;
- Barriers to entry;
- Threat of substitute products;
- Rivalry among firms in the industry.

Industry Cost Structure

The cost structure is important for identifying key factors for success. To this end,

Porter's value chain model is useful for determining where value is added and for isolating the costs.

The cost structure also is helpful for formulating strategies to develop a competitive advantage. For example, in some environments the experience curve effect can be used to develop a cost advantage over competitors.

Distribution Channels

Examining the following aspects of the distribution system may help with a market analysis:

- Existing distribution channels - can be described by how direct they are to the customer.

- Trends and emerging channels - new channels can offer the opportunity to develop a competitive advantage.

- Channel power structure - for example, in the case of a product having little brand equity, retailers have negotiating power over manufacturers and can capture more margin.

Success Factors

The key success factors are those elements that are necessary in order for the firm to achieve its marketing objectives. A few examples of such factors include:

- Access to essential unique resources;

- Ability to achieve economies of scale;

- Access to distribution channels;

- Technological progress.

It is important to consider that key success factors may change over time, especially as the product progresses through its life cycle.

Environmental Analysis

The environmental analysis can be divided into two parts which are external and internal factors. External factors. Political issues, social potential force, and local economy called external environmental factors. Internal environmental factors belongs to company's internal position such as employees, department structure, budget and so forth (Christina). How environmental effect markets. According to the Parry, the government limit pollution emission, they mention environmental taxes to prevent company which produce pollution substance. In other words, the government drives the organization. On the contrary, the cost of products increase due to the environmental taxes. It means that company may take measure of re-ducing production which may grow unemployment rate by emission tax. Therefore, the environmental taxes leads a income equality. It is not an excuse ignore our seri-ous environmental problem. Even though the higher income group also can benefit from windfall gains.

Competitive Analysis

According to the Christina, competitive analysis is that company must know their com-petitors which have the same common services and products. The business can use like product cost, operational efficiency, brand recognition and market Dimensions of market analysis

Except for David A. Aaker's 7 main dimension of a market analysis including mar-ket size, market growth rate, market profitability, industry cost structure, distribution channel, market trends, and key success factor, there is another analysis of dimension market analysis. Based on Christina Callaway, dimension of market analysis can be divided into four parts which is environmental analysis, competitive analysis, target audience analysis, and SWOT analysis. The market analysis is to help company to il-lustrate current trend in the market and may affect the profitability. At the same time, market analysis is also to determine the attractiveness in the market. A good marketing analysis can improve organization investment decision accurately, they can based on the attractiveness to change investment tactical.

The market analysis is to help company to illustrate current trend in the market and may affect the profitability for the business. It can be seen as a part of industry analysis with using global environmental analysis. Company can identify strengths, weakness, opportunities and threats so that the business can define the business strategy. The market analysis is also reference for company's activity, like decisions of inventory, purchase, work force, facility expansion and many aspects of company.

Penetration to find the difference or competitive advantages between two similar-ly companies. How can we find the competitive advantage? Kevin (2016) says that "Anticipating and reading market needs can help business leaders take significant steps towards changing the game and obtaining competitive advantage." How can we sustain competitive advantages? In terms of Richard research, The company should focus on sustaining competitive advantage due to the swift growth global competi-tion. Therefore, Business practice management is the follow principle to maintain competitive advantage.

Target Audience Analysis

In the Christina contribution, target audience is for company to target their customer group who most likely to buy their products. The group can be classified with location, age, gender, income, ethnicity, and behaviors. And people who make a decision of purchase can also be divided in the target audience. How identify market in accordance with Women's enterprise centre the market can be classified in three types which are consumer market, industrial market, and reseller market. The company segment their market, research market, and identify why customer would like to buy their products.

SWOT Analysis

SWOT is strengths, weakness, opportunities, and threats. It matches internal strengths and weaknesses up against opportunities and threats. Strengths and weakness are internal factors which we can control. Opportunities and threats are external factors that businesses can't control, but can however impact on. When using strengths and weakness, businesses need to collect raw data to get information. Businesses can get information by customer feedback, employee surveys. Furthermore, businesses also can identify the capability if it is weakness or strengths, resources and process. Opportunities and threats are the external factors. Business can get information from secondary data like environmental information, industry information and competitive data. The purpose of the business use the SWOT analysis is to get the information from it and match each other to develop the ideas and get into goal statement to form strategic development.

Market communication has significant impact on building and maintaining the relationship of stakeholders. Market analysis elements is to form a strategic planning and the information is responsiveness, intelligence generation, and dissemination. Besides, market communication provide the information focus on the customer needs and competitive advantage. At the same time, these information spread to customers means the company spread its brand value so that customer can make awareness of the company's products. It is the communication channel between business and customers.

Market Segmentation

Market segmentation is one of the important ways to find competitive advantage with its differentiation in market analysis. Market segmentation concentrates on market energy and power to gain competitive advantage. In other words, market segmentation is the concept tool to get the force. In the market analysis, we need a lot of market knowledge to analyze market structure and process. Since segmentation needs to do a lot of market research so that we can get the information from it. Market segmentation recommends the market strategy. Market segmentation can identify customer needs and wants and develop products to satisfy them. Market segmentation can identify different products for different groups, better match between customer wants and product benefits, maximize the use of available resources, focuse marketing expenditures and competitive advantages.

There is no perfect way to segment market but business can follow some rules like geographic, demographic, psychographic, and behavioral. A good market segmentation should be sustainable, accessible, actionable, measurable, and differentiable.

Global Market Segmentation

Since the globalization more and more developed, the global market become indispensability part of the business thinking. In order to explore global market, how market segmentation can be used in the global market. There are some aspects of defining the global market so which is more efficient to segment global market. Some researchers mention about Cross-National and Cross-Cultural Approach to segment global market. To differentiate country and culture, the company have to identify two areas which is vertical market segment existing internal area. Another area is external market segments which a group of countries has relationship of each other and share their characteristics. Compared with cross- cultural approach and cross-national approach, cross-cultural approach has its cultural stability of traditional values. cultural stability has a wide range of shared national-cultural values features, due to group solidarity, interpersonal harmony and so forth. However, cross-cultural approach has challenge of environmental changes, cultural change and some other unstable factors. Therefore, the main principle of looking at cross-cultural approach and cross- national approach base on perceive service quality. In the global service marketing, the marketing manager face a challenge of international services on account of the intangibility of services, unification standardizing services across national borders and difference of preference for customized services in different countries and culture. Therefore, it is significance for business to have a deep understanding service quality in facing across different countries, regions and cultures.

In the software market, the trend of software is the price is high and coverage is low. In order to improve the trend, there is some problems of software market:

- What possibly discourages product differentiation in such a competitive market?

- Why is versioning absent here?

- How does the presence of free alternatives in this market impact its structure?

In order to improve these problems, Zhang mention that quality competition and market segmentation apply to the software market. In Zhang's research, the software company lack of developed the method of quality competition, market segmentation, and versioning. In terms of market segmentation, software company think segmentation consumer market is not useful. Therefore, even though versioning is the least costless way of spread product information, the company still ignore it.

The relationship between market segmentation and communication in marketing is interaction. For example, market segmentation is important in the social media. There is three perspectives supplier perspectives, interaction perspectives, and buyer perspectives. In order to balance these three relationships, business must do segment well. Otherwise, the buyer perspective and supplier perspective cannot interact very well may lead loss of promotion. Therefore, social media is important method of communication in the market and market segmentation also unnecessary before the business use social media channel.

Applications

The literature defines several areas in which market analysis is important. These include: sales forecasting, market research, and marketing strategy. Not all managers will need to conduct a market analysis. Nevertheless, it would be important for managers that use market analysis data to know how analysts derive their conclusions and what techniques they use to do so.

B2B Branding

A brand has grown to mean much more than a logo. Branding begins with the consistency of presentation that becomes the identity of a company. Beyond this it represents a consistent value system that a company presents to the world and that is seen to be that company's way of doing things. On this branding ladder, the challenge is to move beyond the graphic symbols and metaphors to get to the more difficult cultural uniformity that customers and potential customers recognize and value.

A good test of branding uniformity is to collect business cards from everyone in a company and lay them on the table. Do the same thing with all pieces of stationery including compliment slips, letterheads and labels. Put all the company's adverts and sales literature on the table. What is the uniformity in layout and presentation? What variable images do they communicate? Do the presentations look messy and all over the place? The enemy of branding is the well meaning person within a company who believes that their concept of a design, image or brand is superior to all others. Within all of us there is a desire to fiddle with brands and layouts and so potentially, everyone is a branding terrorist. Whenever you see a good and strong brand you can be sure that behind it there will be a brand champion who is prepared to be unpopular if necessary in enforcing the branding rules of that company.

The starting point of any b2b brand strategy research is to work out what the company stands for. What is the single most important value that the company presents to the world? Think of it this way − if the company's back is to the wall, how would it react to a demanding customer? And, now think through every contact with the outside world and question whether or not it presents these values. What does it sound like when the phone is answered? What consistency of messages comes from the appearance of the sales and technical team? Do the cars that people drive when they visit customers, do their clothes and do the words that come from their mouths correspond with the values of the company? Does the response that a company makes to a customer or potential customer fit with the position it thinks it holds. These are the acid tests that a company needs to apply to determine where it sits on the B2B branding ladder.

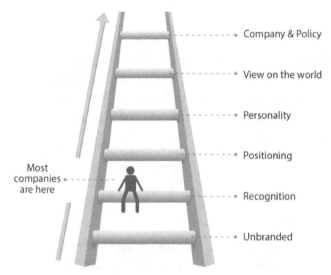

To finish this question about branding definition, we should consider for a minute the difference between a product and a brand. The two often get confused with many an industrial company giving names to their products, believing that these are brands that are recognized by the market. However, a product is only a brand if people think of imagery and associations when they think of that product. Most so called industrial brands are just labels for products which could just as easily be referred to by a generic description or a number or any other such code for the purpose of ordering.

It would be easy to generalize and to say that in most circumstances there are few real opportunities for product brands in industrial companies. The small and specialized nature of most industrial companies' markets means that they cannot support the cost and attention required for a number of such sub brands. Indeed, every B2B brand promoted by a company needs strong promotional support and expense. The proliferation of brands end up either doing nothing useful (the more usual case) or sucking the blood from the corporate brand (less usual because brands are created on a whim and then not supported). In most cases, the corporate brand is the only one that really matters – e.g. Dow acrylic monomers or Lafarge plasterboard; the emphasis being on the corporate names of Dow or Lafarge. Such is the confusion about b2b branding, most companies have a plethora of so called brands that do not pass the following test:

A B2B Brand Is	A Product Is
• Something customers ask for by name.	• A convenient locator in a product range.
• The name people use when talking about the product to someone else.	• Something which could just as easily be ordered by description.
• When people think of the brand rather than the product.	• A level which could be changed without any loss of loyalty to the customer.
• Something which has developed a personality beyond the product.	• A label which customers have to look up and don't really care about.
• Something people would pay a premium for under that and no other name.	

It bears repeating: in most business to business markets, the B2B brand of any value is most often the name of the company itself and the product labels that try to pass as brands could just as easily be numbers or codes. The company name is the brand that customers think of. It is the brand that has a value. And more worryingly, it is the brand that is allowed to grow without direction, without support and without any recognition of its importance to the company.

Two companies, whose products are virtually indistinguishable. In fact, the two companies compete in a large market in which there are dozens of competitors. However the two companies regularly obtain a 30% premium on their competitors.

This is because Coca-Cola and Pepsi-Cola have persuaded us that the phosphoric acid, the H2O, flavourings, colourings, sugar and what ever else they throw into the dark sticky brew is better than that mixed by others and indeed better than simple H_2O itself.

So, if branding works for Coca-Cola, will it work for a manufacturer of industrial hose or a company pressing metal pieces? "Of course" Business-to-business branding is already working for industrial companies, but not with the efficiency it could. Many industrial companies have customers they have supplied for years. These loyal customers buy trust, they have friendships and are affected by any number of other intangibles that have a value as well as the functional properties of the product. Very few industrial buyers will change their supplier if an unknown somebody or other knocks on their door offering the same goods for 10% less.

There is no question that the essence of marketing is having the right product in the right place at the right price. Good marketing will ensure that customers and potential customers are aware of the product and, indeed, have been persuaded to want it to the exclusion of all others.

But, this simplistic view begs the question, "what makes someone want a product (or service) to the exclusion of all others?" We would be naïve in believing that people drink Coke to quench their thirst or drive a Mercedes because it offers best value for money. Coke may be thirst quenching but so is water. Mercedes cars are good value but a second hand Ford could be even better value. Something else is going on.

These examples are taken from consumer products and our interest is in industrial markets. Let us consider for a minute someone who buys lubricants to go in the sump of a packaging machine. Can they really be influenced by the brand? When they are asked in a typical market research survey why they choose a certain supplier, they rationalise their decision with all the usual "hard" or tangible factors. They say it's the performance of the product, its price, the availability, the guarantee etc. If this is true, how is it possible that most buyers of lubrication oils stay loyal to the B2B brand they use for years and years? One reason could be inertia – like it isn't worth the effort to change. Another could be trust in the product – like the present one works and another one may not? So why change if the price of the product in the context of all other purchases is so minimal? In other words, when you dig below the surface, the reasons for choosing a brand of lubrication oil may be something beyond the price, product and availability that were mentioned at first pass. This suggests that brands have a much greater influence than is initially acknowledged.

If we are to attach a value to a brand, we need to know what the values are that are seen in that brand. The brand name and its associations are a shorthand for everything that is on offer. The product quality, the reliability of delivery, the value for money, are all wrapped up in people's perceptions of that brand. This means that when people say that a Mercedes offers good value for money, they really believe that this is the case and don't want or need to confuse the situation by weighing up the many alternatives that could be equal or better value. So too, someone buying a Shell lubricant is synthesizing their decision to the point that they can think only Shell and worry no more.

Market researchers try to get beyond the obvious values attached to a brand by using projective questions in which the respondent is asked to think of a scenario outside or beyond the direct and obvious. Word associations using Freudian psychology are used to tease out simple brand values. Another favourite is to ask respondents to make an association between the brand and a car or the brand and an animal. Such associations can be pushed further by asking what music a brand would listen to, where the brand would go on holiday, what job it would do. In a recent study which tested the brand values attached to a university, people were asked to sketch something that represented how they saw that University. There were many portrayals but most suggested warmth, comfort and security as represented by the three following examples of the armchair, the foetus and the home. Simply asking the question "what does the name of this university mean to you?" would not have flushed out the same depth of answer.

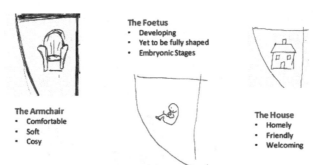

Psycho Drawing As An Aid To Understanding A University's Brand Values

Working out what people associate with a brand is only one part of the equation. It is necessary to go a step further and put a monetary figure on those brand values. In consumer markets there are many sophisticated attempts to get at these values because to do so enables the owner of the brand to include the figure on the balance sheet. This is more difficult in industrial markets because the principal brand is the name of the company itself and one measure of this value is the premium that someone will pay for the company beyond the tangible assets and beyond the "typical" price earnings multiple in that sector. The complications arise when the premium is partly due to the brand and partly due to patents or a charismatic CEO or some other intangible but valuable issue.

Take three brands of computer – Dell, Sony and IBM – each does the same thing. However, prospective buyers may see one standing for flexibility, another for innovation and yet another for quality. All of them possess all three values but the high ground for each value is owned by just one of the companies. This provides them with the opportunity for gaining a competitive advantage. Three different trucks, three different packaging machines, three different brands of polyurethane. In each case the brand will be seen to be different and therefore it could form the centre piece of a differentiating opportunity.

This is almost self evident and yet so few industrial companies have strategic plans for managing their company brand. Returning to one of the first issues we discussed in this white paper, most industrial companies are low on the b2b branding ladder, struggling to ensure a common template for its stationery and adverts, let alone having a brand essence that is reflected in every thing that the company does.

This is not always easy. Inside the company some people will suggest values or a position that is aspirational while others will want something that is more reflective of the here and now. Some will want a complicated essence while others will try to find simplicity. Some will be happy to run with internal opinion while others will insist on an independent view. A company that gets this wrong will lose its single most important differentiating opportunity.

In arriving at the brand essence of a company, it may be helpful to use a "bull's eye" tool. This sets the brand essence in the context of what customers say and think about a supplier, what evidence there is that the essence is being delivered and the personality of the company. The diagram below shows a worked example.

B2B Brand Bull's Eye Tool For Arriving At A Company Brand Essence

In a world where everything increasingly looks the same, brands are one of the few opportunities for making a difference. When industrial companies benefit from business to business branding, it is often by accident rather than design. However, with a little extra effort and cost, the effect could be much improved loyalty and greater profitability. Let's imagine that the effect of the brand could be separated out from the utility of an industrial product, we could find that it accounts for only around 5% of the influence to select a supplier. Now let's also imagine that with a little bit of pushing, shoving and promotional effort the brand could be more precisely positioned. With this positioning, the influence of the brand on the selection of the supplier would surely be increased. Assuming this repositioning of the brand resulted in raising the brand influence a modest 2% points to 7%, this would enable the supplier to achieve an increase in price or, if the price remains the same, a larger market share. This has got to be worthwhile.

Some companies have been highly successful in this mission. RS Components, suppliers of thousands of electronic, electrical and mechanical products from its CD-ROMs, catalogues and web site obtains a high premium for products because it offers one stop shopping with unfailing delivery to your door in the morning post. Dow Chemical has built a brand with a reputation for high technology and a low cost to serve in a wide range of plastics. Eddie Stobbart used to operate an ordinary trucking company until he ensured that the reliability of his operation is always supported by clean trucks and smart drivers. His drivers green shirts and their mandatory ties, have become hallmarks of the brand which justifies a substantial premium over Joe Soap Transport.

B2B branding is certainly not the holy grail. It is not the be all and end all of a successful business. Branding is just one aspect of marketing. But if a company gets its industrial brand right, the likelihood is that all the other parts of the marketing mix will fall into place.

Target Market

Target market is the end consumer to which the company wants to sell its end products too. Target marketing involves breaking down the entire market into various segments and planning marketing strategies accordingly for each segment to increase the market share.

In simple words, not all products can be consumed by all customers and each product has a different set of consumers who want to purchase the product. In order to attract a particular segment of the market, the company at times, modifies the product accordingly. Creating the target market involves conceptualizing the product, understanding the need of the product in a market, studying its target audience etc. Target marketing would revolve around deploying marketing techniques for a particular segment of markets which could be key to attract new customers, expand business opportunities across geographies and expand distribution network to widen the reach.

There are various steps involved in defining the target market. The first is to understand the problem of a customer whom you are addressing. Once it is done, the customers can be identified who are interested in that product. For example, you make water purifiers – so you address the problem of contaminated water quality. We know that farm houses do not have a regular water connection and the water they get from underground is hard. So, there is a wide opportunity for water-purifier makers to enter into this segment and tap the market. The next step is to understand your customer according to the region, income level, etc. Always think about the market, know your competition and the pricing of the product. It will help you in creating a benchmark.

There are two important features, which the company should always consider before it decides to capture a separate market segment. First is the attractiveness of the segment, which means that it has less competition, high margin business etc. The second is that it falls in line with the company's objective, vision etc.

Importance of Identifying the Target Market

Identifying a target market helps the company develop effective marketing communication strategies. A target market is a set of individuals sharing similar needs or characteristics that the company hopes to serve. These individuals are usually the end users most likely to purchase the product.

Craft Specific Messages

Selecting a target market allows one to craft messages that appeal specifically to them. A lipstick marketer using a target marketing approach aims the message at female users, as men typically do not wear lipstick. Within the female audience, women wear lipstick for varying reasons. A savvy marketer reaches a younger audience with a lifestyle message that wearing the lipstick is cool. A mature woman may respond to a bene-fit-based message that the lipstick reduces chapped lips.

Focus on Potential

Organizations don't have the time or resources to be able to reach everyone with a product message. Identifying a target market allows marketers to focus on those most likely to purchase the product. Limiting the population funnels research and budgets to the customers with the highest profit potential.

Reach the Right Audience

Once one has identified the target market, the target audience, the intended recipient of the advertising message can be defined. Many times the market and the audience are the same. When one person is the end user and another is the purchaser, the target market and target audience differ. There are quite a few products used by men that are purchased primarily by their wives. In these instances, the target market is male and the target audience is the female who makes the purchase. Marketers design strategies to meet the needs of the target market and use media channels and other touch points to best reach the purchaser.

Cost-effective Strategies

Once one know who one are targeting, it is much easier to make decisions on media allocations. If the target market is young women, there is no need to purchase ad space in every magazine. One can advertise only in those popular with that audience. One will save money and get a better return on investment by using a target market plan. Media buys will be more efficient as wasted audience those unlikely to purchase the product is greatly reduced.

Compete Successfully

Businesses of any size can compete effectively by identifying an under-served market. One no longer have to worry about trying to reach every customer who could use the product and can focus a marketing plan to fit a smaller, like minded part of the total market. By focusing resources on a specific customer segment, a small business may be able to better serve a target market than its larger competitors.

Types of Target Markets on the Basis of Demography

1. Age: The target market can be on the basis of age. Best example is clothes which are different based on the age of the individual.

2. Gender: Taking the same clothes example, if you have decided that you want to market to only one gender, then your target market will differ based on the 2 genders out there. Naturally, your products will differ accordingly.

3. Race: A lot of decisions are made by an individual based on where he originates from. Race makes a lot of influence on purchasing decisions. So an Asian customer will have a different purchasing behavior then an American.

4. Income: Rolex is a good example of making generic products but keeping the target market based on income. Off course, income can be a psychographic factor too.

5. Religion: Many people get confused between race and religion and you should not confuse the same. Taking the above example, Asians have diverse religions and each country you go to will have different religions. Similarly, thinking that Christians are one religion is also wrong. You will find many sub religions of Christianity. So if your target market is based on religion, you have to take decisions accordingly.

6. Occupation: A medicine for allergy is not marketed to an engineer and similarly, a product which is targeted towards one occupation should not be targeted towards the other. This is where you should adhere to your target market.

7. Family size: The Scorpio, Renault Duster or Toyota innova is mostly marketed to families which are large in size. Where you have to travel in groups? Family size is another target market group.

8. Geographic location: If a restaurant from which is close to your home, is marketing to people who are far away from you, then the restaurant will fail in its business. It has to reach to the people who are closer because traveling time is important when considering which restaurant to have dinner in.

9. Zip code: Many FMCG companies or small retailers and dealers target their customers based on zip code. Beyond that zip code is the territory of the competitor and they do not target that area.

Above were all the types of Target markets which are based on demography. But with rise in competition, there are other types of Segmentation which have gained prominence. Based on these types of segmentation, the target market varies too.

Target Markets based on Psychographic Segmentation

1. Consumer activities: Adidas, Reebok and Nike all market based on one consumer activity – Staying physically fit. With this ideology, Nike and Reebok have penetrated the market strongly for their sports shoes. These 3 are the top brands for this activity.

2. Interests: If we continue with the shoes examples, then anyone who buys Jimmy Choo has the earnings to buy such premium brands and he is interested in collecting shoes as a commodity. Similarly, many people are interested in

collecting antiques or stamps. In fact, If you target based on consumer interests, it can be a very profitable venture.

3. Opinions: Which magazine do you read or blog you follow? If you ask this to every person out there, each one will answer different. This is because people follow things which in their opinion are good and people opinion varies at all time. Some people might thing Hollywood based magazines are crap whereas others might thing science and tech based blogs are useless.

Target Markets Based on Product Usage

1. Use on occasions: One of the best brands which markets on the basis of Occasions is Cadbury Dairy milk. Think of a celebration and you will remember cadbury's celebration chocolates. Cadbury has covered the gifting niche perfectly. Similarly, you can think of Archies and Hallmark cards which are used on Occasions and this is their target market.

2. Use on situations: When do you use an Umbrella? Or when do you use a Sun screen? Both of them are used based on situations. You use an Umbrella when it is raining outside, and you use a sun screen when it is hot or too much sunny outside. So these are target markets based on situational usage.

3. Usage type: Many customers use certain products lightly whereas others use it heavily. A residential printer of Hewlett packard will be much different and will have a different refilling mechanism then a printer being used by corporates (which has a drum cartridge mechanism) So based on different usage types, the target market can vary.

Target Market based on Brand Preference

Example, I prefer only Dell Laptops. I have purchased 4 laptops till date and all have been from Dell. I have used different laptops which were owned by my friends, but I always liked the speed and usefulness of Dell. Now this is excellent brand loyalty from my part.

So based on the brand preference, there are 3 types of customers you can market to:

1. Brand loyal customers: Customers like me, who stick to a brand which is good and don't keep changing.

2. Brand aware customers: There are some customers who just keep changing at all times, and you need to target these customers to bring them back.

3. Unaware customers: When you are yet to established yourself as a brand, this is your target market. Baidu is known in China, but it is unknown in many other countries.

Target Market based on Decision Process

The target market also varies on the type of decision. For example – the water purifiers which are marketed to businesses as well as to individuals. In case of individuals, they are consumer products and in case of individuals, the target market is Usage based.

In case of organization however, the decision process is completely different and might take some time. Marketing to OEM's and Government is a type of target market which is based on decision making. Here the decisions are big and the order value is large.

Pricing

Pricing is the method of determining the value a producer will get in the exchange of goods and services. Simply, pricing method is used to set the price of producer's offerings relevant to both the producer and the customer.

Every business operates with the primary objective of earning profits, and the same can be realized through the Pricing methods adopted by the firms.

While setting the price of a product or service the following points have to be kept in mind:

- Nature of the product/service.

- The price of similar product/service in the market.

- Target audience i.e. for whom the product is manufactured (high, medium or lower class).

- The cost of production viz. Labor cost, raw material cost, machinery cost, inventory cost, transit cost, etc.

- External factors such as Economy, Government policies, Legal issues, etc.

Pricing Objectives

The objective once set gives the path to the business i.e. in which direction to go. The following are the pricing objectives that clears the purpose for which the business exists:

1. Survival: The foremost Pricing Objective of any firm is to set the price that is optimum and help the product or service to survive in the market. Each firm faces the danger of getting ruled out from the market because of the intense competition, a mature market or change in customer's tastes and preferences, etc. Thus, a firm must set the price covering the fixed and variable cost incurred without adding any profit margin to it. The survival should be the short term objective

once the firm gets a hold in the market it must strive for the additional profits. The New Firms entering into the market adopts this type of pricing objective.

2. Maximizing the current profits: Many firms try to maximize their current profits by estimating the Demand and Supply of goods and services in the market. Pricing is done in line with the product's demand in the customers and the substitutes available to fulfill that demand. Higher the demand higher will be the price charged. Seasonal supply and demand of goods and services are the best examples that can be quoted here.

3. Capturing huge market share: Many firms charge low prices for their offerings to capture greater market share. The reason for keeping the price low is to have an increased sales resulting from the Economies of Scale. Higher sales volume lead to lower production cost and increased profits in the long run. This strategy of keeping the price low is also known as Market Penetration Pricing. This pricing method is generally used when competition is intense and customers are price sensitive. FMCG industry is the best example to supplement this.

4. Market Skimming: Market skimming means charging a high price for the product and services offered by the firms which are innovative, and uses modern technology. The prices are comparatively kept high due to the high cost of production incurred because of modern technology. Mobile phones, Electronic Gadgets are the best examples of skimming pricing that are launched at a very high cost and gets cheaper with the span of time.

5. Product – Quality Leadership: Many firms keep the price of their goods and services in accordance with the Quality Perceived by the customers. Generally, the luxury goods create their high quality, taste, and status image in the minds of customers for which they are willing to pay high prices. Luxury cars such as BMW, Mercedes, Jaguar, etc. create the high quality with high-status image among the customers.

Pricing Strategies

Marketers develop an overall pricing strategy that is consistent with the organisation's mission and values. This pricing strategy typically becomes part of the company's overall long -term strategic plan. The strategy is designed to provide broad guidance to price-setters and ensures that the pricing strategy is consistent with other elements of the marketing plan. While the actual price of goods or services may vary in response to different conditions, the broad approach to pricing (i.e., the pricing strategy) remains a constant for the planning outlook period which is typically 3–5 years, but in some industries may be a longer period of 7–10 years.

Broadly, there are six approaches to pricing strategy mentioned in the marketing literature:

- Operations-oriented pricing: Where the objective is to optimize productive capacity, to achieve operational efficiencies or to match supply and demand through varying prices. In some cases, prices might be set to de-market.

- Revenue-oriented pricing: (Also known as profit-oriented pricing or cost-based pricing) - where the marketer seeks to maximise the profits (i.e., the surplus income over costs) or simply to cover costs and break even. For example, dynamic pricing (also known as yield management) is a form of revenue oriented pricing.

- Customer-oriented pricing: Where the objective is to maximise the number of customers; encourage cross-selling opportunities or to recognise different levels in the customer's ability to pay.

- Value-based pricing: (Also known as *image-based pricing*) occurs where the company uses prices to signal market value or associates price with the desired value position in the mind of the buyer. The aim of value-based pricing is to reinforce the overall positioning strategy e.g. premium pricing posture to pursue or maintain a luxury image.

- Relationship-oriented pricing: Where the marketer sets prices in order to build or maintain relationships with existing or potential customers.

- Socially-oriented pricing: Where the objective is to encourage or discourage specific social attitudes and behaviours. e.g. high tariffs on tobacco to discourage smoking.

Pricing Tactics

When decision-makers have determined the broad approach to pricing (i.e., the pricing strategy), they turn their attention to pricing tactics. Tactical pricing decisions are shorter term prices, designed to accomplish specific short-term goals. The tactical approach to pricing may vary from time to time, depending on a range of internal considerations (e.g. such as the need to clear surplus inventory) or external factors (e.g. a response to competitive pricing tactics). Accordingly, a number of different pricing tactics may be employed in the course of a single planning period or across a single year. Typically line managers are given the latitude necessary to vary individual prices providing that they operate within the broad strategic approach. For example, some premium brands never offer discounts because the use of low prices may tarnish the brand image. Instead of discounting, premium brands are more likely to offer customer value through price-bundling or give-aways.

When setting individual prices, decision-makers require a solid understanding of pricing economics, notably break-even analysis, as well as an appreciation of the psychological aspects of consumer decision-making including reservation prices, ceiling prices and floor prices. The marketing literature identifies literally hundreds of pricing tactics. It is difficult to do justice to the variety of tactics in widespread use. Rao and Kartono carried out a cross-cultural study to identify the pricing strategies and tactics that are most widely used. The following listing is largely based on their work.

ARC/RRC Pricing

A traditional tactic used in outsourcing that uses a fixed fee for a fixed volume of services, with variations on fees for volumes above or below target thresholds. Charges for additional resources ("ARC's") above the threshold are priced at rates to reflect the marginal cost of the additional production plus a reasonable profit. Credits ("RRC's") granted for reduction in resources consumed or provided offer the enterprise customer some comfort, but the savings on credits tend not to be equivalent to the increased costs when paying for incremental resources in excess of the threshold.

Complementary Pricing

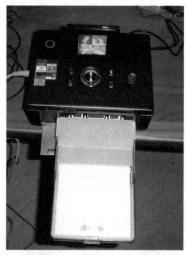

The purchase of a printer leads to a lifetime of purchases of replacement parts.
In such cases, complementary pricing may be considered

Complementary pricing is a collective term used to describe `captive-market' pricing tactics. It refers to a method in which one of two or more complementary products (a deskjet printer, for example) is priced to maximise sales volume, while the complementary product (printer ink cartridges) are priced at a much higher level in order to cover any shortfall sustained by the first product.

Contingency Pricing

Contingency pricing describes the process where a fee is only charged contingent on certain results. Contingency pricing is widely used in professional services such as legal services and consultancy services. In the United Kingdom, a contingency fee is known as a conditional fee.

Differential Pricing

Differential pricing is also known as flexible pricing, multiple pricing or price discrimination is where different prices dependent on the service provider's assessment of the customer's willingness or ability to pay. There are various forms of price difference including: the type of customer, quantity ordered, delivery time, payment terms, etc.

Discrete Pricing

Discrete Pricing occurs when prices are set at a level that the price comes within the competence of the decision making unit (DMU). This method of pricing is often used in B2B contexts where the purchasing officer may be authorized to make purchases up to a predetermined level, beyond which decisions must go to a committee for authorization.

Discount Pricing

A discount is any form of reduction in price

Discount pricing is where the marketer or retailer offers a reduced price. Discounts in a variety of forms - e.g. quantity rebates, loyalty rebates, seasonal discounts, periodic or random discounts etc.

Diversionary Pricing

Diversionary Pricing is a variation of loss leading used extensively in services; a low price is charged on a basic service with the intention of recouping on the extras; can also refer to low prices on some parts of the service to develop an image of low price.

Everyday Low Prices (EDLP)

"Everyday Low Prices" are widely used in supermarkets

Everyday low prices refers to the practice of maintaining a regular low price-low price - in which consumers are not forced to wait for discounting or specials. This method is used by supermarkets.

Exit Fees

Exit Fees refer to a fee charged for customers who depart from the service process prior to natural completion. The objective of exit fees is to deter premature exit. Exit fees are often round in financial services, telecommunications services and aged care facilities. Regulatory authorities, around the globe, have often expressed their discontent with the practice of exit fees as it has the potential to be anti-competitive and restricts consumers' abilities to switch freely, but the practice has not been proscribed.

Experience Curve Pricing

Experience curve pricing occurs when a manufacturer prices a product or service at a low rate in order to obtain volume and with the expectation that the cost of production will decrease with the acquisition of manufacturing experience. This approach which is often used in the pricing of high technology products and services, is based on the insight that manufacturers learn to trim production costs over time in a phenomenon known as experience effects.

Geographic Pricing

Geographic pricing occurs when different prices are charged in different geographic markets for an identical product. For example, publishers often make text-books available at lower prices in Asian countries because average wages tend to be lower with implications for the customer's ability to pay.

Guaranteed Pricing

Guaranteed pricing is a variant of contingency pricing. It refers to the practice of including an undertaking or promise that certain results or outcomes will be achieved. For instance, some business consultants undertake to improve productivity or profitability by 10%. In the event that the result is not achieved, the client does not pay for the service.

High-low Pricing

High-low pricing refers to the practice of offering goods at a high price for a period of time, followed by offering the same goods at a low price for a predetermined time. This practice is widely used by chain stores selling homewares. The main disadvantage of the high-low tactic is that consumers tend to become aware of the price cycles and time their purchases to coincide with a low-price cycle.

Honeymoon Pricing

Honeymoon Pricing refers to the practice of using a low introductory price with subsequent price increases once relationship is established. The objective of honeymoon pricing is to "lock" customers into a long-term association with the vendor. This approach is widely used in situations where customer switching costs are relatively high such as in home loans and financial investments. It is also common in categories where a subscription model is used, especially if this is coupled with automatic regular payments, such as in newspaper and magazine subscriptions, cable TV, broadband and cell phone subscriptions and in utilities and insurance.

Loss Leader

A loss leader is a product that has a price set below the operating margin. Loss leadering is widely used in supermarkets and budget-priced retail outlets where the store as a means of generating store traffic. The low price is widely promoted and the store is prepared to take a small loss on an individual item, with an expectation that it will recoup that loss when customers purchase other higher priced-higher margin items. In service industries, loss leading may refer to the practice of charging a reduced price on the first order as an inducement and with anticipation of charging higher prices on subsequent orders.

Offset Pricing

Offset pricing (also known as *diversionary pricing*) is the service industry's equivalent of loss leadering. A service may price one component of the offer at a very low price with an expectation that it can recoup any losses by cross-selling additional services. For example, a carpet steam cleaning service may charge a very low basic price for the first three rooms, but charges higher prices for additional rooms, furniture and curtain cleaning. The operator may also try to cross-sell the client on additional services such as spot-cleaning products, or stain-resistant treatments for fabrics and carpets.

Parity Pricing

Parity pricing refers to the process of pricing a product at or near a rival's price in order to remain competitive.

Price Bundling

Xbox price bundle price

Price bundling (also known as product bundling) occurs where two or more products or services are priced as a package with a single price. There are several types of bundles: pure bundles where the goods can only be purchased as package or mixed bundles where the goods can be purchased individually or as a package. The prices of the bundle is typically less than when the two items are purchased separately.

Peak and off-Peak Pricing

Peak and off-peak pricing is a form of price discrimination where the price variation is due to some type of seasonal factor. The objective of peak and off peak pricing is to use prices to even out peaks and troughs in demand. Peak and off-peak pricing is widely used in tourism, travel and also in utilities such as electricity providers. Peak pricing has caught the public's imagination since the ride-sharing service provider, Uber, commenced using *surge pricing* and has sought to patent the technologies that support this approach.

Price Discrimination

Price discrimination is also known as variable pricing or differential pricing.

Price Lining

Price lining is the use of a limited number of prices for all product offered by a business. Price lining is a tradition started in the old five and dime stores in which everything cost either 5 or 10 cents. In price lining, the price remains constant but quality or extent of product or service adjusted to reflect changes in cost. The underlying rationale of this tactic is that these amounts are seen as suitable price points for a whole range of products by prospective customers. It has the advantage of ease of administering, but the disadvantage of inflexibility, particularly in times of inflation or unstable prices. Price lining continues to be widely used in department stores where customers often note racks of garments or accessories priced at predetermined price points e.g. separate racks of men's ties, where each rack is priced at $10, $20 and $40.

Penetration Pricing

Penetration pricing is an approach that can be considered at the time of market entry. In this approach, the price of a product is initially set low in an effort to penetrate the market quickly. Low prices and low margins also act as a deterrent, preventing potential rivals from entering the market since they would have to undercut the low margins to gain a foothold.

Prestige Pricing

Premium brands rarely discount due to the potential to tarnish the brand.
Instead they offer gift packs to provide customers with value

Prestige pricing is also known as *premium pricing* and occasionally *luxury pricing* or *high price maintenance* refers to the deliberate pursuit of a high price posture to create an image of quality.

Price Signalling

Price signalling is where the price is used as an indicator of some other attribute. For example, some travel resorts promote that when two adults make a booking, the kids stay for free. This type of pricing is designed to signal that the resort is a family friendly operation.

Price Skimming

Price skimming, also known as *skim-the-cream pricing* is a tactic that might be considered at market entry. The objective is to charge relatively high prices in order to recoup the cost of product development early in the life-cycle and before competitors enter the market.

Promotional Pricing

Promotional pricing is a temporary measure that involves setting prices at levels lower than normally charged for a good or service. Promotional pricing is sometimes a reaction to unforeseen circumstances, as when a downturn in demand leaves a company with excess stocks; or when competitive activity is making inroads into market share or profits.

Two-part Pricing

Two-part pricing is a variant of captive-market pricing used in service industries. Two part pricing breaks the actual price into two parts; a fixed service fee plus a variable consumption rate. Two- part pricing tactics are widely used by utility companies such as electricity, gas and water and services where there is a quasi- membership type relationship, credit cards where an annual fee is charged and theme parks where an entrance fee is charged for admission while the customer pays for rides and extras. One part of the price represents a membership fee or joining fee, while the second part represents the usage component.

Psychological Pricing

Psychological pricing is a range of tactics designed to have a positive psychological impact. Price tags using the terminal digit "9", ($9.99, $19.99 or $199.99) can be used to signal price points and bring an item in at just under the consumer's reservation price. Psychological pricing is widely used in a variety of retail settings.

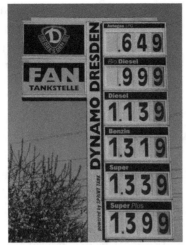

Extensive use of the terminal digit 'nine' suggests that psychological pricing is at play

Premium Pricing

Premium pricing (also called prestige pricing) is the strategy of consistently pricing at, or near, the high end of the possible price range to help attract status-conscious consumers. The high pricing of a premium product is used to enhance and reinforce a product's luxury image. Examples of companies which partake in premium pricing in the marketplace include Rolex and Bentley. As well as brand, product attributes such as eco-labelling and provenance (e.g. 'certified organic' and 'product of Australia') may add value for consumers and attract premium pricing. A component of such premiums may reflect the increased cost of production. People will buy a premium priced product because:

- They believe the high price is an indication of good quality;

- They believe it to be a sign of self-worth - "They are worth it;" it authenticates the buyer's success and status; it is a signal to others that the owner is a member of an exclusive group;

- They require flawless performance in this application - The cost of product malfunction is too high to buy anything but the best - for example, a heart pacemaker.

The old association of luxury only being for the kings and queens of the world is almost non-existent in today's world. People have generally become wealthier, therefore the mass marketing phenomenon of luxury has simply become a part of everyday life, and no longer reserved for the elite. Since consumers have a larger source of disposable income, they now have the power to purchase products that meet their aspirational needs. This phenomenon enables premium pricing opportunities for marketers in luxury markets. Luxurification in society can be seen when middle class members of society, are willing to pay premium prices for a service or product of the highest quality when compared with similar goods. Examples of this can be seen with items such as clothing and electronics. Charging a premium price for a product also makes it more inaccessible and helps it gain an exclusive appeal. Luxury brands such as Louis Vuitton and Gucci are more than just clothing and become more of a status symbol.

Prestige goods are usually sold by companies that have a monopoly on the market and hold competitive advantage. Due to a firm having great market power they are able to charge at a premium for goods, and are able to spend a larger sum on promotion and advertising. According to Han, Nunes and Dreze figure on "signal preference and taxonomy based on wealth and need for status" two social groups known as "Parvenus" and "Poseurs" are individuals generally more self-conscious, and base purchases on a need to reach a higher status or gain a social prestige value. Further market research shows the role of possessions in consumer's lives and how people make assumptions about others solely based on their possessions. People associate high priced items with success. Marketers understand this concept, and price items at a premium to create the illusion of exclusivity and high quality. Consumers are likely to purchase a product at a higher price than a similar product as they crave the status, and feeling of superiority as being part of a minority that can in fact afford the said product.

A price premium can also be charged to consumers when purchasing eco-labelled products. Market based incentives are given in order to encourage people to practice their business in an eco-friendly way in regard to the environment. Associations such as the MSC's fishery certification programme and seafood ecolabel reward those who practice sustainable fishing. Pressure from environmental groups have caused the implementation of Associations such as these, rather than consumers demanding it. The value consumer's gain from purchasing environmentally conscious products may create a premium price over non eco-labelled products. This means that producers have some sort of incentive for supplying goods worthy of eco-labelling standard. Usually more costs are incurred when practicing sustainable business, and charging at a premium is a way businesses can recover extra costs.

Methods of Setting Prices

Demand-based Pricing

Demand-based pricing, also known as dynamic pricing, is a pricing method that uses consumer demand - based on perceived value - as the central element. These include price skimming, price discrimination and yield management, price points, psychological pricing, bundle pricing, penetration pricing, price lining, value-based pricing, geo and premium pricing.

Pricing factors are manufacturing cost, market place, competition, market condition, quality of product.

Price modeling using econometric techniques can help measure price elasticity, and computer based modeling tools will often facilitate simulations of different prices and the outcome on sales and profit. More sophisticated tools help determine price at the SKU level across a portfolio of products. Retailers will optimize the price of their private label SKUs with those of National Brands.

Uber's pricing policy is an example of demand-based dynamic pricing. It uses an automated algorithm to increase prices to surge price levels, responding rapidly to changes of supply and demand in the market. By responding in real time, an equilibrium between demand and supply of drivers can be approached. Customers receive notice when making an Uber reservation that prices have increased. The company applied for a U.S. patent on surge pricing in 2013, though airlines are known to have been using similar techniques in seat pricing for years.

The practice has often caused passengers to become upset and invited criticism when it happens as a result of holidays, inclement weather, natural disasters or other factors. During New Year's Eve 2011, Uber prices were as high as seven times normal rates, causing outrage. During the 2014 Sydney hostage crisis, Uber implemented surge pricing, resulting in fares of up to four times normal charges; while it defended the surge pricing at first, it later apologized and refunded the surcharges. Uber CEO Travis Kalanick has responded to criticism by saying: "because this is so new, it's going to take some time for folks to accept it. There's 70 years of conditioning around the fixed price of taxis."

Multidimensional Pricing

Multidimensional pricing is the pricing of a product or service using multiple numbers. In this practice, price no longer consists of a single monetary amount (e.g., sticker price of a car), but rather consists of various dimensions (e.g., monthly payments, number of payments, and a down payment). Research has shown that this practice can significantly influence consumers' ability to understand and process price information.

Micromarketing

Micromarketing is the practice of tailoring products, brands (microbrands), and promotions to meet the needs and wants of microsegments within a market. It is a type of market customization that deals with pricing of customer/product combinations at the store or individual level.

Theoretical Considerations in Pricing

Price/Quality Relationship

The price/quality relationship comprises consumers' perceptions of value. High prices are often taken as a sign of quality, especially when the product or service lacks search qualities that can be inspected prior to purchase. Understanding consumers' perceptions of the price/quality relationship is most important in the case of complex products that are hard to test, and experiential products that cannot be tested until used (such as most services). The greater the uncertainty surrounding a product, the more consumers depend on the price/quality signal and the greater premium they may be prepared to pay.

News report by Voice of America about ticket prices at the 2016 World Series, the first world series game.

Consumers can have different perceptions on premium pricing, and this factor makes it important for the marketer to understand consumer behaviour. According to Vigneron and Johnson's figure on "Prestige-Seeking Consumer Behaviours", Consumers can be categorised into four groups. These groups being; Hedonist & Perfectionist, snob, bandwagon and veblenian. These categories rank from level of self-consciousness, to importance of price as an indicator of prestige. The Veblen Effect explains how this group of consumers makes purchase decisions based on conspicuous value, as they tend to purchase publicly consumed luxury products. This shows they are likely to make the purchase to show power, status and wealth. Consumers that fall under the "Snob Effect" can be described as individuals that search for perceived unique value, and will purchase exclusive products in order to be the first or very few who has it. They will also avoid purchasing products consumed by a general mass of people, as it is perceived that items in limited supply hold a higher value than items that do not. The bandwagon effect explains that consumers that fit into this category make purchasing decisions to fit into a social group, and gain a perceived social value out of purchasing popular products within said social group at premium prices. Research shows that people will often conform to what the majority of the group they are a member of thinks when it comes to the attitude of a product. Paying a premium price for a product can act as a way of gaining acceptance, due to the pressure placed on them by their peers. The Hedonic effect can be described as a certain group of people whose purchasing decisions are not affected by the status and exclusivity gained by purchasing a product at a premium, nor susceptible to the fear of being left out and peer pressure. Consumers who fit into this category base their purchasing decisions on a perceived emotional value, and gain intangible benefits such as sensory pleasure, aesthetic beauty and excitement. Consumers of this type have a higher interest on their own wellbeing. The last category on Vigneron and Johnson's figure of

"Prestige-Seeking Consumer Behaviours" is the perfectionism effect. Prestige brands are expected to show high quality, and it's this reassurance of the highest quality that can actually enhance the value of the product. According to this effect, those that fit into this group value the prestige's brands to have a superior quality and higher performance than other similar brands. Research has indicated that consumer's perceive quality of a product to be relational to its price. Consumers often believe a high price of a product indicates a higher level of quality.

Even though it is suggested that high prices seem to make certain products more desirable, consumers that fall in this category have their own perception of quality and make decisions based upon their own judgement. They may also use the premium price as an indicator of the product's level of quality.

Price Sensitivity and Consumer Psychology

In their book, *The Strategy and Tactics of Pricing*, Thomas Nagle and Reed Holden outline nine laws or factors that influence how a consumer perceives a given price and how price-sensitive she/he is likely to be with respect to different purchase decisions:

- Reference price effect: Buyer's price sensitivity for a given product increases the higher the product's price relative to perceived alternatives. Perceived alternatives can vary by buyer segment, by occasion, and other factors.

- Difficult comparison effect Buyers are less sensitive to the price of a known/ more reputable product when they have difficulty comparing it to potential alternatives.

- Switching costs effect: The higher the product-specific investment a buyer must make to switch suppliers, the less price sensitive that buyer is when choosing between alternatives.

- Price-quality effect: Buyers are less sensitive to price the more that higher prices signal higher quality. Products for which this effect is particularly relevant include: image products, exclusive products, and products with minimal cues for quality.

- Expenditure effect: Buyers are more price sensitive when the expense accounts for a large percentage of buyers' available income or budget.

- End-benefit effect: The effect refers to the relationship a given purchase has to a larger overall benefit, and is divided into two parts:

  o Derived demand: The more sensitive buyers are to the price of the end benefit, the more sensitive they will be to the prices of those products that contribute to that benefit.

- o Price proportion cost: The price proportion cost refers to the percent of the total cost of the end benefit accounted for by a given component that helps to produce the end benefit (e.g., think CPU and PCs). The smaller the given components share of the total cost of the end benefit, the less sensitive buyers will be to the component's price.

- Shared-cost effect: The smaller the portion of the purchase price buyers must pay for themselves, the less price sensitive they will be.

- Fairness effect: Buyers are more sensitive to the price of a product when the price is outside the range they perceive as "fair" or "reasonable" given the purchase context.

- Framing effect: Buyers are more price sensitive when they perceive the price as a loss rather than a forgone gain, and they have greater price sensitivity when the price is paid separately rather than as part of a bundle.

Approaches

Pricing is the most effective profit lever. Pricing can be approached at three levels: the industry, market, and transaction level:

- Pricing at the industry level focuses on the overall economics of the industry, including supplier price changes and customer demand changes.

- Pricing at the market level focuses on the competitive position of the price in comparison to the value differential of the product to that of comparative competing products.

- Pricing at the transaction level focuses on managing the implementation of discounts away from the reference, or list price, which occur both on and off the invoice or receipt.

A "price waterfall" analysis helps businesses and sales personnel to understand the differences which arise between the reference or list price, the invoiced sale price and the actual price paid by a customer taking account of contract, sales and payment discounts.

Pricing Mistakes

Many companies make common pricing mistakes. Jerry Bernstein's, *Use Suppliers' Pricing Mistakes* outlines several sales errors, which include:

- Weak controls on discounting (price override);

- Inadequate systems for tracking competitors' selling prices and market share (Competitive intelligence);

- Cost-plus pricing;

- Price increases poorly executed;

- Worldwide price inconsistencies;

- Paying sales representatives on sales volume vs. addition of revenue measures.

Promotion

Promotion is the marketing term used to describe all marketing communications activities and includes personal selling, sales promotion, public relations, direct marketing, trade fairs and exhibitions, advertising and sponsorship. Promotion needs to be precisely coordinated and integrated into the businesses global communications message, and this is called Integrated Marketing Communications (IMC). IMC integrates the message through the available channels to deliver a consistent and clear message about your company's brands, products and services. Any movement away from the single message confuses the consumer and undermines the brand.

The promotions mix (the marketing communications mix) is the specific blend of promotion tools that the company uses to persuasively communicate customer value and build customer relationships.

Promotion is the element of the marketing mix which is entirely responsible for communicating the marketing proposition. Marketers work hard to create a unique marketing proposition for their product or service. McDonald's is about community, food and enjoyment. Audi is about the driver experience and technology.

Think of it like a cake mix, the basic ingredients are always the same. However if you vary the amounts of one of the ingredients, the final outcome is different. It is the same with promotions. You can integrate different aspects of the promotions mix to deliver a unique campaign. Now let's look at the different elements of the promotions mix.

The elements of the promotions mix are:

- Personal Selling.

- Sales Promotion.

- Public Relations.

- Direct Mail.

- Trade Fairs and Exhibitions.

- Advertising.

- Sponsorship.

And also online promotions.

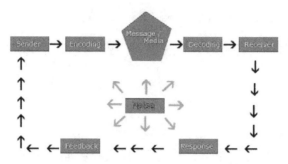

Communications Process / Marketing Communications Process

The elements of the promotions mix are integrated to form a coherent campaign. As with all forms of communication, the message from the marketer follows the 'communications process' as illustrated above. For example, a radio advert is made for a car manufacturer. The car manufacturer (sender) pays for a specific advert with contains a message specific to a target audience (encoding). It is transmitted during a set of commercials from a radio station (message/medium).

The message is decoded by a car radio (decoding) and the target consumer interprets the message (receiver). He or she might visit a dealership or seek further information from a web site (Response). The consumer might buy a car or express an interest or dislike (feedback). This information will inform future elements of an integrated promotional campaign. Perhaps a direct mail campaign would push the consumer to the point of purchase. Noise represents the thousands of marketing communications that a consumer is exposed to everyday, all competing for attention.

The Promotions Mix

Let us look at the individual components of the promotions mix in more detail. Remember all of the elements are 'integrated' to form a specific communications campaign.

Personal Selling

Personal Selling is an effective way to manage personal customer relationships. The sales person acts on behalf of the organization. They tend to be well trained in the approaches and techniques of personal selling. However sales people are very expensive and should only be used where there is a genuine return on investment. For example salesmen are often used to sell cars or home improvements where the margin is high.

Sales Promotion

Sales promotions tend to be thought of as being all promotions apart from advertising, personal selling, and public relations. For example, the BOGOF promotion, or Buy One Get One Free. Others include couponing, money-off promotions, competitions, free accessories (such as free blades with a new razor), introductory offers (such as buy digital TV and get free installation), and so on. Each sales promotion should be carefully costed and compared with the next best alternative.

Public Relations (PR)

Public Relations is defined as 'the deliberate, planned and sustained effort to establish and maintain mutual understanding between an organization and its publics' (Institute of Public Relations). PR can be relatively cheap, but it is certainly not free. Successful strategies tend to be long-term and plan for all eventualities. All airlines exploit PR; just watch what happens when there is an incident. The pre-planned PR machine clicks in very quickly with a very effective rehearsed plan.

Direct Marketing

Direct marketing is any marketing undertaken without a distributor or intermediary. In terms of promotion it means that the marketing company has direct communication with the customer. For example, Nintendo distributes via retailers, although you can register directly with them for information which is often delivered by e-mail or mail.

Direct mail is very highly focussed upon targeting consumers based upon a database. As with all marketing, the potential consumer is targeted based upon a series of attributes and similarities. Creative agencies work with marketers to design a highly focussed communication in the form of a mailing. The mail is sent out to the potential consumers and responses are carefully monitored. For example, if you are marketing medical text books, you would use a database of doctors' surgeries as the basis of your mail shot.

Similarly e-mail is a form of online direct marketing. You register, or opt in, to join a mailing list for your favourite website. You confirm that you have opted in, and then you will receive newsletters and e-mails based upon your favourite topics. You need to be able to unsubscribe at any time, or opt out. Mailing lists which generate sales are like gold dust to the online marketer. Make sure that you use a mailing list with integrity just as you would expect when you sign up. The mailing list needs to be kept up-to-date, and often forms the basis of online Customer Relationship Management (CRM).

Trade Fairs and Exhibitions

Such approaches are very good for making new contacts and renewing old ones. Companies will seldom sell much at such events. The purpose is to increase awareness and to encourage trial. They offer the opportunity for companies to meet with both the trade and the consumer.

Advertising

Advertising is a 'paid for' communication. It is used to develop attitudes, create awareness, and transmit information in order to gain a response from the target market. There are many advertising 'media' such as newspapers (local, national, free, trade), magazines and journals, television (local, national, terrestrial, satellite) cinema, outdoor advertising (such as posters, bus sides). There is much more about digital, online and Internet advertising further down this pages, as well as throughout Marketing Teacher and the Marketing Teacher Blog.

Sponsorship

Sponsorship is where an organization pays to be associated with a particular event, cause or image. Companies will sponsor sports events such as the Olympics or Formula One. The attributes of the event are then associated with the sponsoring organization.

The elements of the promotional mix are then integrated to form a unique, but coherent campaign.

Online Promotions

Online promotions will include many of the promotions mix elements which we considered above. For example advertising exists online with pay per click advertising which is marketed by Google. You can sponsor are website for example. Online businesses regularly send out newsletters which are targeted using e-mail and mailing lists, which is a form of direct marketing. Indeed websites are premium vehicle in the public relations industry to communicate particular points of view to relevant publics.

Online promotions field is indeed emerging. The field will soon spread into Geo targeting of adverts to people in specific locations via smart phones. Another example would be how social media targets adverts to you whilst you socialising online. Take a look at Marketing Teacher's Blog for more up-to-date examples of the emerging online promotions space.

Importance of Promotion

Market Share

If you increase advertising and promotion expenditures, you stand a good chance of capturing market share, especially if your competition is cutting back on ad spending. You let the buying customer know that you are maintaining a robust effort to remain vital in the marketplace.

Higher Sales Growth

Businesses that increase advertising and promotion during recessions actually experience higher sales growth during the recession and for three years after, according to Paul Dunay of Marketing Profs. This could be because customers are more willing to shop around during tough economic times.

Increasing Value to the Customer

Increasing your advertising and promotions forces you to think about offering more value to the customer. You need something to advertise, and the best thing to advertise is better value. If you can find a way to put goods and services on sale, bundle services to customers who spend more and promote special offers, you can increase value to the customer and drive sales higher.

Improved Reputation

Your visibility through advertising and promotion builds your reputation with the customer. You draw customers to you, because they read the signal of increased advertising and promotion as increased success of your business. Although most advertising is through word of mouth, that word of mouth starts with awareness that customers have gained about you through your advertising and promotions.

Innovation

Trying to increase your advertising and promotions can be an inspiration to get more creative, especially if money is tight. For example, you could add labels to your products with your contact information. This allows the customer to contact you or pass your name along to potential customers. You can also write articles online, participate in community fairs and hold drawings. These relatively inexpensive advertising and promotion methods arise out of your desire to increase advertising when you don't have the budget for it.

Effective Communication

Marketing communication (MarCom) is a fundamental and complex part of a company's marketing efforts. Loosely defined, MarCom can be described as all the messages and media you deploy to communicate with the market.

Marketing communication includes advertising, direct marketing, branding, packaging, your online presence, printed materials, PR activities, sales presentations, sponsorships, trade show appearances and more.

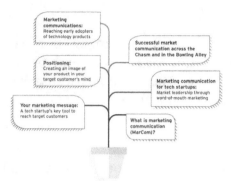

marketing communication series

The complexity of the MarCom topic makes it too broad to cover in this topic. This is one in a series of six that covers the field of marketing communication. The full list of the titles in this series includes:

- What is marketing communication (MarCom)?—outlines the basic marketing communication concepts and provides the foundation for rest of the series;

- Positioning—discusses the ins and outs and importance of claiming the most attractive position in your customer's mind;

- Your marketing message—provides the framework for planning your marketing message throughout the technology adoption lifecycle (TALC);

- Marketing communication for tech startups—describes the process and methods to develop word-of-mouth marketing in the marketplace;

- Marketing communications: Reaching early adopters of technology products—focuses on how (and why) you should tailor your message for technology enthusiasts and visionaries;

- Successful market communication across the Chasm and in the Bowling Alley—explains the tactics that will help you cross the Chasm.

Marketing Communication Objectives

Marketing communication has two objectives: One is to create and sustain demand and preference for the product. The other is to shorten the sales cycle.

Creating Preference

Creating preference is often a longer-term effort that aims at using communication tools to help position your product or company in the minds of the target customer.

Positioning and building a brand takes time and requires a certain consistency (not just in the communication efforts themselves, but also in regards to the core elements of product, pricing, and distribution) and therefore represents a significant commitment for the company.

Remember, establishing preference by building a brand will impact market share, profitability and even your access to talent—and thus provides long-term value for the company.

From positioning to communication

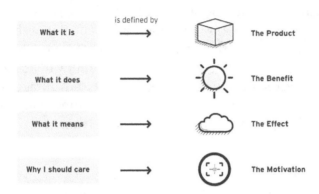

	is defined by	
What it is	→	The Product
What it does	→	The Benefit
What it means	→	The Effect
Why I should care	→	The Motivation

Shortening the Sales Cycle

Shortening the sales cycle means assisting your sales and channel partners in their efforts to identify, engage and deliver a customer. Understanding the customer's buying process brings critical insight into how one can shorten the sales cycle.

The figure below illustrates the process the buyer goes through when buying a product. Through market research and conversations with salespersons, MarCom staff must identify how they can help speed up the process.

In the case of high-tech products, the sales cycle involves considerable amounts of customer education in the early stages of the process. MarCom must focus on creating, packaging and delivering relevant information to the buyer throughout the buying process in order to sales meet this education need.

The buying process

Problem recognition › Information searches › Evaluate alternatives › Purchase decision › Post-purchase evaluation

In general, the communication techniques employed to shorten the sales cycle are by nature more tactical than those used in building a brand. Nevertheless, your strategy to achieve the two MarCom objectives must be balanced, or the legitimacy of your plan will be questioned if one objective takes priority over the other.

Direct Marketing

In direct marketing the producer communicates directly with potential customers, instead of through third party media. Individual customer's responses and transactions are recorded. Direct marketing is a growing form of marketing communication. It is designed to build the relationship between the customer and the brand, known as customer relationship management (CRM). Organizations use customer accounts in order to monitor and understand their needs. They manage detailed information about the customer's touch points with the objective to maximize satisfaction and loyalty. The communication can be in person, by telephone, mail, email or website. The interaction between the organization and the customer is usually a two-way communication. Direct marketing relies on CRM databases which contain valuable customer information. Good quality databases can provide a competitive advantage and increase profitability. Treating the customer database as an expense rather than an investment, or not continuously maintaining or updating them can be detrimental.

Direct Mail

Direct mail is a letter, card, catalogue, or sample sent through post, email, fax, or courier. This communication is most effective when the recipient has shown interest in or has previously purchased from the organization. Advantages of direct mail are personalisation, careful targeting, creativity and flexibility. Email is low-cost, but can be lost through spam and junk email filters. Direct mail is dependent on accurate databases.

Telemarketing

Telemarketing is marketing communication via telephone. There are two types of telemarketing: outbound and inbound, outbound telemarketing is used by organizations to reach out to potential customers, generate sales, make appointments with salespeople and introduce new products. Inbound telemarketing is where people call the organization to complain or inquire about products. Both outbound and inbound can be used as a customer service strategy to boost sales and receive suggestions for improvement. Advantages of telemarketing include targeted communications, flexible and direct interaction between the organization and the customer, it can be an effective personal selling partner and it is cost effective compared to face-to-face contact. A disadvantage is that call centres are usually used to handle outbound and inbound telemarketing, which need to be implemented, managed and financed.

Mail Order

Mail order marketing is a catalogue of products that customers can order to receive in the mail. This form of direct marketing dates back over 100 years. Home shopping, online shopping and teleshopping now accompany it. With current technology mail order has improved. Now there can be a larger range in catalogue, delivery is faster, and complaints are dealt with professionally. Mail order exerts less pressure on the customer than telemarketing and sales are easy to manage, however costly infrastructure is required in maintaining the back-end.

Direct-response Advertising

Direct-response advertising is partially direct marketing. It is a message transmitted through traditional communications media that requires the reader, viewer, listener or customer to respond directly to the organization. The audience may respond to receive more information or to purchase a product. A common example of direct response advertising is in television "home shopping immediately to receive a particular deal or discount. Disadvantages are that focus can be lost because of the medium of communication and the targeting can be less narrow compared to direct mail. Organizational messages can get cluttered and crowded.

Cellular Marketing

Cellular marketing uses audience's mobile phone and SMS to promote a product or brand. Advantages are a high level of flexibility and easy integration through computer systems using the Internet to send mass text messages. This marketing communications platform allows organizations to directly target customers to remind them to renew subscriptions, give exclusive product discounts, or build brand reputation through competitions or sweepstakes. The disadvantage is that some customers are charged to receive SMS, so opt-in permission is required.

CD/DVD Technology

CD and DVD discs can be used as part of e-communications. Entire marketing presentations, catalogues, brochures and price lists can be stored on a CD. CDs are small and simple to hand out to target audiences and most modern computers have CD drive readers, however most of the same information can be presented on a website or email.

Integrated Marketing Communications

Integrated marketing communications (IMC) is the use of marketing strategies to optimise the communication of a consistent message of the company's brands to stakeholders. Coupling methods together improves communication as it harnesses the benefits of each channel, which when combined together builds a clearer and vaster impact than if used individually. IMC requires marketers to identify the boundaries around the promotional mix elements and to consider the effectiveness of the campaign's message.

In the mid to late 1980s, the marketing environment was undergoing profound environmental changes with implications for marketing communications. Media proliferation, audience fragmentation, globalisation of markets, the advent of new communications technologies, the widespread use of databases meant that the old methods, and practices used in mass marketing were no longer relevant. In particular, the rise of digital and interactive media meant that marketers were relying less on advertising as the dominant form of marketing communications. Amongst practitioners and scholars, there was an increasing recognition that new approaches to marketing communications were required. That new approach would become known as *integrated marketing communications*. A number of empirical studies, carried out in the early 1990s, found that the new IMC was far from a "short-lived managerial fad, but rather was a very clear reaction by advertisers and marketers to the changing external environment.

Integrated marketing communications is a holistic planning process that focuses on integrating messages across communications disciplines, creative executions, media, timing and stakeholders. An integrated approach has emerged as the dominant approach used by companies to plan and execute their marketing communication programs and has been described as a *paradigm shift*.

IMC unifies and coordinates the organizations marketing communications to promote a consistent brand message. Coordinating the brands communications makes the brand seem more trustworthy and sound as it is seen as a 'whole' rather than a mixture of different messages being sent out. The IMC perspective looks at the 'big picture' in marketing, advertising and promotions.

The impetus to rethink marketing communications came from a number of environmental changes that were becoming increasingly apparent throughout the mid to late 1980s. Media was proliferating and at the same time converging, audiences were fragmenting and many new communications disciplines were emerging. Few advertising agencies provided the full suite of services in terms of the varied communications disciplines. Companies were reliant on a multiplicity of service providers for assistance with advertising, public-relations, branding, packaging, sales promotion, event organisers and other promotional activities. Each of these communications disciplines was treated as a "silo"; with little thought to the synergies between them,with the result that many different stakeholders involved in presenting the company's external image throughout the breadth and length of a campaign. In that environment, both practitioners and theorists recognised the potential for confusing or inconsistent brand images to develop across media and across different communications disciplines. The fragmentation of audiences presented marketers with particular challenges. No longer were they able to communicate with mass markets via mass media; instead they needed to communicate with increasingly tightly defined market segments, using highly specialist media and communications disciplines. New media and the use of databases were enabling marketers to communicate with customers on a one-to-one basis. The old methods and practices associated with mass communications were failing to serve the realities of the new era. The imperative to present a clear, coherent and unified narrative in both internal and external communications was becoming increasingly apparent by the late 1980s.

In 1989, two discrete events served to draw attention to the fact that industry attitudes to marketing communications were shifting. Firstly, the consulting firm, Shearson-Lehman Hutton published a report on the subject of consumer advertising, signalling that a number of market-place changes would force packaged goods marketers to adopt a more integrated approach to marketing communications. Their report also noted that high-end manufacturers (e.g. automobiles) and up-market services (e.g. cruise vacations) were more inclined to use integrated promotions. Secondly, the American Association of Advertising Agencies (4A's), instituted a task-force to investigate integrated marketing communications (IMC), with the result that the first official definition was published. The AAAA defined IMC as, "a concept of marketing communications planning that recognizes the added value of a comprehensive plan that evaluates the strategic roles of a variety of communication disciplines (e.g. general advertising, direct response, sales promotion, and public relations) and combines these disciplines to provide clarity, consistency, and maximum communication impact." At this stage, the development of IMC, focused primarily on the need for organisations to offer more than just standard advertising and to integrate the various communications disciplines. The 4As originally coined the term the new advertising; however, this title did not appropriately incorporate many other aspects included in the term IMC – most notably, those beyond traditional advertising process aside from simply advertising.

In 1991, the faculty of Medill School of Journalism, Northwestern University in conjunction with the AAAA, began the first empirical research study designed to investigate how IMC was being used. The study focused around understanding the concept and the importance of IMC and also to analyse the extent in which IMC was practiced in all major U.S advertising agencies.

The Medill School at Northwestern was the first university to teach course in integrated marketing communications

This initial study was then replicated by other studies with a view to examining how IMC was being used in other countries; New Zealand, UK, US, Australia, India, Thailand, South Africa and the Philippines, etc. The findings from these studies demonstrated that the new IMC was far from a "short-lived managerial fad" but rather was "a very clear reaction by advertising agencies and their clients as they are affected by a multitude of factors such as new forms of information technology including development and usage of databases, media fragmentation, client desires for interaction/synergy, and global and regional coordination." This was the second stage of IMC's development, where the focus shifted to documenting the practice of IMC as a global phenonenon. In other words, researchers were attempting to codify practices that had been used for some time.

In 1993, Don Schultz and his team published the first text-book dedicated to IMC. Their work, simply entitled, Integrated Marketing Communications, described IMC as a totally new way of looking at the whole of marketing communications, rather than looking at each of the parts separately. And, in the same year, the Medill School at Northwestern University changed their curriculum to include a focus on this new idea of integrated marketing communications rather than the traditional program which had emphasised advertising. IMC emerged from an "academic department that, for several decades, had been recognized as the number one advertising program. Since the mid-1990s, virtually every text-book on the subject of marketing communications has adopted an integrated perspective or has added chapters on IMC in new editions of standard works. Collectively these books focus on the IMC planning processes and this represents the third distinct stage in the evolution of IMC – an emphasis on managing and organising IMC.

Over time, scholars have advanced different definitions of IMC, with each definition exhibiting a slightly different emphasis. Yet, in spite of the variety of definitions in circulation, there is general consensus that integrated marketing communications should be viewed as a planning process. Some scholars have pointed out that because IMC is both a process and a concept, it is exceedingly difficult to define.

Some of the key definitions that have been advanced during IMC's evolution are outlined here:

- "IMC is the process of all sources and information managed so a consumer or prospect is exposed which behaviorally moves the customer more towards a sale."

- "The strategic co-ordination of all messages and media used by an organisation to influence its perceived brand value."

- "The process of strategically controlling or influencing all messages and encoring purposeful dialogue to created and nourish profitable relationships with consumers and other stakeholders."

- One-voice marketing communications is integration that creates a clear and consistent image, position, message, or theme across all marketing communication disciplines or tools. Integrated communications refers to the creation of both a brand image and a behavioural response that emanate directly from marketing communications materials such as advertisements. Coordinated marketing communications associates 'integrated' with the concept of 'coordination'.

- "IMC is a strategic business process used to plan, develop, execute and evaluate coordinate measurable persuasive brand communication programs over time with consumers, customers and prospects, and other that are targeted, relevant internal and external audiences."

- "IMC is the concept and process of strategically managing audience-focused, channel-centred, and results-driven brand communication programmes over time."

- "An IMC program plans and executes various marketing activities with consistency so that its total impact exceeds the sum of each activity. It is a strategy in which different communication tools like advertising, public relations, sales promotion, direct marketing and personal selling work together to maximize the communication impact on target consumers."

- "IMC is the planning and execution of all types of advertising-like and promotion-like messages selected for a brand, service, or company, in order to meet a common set of communication objectives, or more particularly, to support a single 'positioning'."

Today, there is general agreement amongst both practitioners and scholars that the emergence of IMC represents "a significant example of development in the marketing discipline that has influenced thinking and acting among all types of companies and organizations facing the realities of competition in an open economy." Belch and Belch argue that IMC has become the dominant approach used by companies to plan and execute their marketing communication programs while other scholars have described IMC as a paradigm shift. Larry Percy argues that "the planning and execution of *all* marketing communication should be integrated".

Meaning of Integration

Integrating the creative and the media can result in imaginative and
powerful messages that grab attention and are noticed

Within the literature there is no absolute agreement about the meaning of "integration" in the concept, "integrated marketing communications". The concept of IMC has evolved during its brief history, and with that different ideas around the meaning of integration have been advanced. The diverse views surrounding IMC and its meaning can be explained by the early state of theoretical development and research on IMC which gives rise to a mulplicity of different perspectives. As the discipline matures, these different views are expected to converge.

The marketing and advertising literature identifies many different types of integration:

- Functional integration

   Functional integration refers to the capacity of the different promotional tools to complement each other and deliver a unified, coherent message. Each of the communications disciplines (advertising, PR, personal selling, sales promotion etc.) has its own strengths and weaknesses. For instance, it is generally recognised that straight advertising is very effective at creating brand awareness, but much less effective at converting awareness into actual sales. As consumers approach the actual purchase, they may turn to other types of promotion such as personal selling or direct marketing. A carefully planned communications program will include a blend of tools in a way that the messages move the customer through the various stages of the purchase decision – from need recognition through to purchase and post-purchase stages. Integrating the communications disciplines addresses the question of how the strengths of one discipline can be used to overcome the weaknesses of a different discipline.

- Message integration

   Message integration is also known as *image integration* or *creative integration*. A key task for IMC is ensuring consistency in executions within and across the different types of marketing communications, as well as over time. Everything connected with an IMC campaign should have a similar 'look and feel', irrespective of the medium or tool. Message integration does not imply that messages need to identical. Rather it means that every piece of promotion – from advertising to direct mail to collateral materials to packaging to posters to corporate vehicles to business cards and office stationery – should be immediately recognisable as part of the same livery.

   Clearly, media releases which are often part of a PR program are very different to persuasive messages used in advertising. However, messages should include a similar tone and at least some common elements so that each message looks like it is part of a coherent, integrated campaign. Every execution is part of the brand's identity. Consistent executions facilitate brand awareness. People associate the 'look' of the brand's marketing communication with the brand itself. Consistent executions are more of a 'feeling' that ties everything together;

a unique look or feel so that the target audience recognizes a brand's marketing communication even before they see the brand name. The key to consistency is the visual feel. This is because the visual memory for the imagery associated with the brand actually elicits faster brand identification than the brand name itself.

- Media integration

Much IMC planning is concerned with co-ordinating different media channels to optimize the effectiveness of marketing communications programmes. If brand communications "reflect implied brand values and imagery that are consistent throughout differing media channels, then clearly these channels act in a mutually reinforcing way with each successive consumer engagement." Certain messages may not translate into other media. For instance, messages containing 'sex appeals' may work well on TV because movement lends itself to eroticism, but may become flat in a static medium such as print. In such cases it is important that the secondary media support the primary media and that messages harmonise.

Research studies suggest that consumers learn more quickly when exposed to messages via different media. The explanation for this is that slight variations in execution create a slight mental perturbation which grabs attention, and results in more elaborate encoding of the main message argument. By exposing consumers to the same message through multiple media, there are more opportunities to engage with consumers. In short, a multi media strategy is more effective.

- Integration of timing

Integration of timing refers to the timing messages so that they operate to support each other and reach potential customers at different junctures, depending on when they are most receptive to different types of message or depending on the consumer's readiness to buy.

Other Types of Integration

- Coordinated integration refers to the ways that different internal and external agencies (e.g web designers, advertising agencies, PR consultants, graphic designers) coordinate to provide a consistent message.

- Stakeholder integration refers to the way that all stakeholders (e.g. employees, suppliers, customers and others) cooperate to communicate a shared understanding of the company's key messages and values.

- Relationship integration refers to the way that communications professionals (e.g. marketing managers, advertising managers) contribute to the company's overall corporate goals and quality management.

Criticisms

Both practitioners and scholars agree that IMC makes practical "good sense". Consequently, the discipline has relatively few critics. Nevertheless, researchers have pointed to areas that are in need of further research, and highlight some of the discipline's deficiencies:

- Some practitioners and scholars argue that IMC is not new. Skeptics point out that the more experienced communications managers, especially national brand managers, have always practiced integration.

- A more serious criticism of IMC concerns the problem of measurement. The value of IMC activities has proved very difficult to measure due to the interactions of different communications tools. A growing number of scholars agree that the lack of rigorous measurement metrics and methods represents a major challenge for the discipline.

Studies have shown that, while managers are familiar with the IMC concept in theory, it is not widely practiced. Such findings suggest that IMC is easy to understand, but difficult to do. One possible explanation for the slow uptake is that organizational barriers to implementation may have become entrenched and are difficult to overcome. A number of organizational characteristics have been cited as possible barriers to implementation. These factors include: a mind-set that has been built up over the years which promotes specialization rather than integration; organizational structure which has been designed to manage specialisms (e.g. advertising, PR as separate branches); manager ability and lack of skills in integration; agency remuneration systems and the adequacy of budgets.

Marketing Communications Framework

The marketing communications planning framework (MCPF) is a model for the creation of an ICM plan. Created by Chris Fill, senior examiner for the Chartered Institute of Marketing, the MCPF is intended to solve the inadequacies of other frameworks.

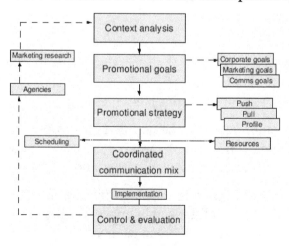

IMC planning Approaches

Inside–out Approach

An "inside-out" approach is the traditional planning approach to marketing communication. Planning begins "inside" the organisation by identifying the goals and objectives which are often based around what has always been done. Communication's task then becomes a process of "selling" the organisation's message to the "outside" or external stakeholders.

The inside–out approach to integrated marketing communications has been criticised as a one sided view point, since it combines the elements of communication and marketing to create a single unified message. Porcu and his team point out that many of the first, tentative attempts to practice IMC were primarily concerned with integrating the message, so that to organisation appeared to speak with "one voice," but failed to adopt a more rounded customer orientation. The inside–out approach is weak due to the stagnant, outdated method.

Outside–in Approach

The outside–in approach of integrated marketing communications seeks to understand the needs and wants of the consumer. In addition to the previous category, this approach establishes significant progression. Organisations can gain in-depth knowledge based on consumers and therefore can accommodate the way they approach to fulfil their requirements. Relationship marketing aids in building up a history of frequent conversation between organisations and stakeholders which contributes to trust. Communication builds rapport that could prove to be profitable as they retain clientele. The outside-in approach offers a unique way to planning, as it operates backwards by concentrating on customers first, then determining the most effective course of marketing and communication methods to implement. Effectively managing the strategic business process is crucial as it defines the steps to follow which ensure brand value is upheld.

Cross-functional Planning Approach

Cross-functional planning approach of integrated marketing communications diverges away from the other two categories, it does not centre around the concept of marketing promotional elements, instead the focus has shifted toward restructuring the organization to increase a customer-centric environment. This approach recognises that messages do not just come from the marketing department, but can come from virtually any department within the organization. Investing for the reorganization sparks change where all departments interconnect to work cohesively toward managing and planning all stages of brand relationship. As a unified organization, the cross-functional process is a competitive advantage as they can achieve profitable relationships with customers and stakeholders. This can be achieved through improving the relation amongst messages sent from all departments through channels to the receivers. By sending strategic messages and monitoring any external reaction, organizations gain feedback data from consumers which can be used to inform subsequent planning or fine-tuning of the communications strategy. The process is circular, not linear, at the beginning organization and consumer communicate by interacting and dialogue which ignites the relationship, over time trust is earned and the consumer may continue to purchase, which in turn increases sales and profitability for the organization and finally, the relationship is strong and the organization retains clientele. Interactive communication is advantageous for a cross-functional approach as the business and consumer are both involved in brand communication.Implementing IMC is a flexible process due to the changing nature of the marketing dynamics therefore by eliminating borders within the organization it allows for this notion.

Barriers to Implementation

The barriers to implementation have been cited as one of the main reasons for the failure to adopt holistic approaches to IMC. The key barriers cited in the literature are:

- No support from senior management

  It is vital for an organization who implements integrated marketing communications to have the commitment from all levels of employees, including senior management. The union between both marketing and corporate goals should coincide and support simultaneously. The lack of involvement from senior management could lead to IMC being deprived of resources which prevents the full potential IMC can deliver for the organization to benefit from. Higher levels of the business need to coincide with the efforts of staff in the strategic planning to grasp that IMC's programme is valuable.

- Clients are confused about the concept

  Some companies such as advertising agencies could possibly take advantage of the integrated marketing communications model, due to the stress they receive from clients and budgets being reduced. The introduction of new technology broadens the boundaries for advertising elements to endeavour with such avenues like the internet. Their focus may stray from the core principles of IMC which is to integrate the elements together, as they're less effective individually. Also, their clients may not grasp the IMC concept as an essential attribute, therefore, they perceive IMC as saving money due to the strategic juxtaposition.

- Organisation is too specialised

  One of the core fundamentals of integrated marketing communications is that of the focus aspires toward a customer orientation. In spite of that, the purpose of some organisations have not adopted the framework and are still task orientated. Examples include public relations, direct marketing and advertising.

- Conflict within organisation

  Trying to implement integrated marketing communications into strong hierarchy structured organisations may cause staff resistance due to the nature of horizontal communication causing disagreements amongst staff. Staff may not perform their tasks and functions which jeopardises the work environment. For IMC to be successful the culture of the organisation needs to accommodate an open perspective where communication amongst the varying departments are managed tactically. Individuals reactions toward the new restructure will differ, as some become custom to the process and enjoy the borderless integration, on the other hand, some may feel threatened from the absence of control that once maintained order and power within the previous structured organisation. A corporate structure may not necessarily invite IMC due to their culture being incompatible for the integration.

- Removing barriers

  Integrated marketing communication is the process of communicating an idea in order to attract customers using an array of tools. It is the process of sending out a message to a receiver. Depending on the company values and the type of product or service they offer, the most appropriate message to deliver will depend on the brand and consumer. To understand how integrated marketing communication can benefit a business, three main areas will be discussed. These areas being who the Sender is? Who is the Receiver? And what tools can the sender use in order to pass a message on to the receiver?

Practical solutions towards improving marketing strategies by using ICM can be done through two differing marketing concepts the four P's or the four C's. Also, the uses of encoding and decoding should be followed, all of which intertwine to form growth in sales financially for a business.

A sender is someone who is aiming to communicate an idea to a receiver, which might be an individual or a group. Marketers must first understand who the receive is in order to successfully implement marketing communications. For example, Staples seeks to identify itself as a 'one-stop' shop for all office needs. It advertises a wide variety of office supplies, safe and on time delivery, competitive pricing and excellent customer service. Staples focuses its marketing efforts on advertising those values. Their slogan "To make more happen, everyday". This theme is the most appropriate because it attracts their target audience. Workers have little time on their hands, the product they offer will give them the ability to make life easier; by doing so, they save time. In today's fast-paced lifestyle, if a service is convenient, customers will most likely use the product. Staples have successfully taken the necessary steps in order to communicate their values to their customers. They have done this through understanding who they are and who they should be targeting.

4C's

Originally, marketing was focused around the 4P's (product, price, place and promotion) which concentrated on companies' internal concepts. The idea of integrated marketing communications was first raised in 1993 by Don E. Schultz, who changed the 4P's concept into the 4C's model. The four parts include consumer, communication, convenience and cost, taking into consideration the needs and wants of consumers. Integrated marketing communications accomplished synergy when each element was executed in accordance with the overall vision of the organization's campaign, which allows the message to be executed efficiently. Finding out who the target market is to answer the 4C's: knowing what products they're willing to purchase, the amount of money they are willing to spend for it, how the product will fulfill their needs and wants, the accessibility of the product and how easily correct information is transmitted. Changing the emphasis onto what consumers desire leads to a higher success being attained through IMC, as it is being influenced by not only internal stakeholders but also external ones.

Communication-based Relationship Marketing

Expanding from this, Tom Duncan and Sandra E. Moriarty formed the concept of communication-based relationship marketing. This model diverged from the concept of the general one way, business influencing consumers what to believe scenario. However, Duncan and Moriarty argued that communication between business and consumers was the key to developing strong establishment for consumer orientated marketing endeavours. The process of IMC through communication-based marketing goes through a sequential three stage process. Organizations begin with choosing an effective mixture of communication methods; then, the marketing methods are selected; thereafter, the best of each element is fused and integrated together which thence is channelled from the organization to the audience. Subsequently, these findings shaped modern marketing, focusing on an interactive two-way approach that builds rapport with stakeholders. Developments from integrated marketing communications have evolved into three categories: inside-out approach, outside-in approach and cross-functional strategic approach.

Branding

Branding goes beyond having a logo; it is how businesses communicate on behalf of their company, verbally and visually. A brand is a conversation — it is how people talk about your company when you are not in the room. Consumers are constantly interacting and meeting with brands. This can be through television or other media advertisements such as event sponsorships, personal selling and product packaging. Brand exposure such as this is known as a brand touch point or brand contact whereby the organization can try impressing its consumer. Without branding, consumers wouldn't be able to decipher between products and decide which one they like most. People may not be able to even tell the differences between some of the brands, they would have to try each brand several times before being able to judge which one was best. In order to help with purchase decisions, marketing communications try to create a distinct image for the brand. Brand associations are made to encourage linkages with places, personalities or even emotions which creates a sophisticated brand personality in the minds of the consumers. This shows how brand communications add value to products and why branding is a crucial aspect to the communication platform.

Advertising

The advertising, as a part of promotion mix, is the basic element of promotion within marketing mix. Advertising is any form of indirect presentation of ideas products or services. The basic purpose of advertising is to stimulate demand and product sales. Therefore advertising is considered to be basic instrument of sales and communication with public.

The advertising can support two different goals of the company. If the goal of advertising is the product or service, with the purpose of sales increase it is called Product Advertising. On the other hand, if the goal is to promote the image of the company, than it is Institutional Advertising.

Product Advertising can have different roles. The most important roles of product advertising are:

- Pioneer Advertising that points to primary demand for the product. It is relevant during the introduction phase of the product. Since the product is new the pioneer advertising is promoting novelty and set a new trends.

- Competitive Advertising is pointing for demand increase for specific product of the company. Since the product is in the phase of growth or maturity, competition is developed and active. Therefore the goal of competitive advertising is to differentiate product from the competition and to increase or protect sales volume.

- Sustainability Advertising has a goal to keep the loyal segment of customers. The Sustainability advertising is reminder advertising that makes sense for established and developed brands.

Institutional Advertising has advertising goal that is much wider than the product advertising. While the product advertising is basic advertising stage, the institutional advertising is advanced level. Institutional advertising cannot be conducted without developed product advertising.

The institutional advertising is developing image of the company, clarifying the mission and vision to population and building the public opinion about the community contribution of the company.

The example of institutional advertising can be promotion of eco & recycling programs, introduction of new additive free food production technology, switching from import to local production etc.

The usual channels for communication of product advertising and institutional advertising are TV, radio, newspapers, internet advertising, mail, e-mail, billboards, etc.

The Advertising activities are planned mostly by the company, with consulting and execution by marketing agencies.

Advertising may be categorized in a variety of ways, including by style, target audience, geographic scope, medium, or purpose. For example, in print advertising, classification by style can include display advertising (ads with design elements sold by size) vs. classified advertising (ads without design elements sold by the word or line). Advertising may be local, national or global. An ad campaign may be directed toward consumers or to businesses. The purpose of an ad may be to raise awareness (brand advertising), or to elicit an immediate sale (direct response advertising). The term above the line is used for advertising involving mass media; other types of advertising and promotion are referred to as below the line.

Traditional Media

An advertisement for a diner. Such signs are common on storefronts

Virtually any medium can be used for advertising. Commercial advertising media can include wall paintings, billboards, street furniture components, printed flyers and rack cards, radio, cinema and television adverts, web banners, mobile telephone screens, shopping carts, web popups, skywriting, bus stop benches, human billboards and forehead advertising, magazines, newspapers, town criers, sides of buses, banners attached to or sides of airplanes ("logojets"), in-flight advertisements on seatback tray tables or overhead storage bins, taxicab doors, roof mounts and passenger screens, musical stage shows, subway platforms and trains, elastic bands on disposable diapers, doors of bathroom stalls, stickers on apples in supermarkets, shopping cart handles (gra-bertising), the opening section of streaming audio and video, posters, and the backs of event tickets and supermarket receipts. Any place an "identified" sponsor pays to deliver their message through a medium is advertising.

A taxicab with an advertisement for Daikin in Singapore. Buses and other vehicles are popular media for advertisers

A DBAG Class 101 with UNICEFads at Ingolstadt main railway station

A Transperth bus, with an advertisement along its side

Hot air balloon displays advertising for GEO magazine

Share of global adspend		
Medium	2015	2017
Television advertisement	37.7%	34.8%
Desktop online advertising	19.9%	18.2%
Mobile advertising	9.2%	18.4%
Newspaper#Advertising	12.8%	10.1%
Magazines	6.5%	5.3%
Outdoor advertising	6.8%	6.6%
Radio advertisement	6.5%	5.9%
Cinema	0.6%	0.7%

Television

Television advertising is one of the most expensive types of advertising; networks charge large amounts for commercial airtime during popular events. The annual Super Bowl football game in the United States is known as the most prominent advertising event on television – with an audience of over 108 million and studies showing that 50% of those only tuned in to see the advertisements. During the 2014 edition of this game, the average thirty-second ad cost US$4 million, and $8 million was charged for a 60-second spot. Virtual advertisements may be inserted into regular programming through computer graphics. It is typically inserted into otherwise blank backdrops or used to replace local billboards that are not relevant to the remote broadcast audience. More controversially, virtual billboards may be inserted into the background where none exist in real-life. This technique is especially used in televised sporting events. Virtual product placement is also possible. An infomercial is a long-format television commercial, typically five minutes or longer. The word infomercial is a portmanteau of the words information and commercial. The main objective in an infomercial is to create an impulse purchase, so that the target sees the presentation and then immediately buys the product through the advertised toll-free telephone number or website. Infomercials describe, display, and often demonstrate products and their features, and commonly have testimonials from customers and industry professionals.

Radio

Radio advertisements are broadcast as radio waves to the air from a transmitter to an antenna and a thus to a receiving device. Airtime is purchased from a station or network in exchange for airing the commercials. While radio has the limitation of being restricted to sound, proponents of radio advertising often cite this as an advantage. Radio is an expanding medium that can be found on air, and also online. According to Arbitron, radio has approximately 241.6 million weekly listeners, or more than 93 percent of the U.S. population.

Online

Online advertising is a form of promotion that uses the Internet and World Wide Web for the expressed purpose of delivering marketing messages to attract customers. Online ads are delivered by an ad server. Examples of online advertising include contextual ads that appear on search engine results pages, banner ads, in pay per click text ads, rich media ads, Social network advertising, online classified advertising, advertising networks and e-mail marketing, including e-mail spam. A newer form of online advertising is Native Ads; they go in a website's news feed and are supposed to improve user experience by being less intrusive. However, some people argue this practice is deceptive.

Domain Names

Domain name advertising is most commonly done through pay per click web search engines, however, advertisers often lease space directly on domain names that generically describe their products. When an Internet user visits a website by typing a domain name directly into their web browser, this is known as "direct navigation", or "type in" web traffic. Although many Internet users search for ideas and products using search engines and mobile phones, a large number of users around the world still use the address bar. They will type a keyword into the address bar such as "geraniums" and add ".com" to the end of it. Sometimes they will do the same with ".org" or a country-code Top Level Domain (TLD such as ".co.uk" for the United Kingdom or ".ca" for Canada). When Internet users type in a generic keyword and add .com or another top-level domain (TLD) ending, it produces a targeted sales lead. Domain name advertising was originally developed by Oingo (later known as Applied Semantics), one of Google's early acquisitions.

Product Placements

Covert advertising is when a product or brand is embedded in entertainment and media. For example, in a film, the main character can use an item or other of a definite brand, as in the movie *Minority Report*, where Tom Cruise's character John Anderton owns a phone with the *Nokia* logo clearly written in the top corner, or his watch engraved with the *Bulgari* logo. Another example of advertising in film is in *I, Robot*, where main character played by Will Smith mentions his *Converse* shoes several times, calling them classics, because the film is set far in the future. *I, Robot* and *Spaceballs*also showcase futuristic cars with the *Audi* and *Mercedes-Benz* logos clearly displayed on the front of the vehicles. Cadillac chose to advertise in the movie *The Matrix Reloaded*, which as a result contained many scenes in which Cadillac cars were used. Similarly, product placement for Omega Watches, Ford, VAIO, BMW and Aston Martincars are featured in recent James Bond films, most notably *Casino Royale*. In "Fantastic Four: Rise of the Silver Surfer", the main transport vehicle shows a large Dodge logo on the front. *Blade Runner* includes some of the most obvious product placement; the whole film stops to show a Coca-Cola billboard.

Print

Print advertising describes advertising in a printed medium such as a newspaper, magazine, or trade journal. This encompasses everything from media with a very broad readership base, such as a major national newspaper or magazine, to more narrowly targeted media such as local newspapers and trade journals on very specialized topics. One form of print advertising is classified advertising, which allows private individuals or companies to purchase a small, narrowly targeted ad paid by the word or line. Another form of print advertising is the display ad, which is generally a larger ad with design elements that typically run in an article section of a newspaper.

Outdoor

Billboards, also known as hoardings in some parts of the world, are large structures located in public places which display advertisements to passing pedestrians and motorists. Most often, they are located on main roads with a large amount of passing motor and pedestrian traffic; however, they can be placed in any location with large numbers of viewers, such as on mass transit vehicles and in stations, in shopping malls or office buildings, and in stadiums. The form known as street advertising first came to prominence in the UK by Street Advertising Services to create outdoor advertising on street furniture and pavements. Working with products such as Reverse Graffiti, air dancers and 3D pavement advertising, for getting brand messages out into public spaces. Sheltered outdoor advertising combines outdoor with indoor advertisement by placing large mobile, structures (tents) in public places on temporary bases. The large outer advertising space aims to exert a strong pull on the observer, the product is promoted indoors, where the creative decor can intensify the impression. Mobile billboards are generally vehicle mounted billboards or digital screens. These can be on dedicated vehicles built solely for carrying advertisements along routes preselected by clients, they can also be specially equipped cargo trucks or, in some cases, large banners strewn from planes. The billboards are often lighted; some being backlit, and others employing spotlights. Some billboard displays are static, while others change; for example, continuously or periodically rotating among a set of advertisements. Mobile displays are used for various situations in metropolitan areas throughout the world, including: target advertising, one-day and long-term campaigns, conventions, sporting events, store openings and similar promotional events, and big advertisements from smaller companies.

The *RedEye* newspaper advertised to its target market at North Avenue Beach with a sailboat billboard on Lake Michigan.

Point-of-sale

In-store advertising is any advertisement placed in a retail store. It includes placement of a product in visible locations in a store, such as at eye level, at the ends of aisles and near checkout counters (a.k.a. POP – point of purchase display), eye-catching displays promoting a specific product, and advertisements in such places as shopping carts and in-store video displays.

Novelties

Advertising printed on small tangible items such as coffee mugs, T-shirts, pens, bags, and such is known as novelty advertising. Some printers specialize in printing novelty items, which can then be distributed directly by the advertiser, or items may be distributed as part of a cross-promotion, such as ads on fast food containers.

Celebrity Endorsements

Advertising in which a celebrity endorses a product or brand leverages celebrity power, fame, money, popularity to gain recognition for their products or to promote specific stores' or products. Advertisers often advertise their products, for example, when celebrities share their favorite products or wear clothes by specific brands or designers. Celebrities are often involved in advertising campaigns such as television or print adverts to advertise specific or general products. The use of celebrities to endorse a brand can have its downsides, however; one mistake by a celebrity can be detrimental to the public relations of a brand. For example, following his performance of eight gold medals at the 2008 Olympic Games in Beijing, China, swimmer Michael Phelps' contract with Kellogg's was terminated, as Kellogg's did not want to associate with him after he was photographed smoking marijuana. Celebrities such as Britney Spears have advertised for multiple products including Pepsi, Candies from Kohl's, Twister, NASCAR, and Toyota.

Aerial

Using aircraft, balloons or airships to create or display advertising media. Skywriting is a notable example.

New Media and Advertising Approaches

Increasingly, other media are overtaking many of the "traditional" media such as television, radio and newspaper because of a shift toward the usage of the Internet for news and music as well as devices like digital video recorders (DVRs) such as TiVo.

Online advertising began with unsolicited bulk e-mail advertising known as "e-mail spam". Spam has been a problem for e-mail users since 1978. As new online communication channels became available, advertising followed. The first banner ad appeared on the World Wide Web in 1994. Prices of Web-based advertising space are dependent on the "relevance" of the surrounding web content and the traffic that the website receives.

In online display advertising, display ads generate awareness quickly. Unlike search, which requires someone to be aware of a need, display advertising can drive awareness of something new and without previous knowledge. Display works well for direct response. Display is not only used for generating awareness, it's used for direct response campaigns that link to a landing page with a clear 'call to action'.

As the mobile phone became a new mass medium in 1998 when the first paid downloadable content appeared on mobile phones in Finland, mobile advertising followed, also first launched in Finland in 2000. By 2007 the value of mobile advertising had reached $2 billion and providers such as Admob delivered billions of mobile ads.

More advanced mobile ads include banner ads, coupons, Multimedia Messaging Servicepicture and video messages, advergames and various engagement marketing campaigns. A particular feature driving mobile ads is the 2D barcode, which replaces the need to do any typing of web addresses, and uses the camera feature of modern phones to gain immediate access to web content. 83 percent of Japanese mobile phone users already are active users of 2D barcodes.

Some companies have proposed placing messages or corporate logos on the side of booster rockets and the International Space Station.

Unpaid advertising (also called "publicity advertising"), can include personal recommendations ("bring a friend", "sell it"), spreading buzz, or achieving the feat of equating a brand with a common noun (in the United States, "Xerox" = "photocopier", "Kleenex" = tissue, "Vaseline" = petroleum jelly, "Hoover" = vacuum cleaner, and "Band-Aid" = adhesive bandage). However, some companies oppose the use of their brand name to label an object. Equating a brand with a common noun also risks turning that brand into a generic trademark – turning it into a generic term which means that its legal protection as a trademark is lost.

From time to time, The CW Television Network airs short programming breaks called Content Wraps, to advertise one company's product during an entire commercial break. The CW pioneered "content wraps and some products featured were Herbal Essences, Crest, Guitar Hero II, CoverGirl, and recently Toyota.

A new promotion concept has appeared, "ARvertising", advertising on augmented realitytechnology.

Controversy exists on the effectiveness of subliminal advertising , and the pervasiveness of mass messages (Propaganda).

Rise in New Media

With the Internet came many new advertising opportunities. Pop-up, Flash, banner, pop-under, advergaming, and email advertisements (all of which are often unwanted or spam in the case of email) are now commonplace. Particularly since the rise of "entertaining" advertising, some people may like an advertisement enough to wish to watch it later or show a friend. In general, the advertising community has not yet made this easy, although some have used the Internet to widely distribute their ads to anyone willing to see or hear them. In the last three quarters of 2009, mobile and Internet advertising grew by 18% and 9% respectively, while older media advertising saw declines: −10.1% (TV), −11.7% (radio), −14.8% (magazines) and −18.7% (newspapers). Between 2008 and 2014, U.S. newspapers lost more than half their print advertising revenue.

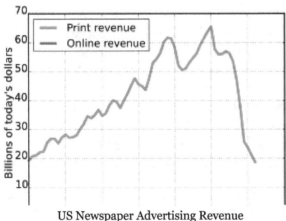

US Newspaper Advertising Revenue
Newspaper Association of America published data

Niche Marketing

Another significant trend regarding future of advertising is the growing importance of the niche market using niche or targeted ads. Also brought about by the Internet and the theory of the long tail, advertisers will have an increasing ability to reach specific audiences. In the past, the most efficient way to deliver a message was to blanket the largest mass market audience possible. However, usage tracking, customer profiles and the growing popularity of niche content brought about by everything from blogs to social networking sites, provide advertisers with audiences that are smaller but much better defined, leading to ads that are more relevant to viewers and more effective for companies' marketing products. Among others, Comcast Spotlight is one such advertiser employing this method in their video on demand menus. These advertisements are targeted to a specific group and can be viewed by anyone wishing to find out more about a particular business or practice, from their home. This causes the viewer to become proactive and actually choose what advertisements they want to view. Niche marketing could also be helped by bringing the issue of color into advertisements. Different colors play major roles when it comes to marketing strategies, for example, seeing the blue can promote a sense of calmness and gives a sense of security which is why many social networks such as Facebook use blue in their logos. Google AdSense is an example of niche marketing. Google calculates the primary purpose of a website and adjusts ads accordingly; it uses key words on the page (or even in emails) to find the general ideas of topics disused and places ads that will most likely be clicked on by viewers of the email account or website visitors.

Crowdsourcing

The concept of crowdsourcing has given way to the trend of user-generatedadvertisements. User-generated ads are created by people, as opposed to an advertising agency or the company themselves, often resulting from brand sponsored advertising competitions. For the 2007 Super Bowl, the Frito-Lays division of PepsiCo held the *Crash the Super Bowl* contest, allowing people to create their own Doritos commercial.Chevrolet held a similar competition for their Tahoe line of SUVs. Due to the success of the Doritos user-generated ads in the 2007 Super Bowl, Frito-Lays relaunched the competition for the 2009 and 2010 Super Bowl. The resulting ads were among the most-watched and most-liked Super Bowl ads. In fact, the winning ad that aired in the 2009 Super Bowl was ranked by the USA Today Super Bowl Ad Meter as the top ad for the year while the winning ads that aired in the 2010 Super Bowl were found by Nielsens BuzzMetrics to be the "most buzzed-about". Another example of companies using crowdsourcing successfully is the beverage company Jones Soda that encourages consumers to participate in the label design themselves.

This trend has given rise to several online platforms that host user-generated advertising competitions on behalf of a company. Founded in 2007, Zooppa has launched ad competitions for brands such as Google, Nike, Hershey's, General Mills, Microsoft, NBC Universal, Zinio, and Mini Cooper. Crowd sourced remains controversial, as the long-term impact on the advertising industry is still unclear.

Global Advertising

Advertising has gone through five major stages of development: domestic, export, international, multi-national, and global. For global advertisers, there are four, potentially competing, business objectives that must be balanced when developing worldwide advertising: building a brand while speaking with one voice, developing economies of scalein the creative process, maximizing local effectiveness of ads, and increasing the company's speed of implementation. Born from the evolutionary stages of global marketing are the three primary and fundamentally different approaches to the development of global advertising executions: exporting executions, producing local executions, and importing ideas that travel.

Advertising research is key to determining the success of an ad in any country or region. The ability to identify which elements and moments of an ad contribute to its success is how economies of scale are maximized. Once one knows what works in an ad, that idea or ideas can be imported by any other market. Market research measures, such as Flow of Attention, Flow of Emotion and branding moments provide insight into what is working in an ad in any country or region because the measures are based on the visual, not verbal, elements of the ad.

Foreign Public Messaging

Foreign governments, particularly those that own marketable commercial products or services, often promote their interests and positions through the advertising of those goods because the target audience is not only largely unaware of the forum as a vehicle for foreign messaging but also willing to receive the message while in a mental state of absorbing information from advertisements during television commercial breaks, while reading a periodical, or while passing by billboards in public spaces. A prime example of this messaging technique is advertising campaigns to promote international travel. While advertising foreign destinations and services may stem from the typical goal of increasing revenue by drawing more tourism, some travel campaigns carry the additional or alternative intended purpose of promoting good sentiments or improving existing ones among the target audience towards a given nation or region. It is common for advertising promoting foreign countries to be produced and distributed by the tourism ministries of those countries, so these ads often carry political statements and depictions of the foreign government's desired international public perception. Additionally, a wide range of foreign airlines and travel-related services which advertise separately from the destinations, themselves, are owned by their respective governments; examples include, though are not limited to, the Emirates airline (Dubai), Singapore Airlines (Singapore), Qatar Airways(Qatar), China Airlines (Taiwan/Republic of China), and Air China (People's Republic of China). By depicting their destinations, airlines, and other services in a favorable and pleasant light, countries market themselves to populations abroad in a manner that could mitigate prior public impressions.

Diversification

In the realm of advertising agencies, continued industry diversification has seen observers note that "big global clients don't need big global agencies any more". This is reflected by the growth of non-traditional agencies in various global markets, such as Canadian business TAXI and SMART in Australia and has been referred to as a revolution in the ad world.

New Technology

The ability to record shows on digital video recorders (such as TiVo) allow watchers to record the programs for later viewing, enabling them to fast forward through commercials. Additionally, as more seasons of pre-recorded box sets are offered for sale of television programs; fewer people watch the shows on TV. However, the fact that these sets are sold, means the company will receive additional profits from these sets.

To counter this effect, a variety of strategies have been employed. Many advertisers have opted for product placement on TV shows like Survivor. Other strategies include integrating advertising with internet-connected EPGs, advertising on companion devices (like smartphones and tablets) during the show, and creating TV apps. Additionally, some like brands have opted for social television sponsorship.

Purposes

Advertising is at the front of delivering the proper message to customers and prospective customers. The purpose of advertising is to inform the consumers about their product and convince customers that a company's services or products are the best, enhance the image of the company, point out and create a need for products or services, demonstrate new uses for established products, announce new products and programs, reinforce the salespeople's individual messages, draw customers to the business, and to hold existing customers.

Sales Promotions and Brand Loyalty

Sales promotions are another way to advertise. Sales promotions are double purposed because they are used to gather information about what type of customers one draws in and where they are, and to jump start sales. Sales promotions include things like contests and games, sweepstakes, product giveaways, samples coupons, loyalty programs, and discounts. The ultimate goal of sales promotions is to stimulate potential customers to action.

Criticisms

While advertising can be seen as necessary for economic growth, it is not without social costs. Unsolicited commercial e-mail and other forms of spam have become so prevalent as to have become a major nuisance to users of these services, as well as being a financial burden on internet service providers. Advertising is increasingly invading public spaces, such as schools, which some critics argue is a form of child exploitation. This increasing difficulty in limiting exposure to specific audiences can result in negative backlash for advertisers. In tandem with these criticisms, the advertising industry has seen low approval rates in surveys and negative cultural portrayals.

One of the most controversial criticisms of advertisement in the present day is that of the predominance of advertising of foods high in sugar, fat, and salt specifically to children. Critics claim that food advertisements targeting children are exploitive and are not sufficiently balanced with proper nutritional education to help children understand the consequences of their food choices. Additionally, children may not understand that they are being sold something, and are therefore more impressionable. Michelle Obama has criticized large food companies for advertising unhealthy foods largely towards children and has requested that food companies either limit their advertising to children or advertise foods that are more in line with dietary guidelines. The other criticisms include the change that are brought by those advertisements on the society and also the deceiving ads that are aired and published by the corporations.

Cosmetic and health industry are the ones which exploited the highest and created reasons of concern.

Regulation

There have been increasing efforts to protect the public interest by regulating the content and the influence of advertising. Some examples include restrictions for advertising alcohol, tobacco or gambling imposed in many countries, as well as the bans around advertising to children, which exist in parts of Europe. Advertising regulation focuses heavily on the veracity of the claims and as such, there are often tighter restrictions placed around advertisements for food and healthcare products.

The advertising industries within some countries rely less on laws and more on systems of self-regulation. Advertisers and the media agree on a code of advertising standards that they attempt to uphold. The general aim of such codes is to ensure that any advertising is legal, decent, honest and truthful. Some self-regulatory organizations are funded by the industry, but remain independent, with the intent of upholding the standards or codes like the Advertising Standards Authority in the UK.

In the UK, most forms of outdoor advertising such as the display of billboards is regulated by the UK Town and County Planning system. Currently, the display of an advertisement without consent from the Planning Authority is a criminal offense liable to a fine of £2,500 per offense. In the US, many communities believe that many forms of outdoor advertising blight the public realm. As long ago as the 1960s in the US there were attempts to ban billboard advertising in the open countryside. Cities such as São Paulohave introduced an outright ban with London also having specific legislation to control unlawful displays.

Some governments restrict the languages that can be used in advertisements, but advertisers may employ tricks to try avoiding them. In France for instance, advertisers sometimes print English words in bold and French translations in fine print.

The advertising of pricing information is another topic of concern for governments. In the United States for instance, it is common for businesses to only mention the existence and amount of applicable taxes at a later stage of a transaction. In Canada and New Zealand, taxes can be listed as separate items, as long as they are quoted up-front. In most other countries, the advertised price must include all applicable taxes, enabling customers to easily know how much it will cost them.

Theory

Hierarchy-of-effects Models

Various competing models of hierarchies of effects attempt to provide a theoretical underpinning to advertising practice:

- The model of Clow and Baack clarifies the objectives of an advertising campaign and for each individual advertisement. The model postulates six steps a buyer moves through when making a purchase;

  ○ Awareness

  ○ Knowledge

  ○ Liking

  ○ Preference

  ○ Conviction

  ○ Purchase

- Means-End Theory suggests that an advertisement should contain a message or means that leads the consumer to a desired end-state.

- Leverage Points aim to move the consumer from understanding a product's benefits to linking those benefits with personal values.

Marketing Mix

The marketing mix was proposed by professor E. Jerome McCarthy in the 1960s. It consists of four basic elements called the "four Ps". Product is the first P representing the actual product. Price represents the process of determining the value of a product. Place represents the variables of getting the product to the consumer such as distribution channels, market coverage and movement organization. The last P stands for Promotion which is the process of reaching the target market and convincing them to buy the product.

In the 1990s, the concept of four Cs was introduced as a more customer-driven replacement of four P's. There are two theories based on four Cs: Lauterborn's Four Cs (*consumer, cost, communication, convenience*), and Shimizu's four Cs (*commodity, cost, communication, channel*) in the 7Cs Compass Model (Co-marketing). Communications can include advertising, sales promotion, public relations, publicity, personal selling, corporate identity, internal communication, SNS, MIS.

Advertising Research

Advertising research is a specialized form of research that works to improve the effectiveness and efficiency of advertising. It entails numerous forms of research which employ different methodologies. Advertising research includes pre-testing (also known as copy testing) and post-testing of ads and campaigns.

Pre-testing includes a wide range of qualitative and quantitative techniques, including: focus groups, in-depth target audience interviews (one-on-one interviews), small-scale quantitative studies and physiological measurement. The goal of these investigations is to better understand how different groups respond to various messages and visual prompts, thereby providing an assessment of how well the advertisement meets its communications goals.

Post-testing employs many of the same techniques as pre-testing, usually with a focus on understanding the change in awareness or attitude attributable to the advertisement. With the emergence of digital advertising technologies, many firms have begun to continuously post-test ads using real-time data. This may take the form of A/B split-testing or multivariate testing.

Continuous ad tracking and the Communicus System are competing examples of post-testing advertising research types.

Semiotics

Meanings between consumers and marketers depict signs and symbols that are encoded in everyday objects. Semiotics is the study of signs and how they are interpreted. Advertising has many hidden signs and meanings within brand names, logos, package designs, print advertisements, and television advertisements. Semiotics aims to study and interpret the message being conveyed in (for example) advertisements. Logos and advertisements can be interpreted at two levels – known as the surface level and the underlying level. The surface level uses signs creatively to create an image or personality for a product. These signs can be images, words, fonts, colors, or slogans. The underlying level is made up of hidden meanings. The combination of images, words, colors, and slogans must be interpreted by the audience or consumer. The "key to advertising analysis" is the signifier and the signified. The signifier is the object and the signified is the mental concept. A product has a signifier and a signified. The signifier is the color, brand name, logo design, and technology. The signified has two meanings known as denotative and connotative. The denotative meaning is the meaning of the product. A television's denotative meaning might be that it is high definition. The connotative meaning is the product's deep and hidden meaning. A connotative meaning of a television would be that it is top-of-the-line.

Apple's commercials used a black silhouette of a person that was the age of Apple's target market. They placed the silhouette in front of a blue screen so that the picture behind the silhouette could be constantly changing. However, the one thing that stays the same in these ads is that there is music in the background and the silhouette is listening to that music on a white iPod through white headphones. Through advertising, the white color on a set of earphones now signifies that the music device is an iPod. The white color signifies almost all of Apple's products.

The semiotics of gender plays a key influence on the way in which signs are interpreted. When considering gender roles in advertising, individuals are influenced by three categories. Certain characteristics of stimuli may enhance or decrease the elaboration of the message (if the product is perceived as feminine or masculine). Second, the characteristics of individuals can affect attention and elaboration of the message (traditionalor non-traditional gender role orientation). Lastly, situational factors may be important to influence the elaboration of the message.

There are two types of marketing communication claims-objective and subjective. Objective claims stem from the extent to which the claim associates the brand with a tangible product or service feature. For instance, a camera may have auto-focus features. Subjective claims convey emotional, subjective, impressions of intangible aspects of a product or service. They are non-physical features of a product or service that cannot be directly perceived, as they have no physical reality. For instance the brochure has a beautiful design. Males tend to respond better to objective marketing-communications claims while females tend to respond better to subjective communications claims.

Voiceovers are commonly used in advertising. Most voiceovers are done by men, with figures of up to 94% having been reported. There have been more female voiceovers in recent years, but mainly for food, household products, and feminine-care products.

Public Relations

Public Relations involves a variety of programs designed to maintain or enhance a company's image and the products and services it offers. Successful implementation of an effective public relations strategy can be a critical component to a marketing plan.

A public relations (PR) strategy may play a key role in an organization's promotional strategy. A planned approach to leveraging public relations opportunities can be just as important as advertising and sales promotions. Public relations is one of the most effective methods to communicate and relate to the market. It is powerful and, once things are in motion, it is the most cost effective of all promotional activities. In some cases, it is free.

The success of well executed PR plans can be seen through several organizations that have made it a central focus of their promotional strategy. Paul Newman's Salad Dressing, The Body Shop, and Ben & Jerry's Ice Cream have positioned their organizations through effective PR strategies. Intel, Sprint and Microsoft have leveraged public relations to introduce and promote new products and services.

Similar to the foundational goals of marketing, effective public relations seeks to communicate information to:

- Launch new products and services.

- Reposition a product or service.

- Create or increase interest in a product, service, or brand.

- Influence specific target groups.

- Defend products or services that have suffered from negative press or perception.

- Enhance the firm's overall image.

- The result of an effective public relations strategy is to generate additional revenue through greater awareness and information for the products and services an organization offers.

Goals and Objectives

Good strategy begins with identifying your goals and stating your objectives. What are the goals and objectives behind your public relations strategy and can they be measured and quantified?

Each of these areas may reflect the goals your public relations campaign may seek to accomplish.

Press Relations

Communicating news and information of interest about organizations in the most positive light.

Product and Service Promotion

Sponsoring various efforts to publicize specific products or services.

Firm Communications

Promoting a better and more attractive understanding of the organization with internal and external communications.

Lobbying

Communicating with key individuals to positively influence legislation and regulation.

Internal Feedback

Advising decision makers within the organization regarding the public's perception and advising actions to be taken to change negative opinions.

Key figures from within an organization will write speeches to be delivered at corporate events, public awards and industry gatherings. PR company officials in liaison with company managers often write speeches and design corporate presentations. They are part of the planned and coherent strategy to build goodwill with publics. Presentations can be designed and pre-prepared by PR companies, ultimately to be delivered by company executives.

Corporate literature includes financial reports, in-house magazines, brochures, catalogues, price lists and any other piece of corporate derived literature. They communicate with a variety of publics. For example, financial reports will be of great interest to investors and the stock market, since they give all sorts of indicators of the health of a business. A company Chief Executive Officer CEO will often write the forward to an annual financial report where he or she has the opportunity to put a business case to the reader. This is all part of Public Relations.

Publics, put simply, are its stakeholders. PR is proactive and future orientated, and has the goal of building and maintaining a positive perception of an organization in the mind of its publics. This is often referred to as goodwill.

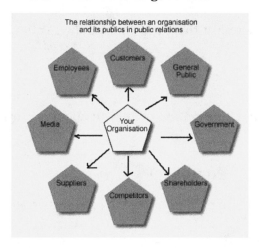

Yes it is difficult to see the difference between marketing communications and PR since there is a lot of crossover. This makes it a tricky concept to learn. Added to this is the fact that PR is often expensive, and not free, as some definitions would have you believe. PR agencies are not cheap. Below are some of the approaches that are often considered under the PR banner.

It is important that company executives are available to generate goodwill for their organisation. Many undertake training in how to deal with the media, and how to behave in front of a camera. There are many key industrial figures that proactively deal with the media in a positive way for example Bill Gates (Microsoft) or Richard Branson (Virgin). Interviews with the business or mass media often allow a company to put its own perspective on matters that could be misleading if simply left to dwell untended the public domain.

The Role of Public Relations in Marketing

Many startups make the mistake of not considering public relations in their strategies as they move out of the blustery launch period and start the long grind toward profitability. Public relations, press outreach and earned media coverage don't stop the week after the launch. It should be part of any growing brand's marketing toolkit, and it may just become a key part of your brand's strategy - as it should.

Here's how to ensure public relations continues to play a role
in your marketing strategy.

Amplify your Message

After you have built your initial campaign and chosen the messaging to use on your site, social pages, paid advertising and content marketing, it's up to the PR team (or whoever is wearing that hat) to amplify your message with press coverage. Tools like Google Trends can help you keep track of the progress you're making during outreach. Make sure to only reach out to journalists who are within your niche and have written articles on similar subjects in the past. Never send out a generic mass email to a list of journalists.

Change the Tone

Launching ads on Facebook or Twitter can generate predictable results from a revenue perspective, but the unique nature of these platforms means your ads are usually open to feedback from the audience you target. Given an open forum, you might receive unpleasant messages from some commenters if they have never heard of your company. Try launching lookalike campaigns from traffic generated from an article you pitched. When you launch your paid media, you can ensure the audience you're targeting is already familiar with your brand.

Improve your SEO

You may not hear about it all that much, but most brands are building backlink profiles and improving their search rankings in Google, Bing, Yahoo or DuckDuckGo. While this shouldn't be why you reach out for press coverage, it is definitely a nice bonus when a prominent site links to yours.

Aim for the Grand Slam

When a company launch is executed well, a good PR strategy can take it to the next level. When done right, landing coverage in major online publications not only serves to benefit the company but also helps the reader. Your goal when pitching should be to bring value to the reader. By contributing value along with your company's message, you can ensure that you are creating content that will last and be utilized by grateful readers for years to come.

Build Recognition

Aside from bolstering your company image, good press outreach can often lead to unexpected results. Don't be surprised if that article about soaring revenues you landed in the *Wall Street Journal* nets you a few calls from interested investors.

It's important to always strive to bring value and communicate effectively to readers and the journalists you're pitching. Make your message a positive one and ensure that comes through in your writing. Blog posts, press releases and status updates should carry your brand persona. Make sure your press outreach does as well.

PR Tools to Build Business's Reputation

Media Relations

Media strategies focus on circulating messages through media channels to manage how your business is portrayed by the media. Your media tools might include releasing media statements and fact sheets, offering on-site media tours to encourage journalists to report positive messages about your business, and using social media to get the attention of journalists and track journalists who report in your market.

By developing good media contact lists and building relationships with key journalists to pitch media releases and story ideas to, you can use local, regional or state media to:

- Promote your business
- Manage risks, issues or crises affecting your business.

Advertorials

Advertorials are advertisements in the form of news stories or reviews in newspapers. Advertorials allow you to associate your advertising with the credibility of the newspaper.

Many businesses employ advertising or marketing professionals to help them develop TV advertorials - which are commonly used as a form of advertising and product placement.

Social Media

Social media lets you bypass the media and go straight to your customers. Using social networking sites such as Facebook and Twitter allows you to follow and be followed by journalists, drive web traffic, manage issues by responding quickly to criticisms or negative perceptions, and increase exposure for your business brand.

Newsletters

Print or emailed newsletters are a good way to promote your business, communicate with customers and keep them informed of new products and services.

Regular newsletters can strengthen your personal connections with customers and reflect your business brand and personality. A well written newsletter offers information of value to your customers.

Brochures and Catalogues

'Take home' or mail-out brochures or catalogues can help keep your customers thinking about your business and its products and services.

Properly designed brochures and catalogues give customers confidence in you and your brand, and help drive customers to your website or store. Information contained in business brochures and catalogues can be effectively reworked for your website, helping you do business online.

Business Events

Events are opportunities for business people to gain exposure for their businesses, promote new products or services and make sure accurate information reaches targeted customers.

From a sales point of view, events are a chance to counter customer doubts and build customer confidence. They can also help you research your market and competitors, and build your mailing list. Make sure you go to the event prepared with marketing materials to disseminate and a way to collect information and customer details.

Trade shows are an opportunity for businesses to compete in their industry and share information with people in similar lines of work.

Speaking Engagements

Speaking at events where customers are likely to attend helps position you as a leader or innovator in your field. As a business owner or leader, building your reputation as an expert also builds the reputation of your business - and draws new customers.

Events are valuable promotional opportunities even if you don't have top billing as a speaker. You will build reputation simply by having your business name or logo on the event listing, or delivering a presentation about a new product or innovation. Additionally, they provide valuable networking opportunities.

Sponsorships or Partnerships

Partnerships and sponsorships are good for business. Supporting a not-for-profit cause can help build feelings of goodwill and loyalty towards your business. Community partnerships may involve an exchange of funds or in-kind benefits to grow a local community organisation in return for benefits that promote your business reputation.

Partnerships can help consumers identify your brand with good business practice and good ethics.

Employee Relations

Your staff are ambassadors for your business and brand. Many larger businesses conduct employee relations - building their business culture and team relationships by sharing information, promoting involvement and instilling a sense of pride in business achievement. This can improve teamwork, staff retention and productivity, and ensure that staff are representing your business consistently and with the right messages.

Community Relations

Building good relationships with members of the community where you do business helps build customer loyalty. Find out where the customers in your community live by collecting postcodes at point of sale.

Engaging local stakeholders and decision makers helps build your profile and level of influence, helping you to attract more customers through word-of-mouth and ensuring your business interests are factored into community decision making.

Search Engine Optimization

SEO is a marketing discipline focused on growing visibility in organic (non-paid) search engine results. SEO encompasses both the technical and creative elements required to improve rankings, drive traffic, and increase awareness in search engines. There are many aspects to SEO, from the words on your page to the way other sites link to you on the web. Sometimes SEO is simply a matter of making sure your site is structured in a way that search engines understand.

SEO isn't just about building search engine-friendly websites. It's about making your site better for people too. At Moz we believe these principles go hand-in-hand.

Need of SEO

The majority of web traffic is driven by the major commercial search engines, Google, Bing, and Yahoo!. Although social media and other types of traffic can generate visits to your website, search engines are the primary method of navigation for most Internet users. This is true whether your site provides content, services, products, information, or just about anything else.

Search engines are unique in that they provide targeted traffic—people looking for what you offer. Search engines are the roadways that make this happen. If search engines cannot find your site, or add your content to their databases, you miss out on incredible opportunities to drive traffic to your site.

Search queries—the words that users type into the search box—carry extraordinary value. Experience has shown that search engine traffic can make (or break) an organization's success. Targeted traffic to a website can provide publicity, revenue, and exposure like no other channel of marketing. Investing in SEO can have an exceptional rate of return compared to other types of marketing and promotion.

Why can't the search engines figure out my site without SEO?

Search engines are smart, but they still need help. The major engines are always working to improve their technology to crawl the web more deeply and return better results to users. However, there is a limit to how search engines can operate. Whereas the right SEO can net you thousands of visitors and increased attention, the wrong moves can hide or bury your site deep in the search results where visibility is minimal.

In addition to making content available to search engines, SEO also helps boost rankings so that content will be placed where searchers will more readily find it. The Internet is becoming increasingly competitive, and those companies who perform SEO will have a decided advantage in visitors and customers.

Sales and Distribution

Sales refers to the exchange of goods/commodities against money or service. It is the only revenue generating function in an organization. It has formed an important part in business throughout history. Even prior to the introduction of money, people used to exchange goods in order to fulfill the needs, which is known as the barter system.

Example of Barter System

A has 100 kg of rice and B has 50 kg of wheat. Here, A needs wheat and B needs rice. They agree to exchange 50 kg of rice and 25 kg of wheat upon mutual understanding.

Conditions of Sales

- There are two parties involved in the transaction, the seller and the buyer.
- The seller is the provider of goods or services and the buyer is the purchaser in exchange of money.

The seller of goods has to transfer the title of ownership of the item to the buyer upon an agreed price. A person who sells goods or services on behalf of the seller is known as the salesman/woman.

Sales management is an art where the sales executive or the salesperson helps the organization or individual to achieve its objective or buy a product with their skills.

The following are some skills that a sales executive needs to possess:

Conceptual Skills

Conceptual skill includes the formulation of ideas. Managers understand abstract relationships, improve ideas, and solve issues creatively. The sales executive should be well versed with the concept of the product he/she is selling.

People Skills

People skills involve the ability to interact effectively with people in a friendly way, especially in business. The term 'people skills' involves both psychological skills and social skills, but they are less inclusive than life skills.

Every person has a different mindset, so a sales executive should know how to present the product depending on the customer's mindset.

Technical Skills

Technical skills are the abilities captured through learning and practice. They are often job or task specific. In simple words, a specific skill set or proficiency is required to perform a specific job or task. As a part of conceptual skills, a sales executive should also have a good grasp on the technical skills of the product.

Decision Skills

Decision skills are the most important because to tackle the questions from consumers, sales executive should always have the knowledge of competitors' products and take a wise decision.

Monitoring Performance

Sales executives should monitor the performance of the employees and report to higher management to improve the performance and fill the loop holes.

Thus, conceptual skills deal with ideas, technical skills deal with things, people skills concern individuals, technical skills are concerned with product-specific skills, and decision skills relate to decision-making.

Importance of Sales Management

Sales management is very crucial for any organization to achieve its targets. In order to increase customer demand for a particular product, we need management of sales.

The following points need to be considered for sales management in an organization:

- The first and foremost importance of sales management is that it facilitates the sale of a product at a price, which realizes profits and helps in generating revenue to the company.

- It helps to achieve organizational goals and objectives by focusing on the aim and planning a strategy regarding achievement of the goal within a time-frame.

- Sales team monitors the customer preference, government policy, competitor situation, etc., to make the required changes accordingly and manage sales.

- By monitoring the customer preference, the salesperson develops a positive relationship with the customer, which helps to retain the customer for a long period of time.

- Both the buyers and sellers have the same type of relationship, which is based on exchange of goods, services and money. This helps in attaining customer satisfaction.

- Sales Management may differ from one organization to the other, but overall, we can conclude that sales management is very important for an organization for achieving its short- and long-term goals.

Objective of Sales Management

Every organization has an objective before initializing functions. We need to understand the goal of managing sales. Here we are discussing Sales Management in terms of its objectives.

Sales Volume

It is the capacity or the number of items sold or services sold in the normal operations of a company in a specified period. The foremost objective of sales management is to increase sales volume to generate revenue.

Contribution to Profit

The sales of the organization should contribute to profit, as it is the only revenue generating department. It can be calculated as the percentage or ratio of gain in total turnover.

Continuing Growth

One of the main objectives of Sales Management is to retain consumers to continue growth of the organization. There should be regular expansion of sales and demand for an item in the market with new advanced formulation.

These are the major objectives a sales executive has to focus on in sales management.

Distribution is the process of making a product or service available for use or consumption to the end consumer or business.

Distribution could be of the following two types:

- Direct Distribution

It can be defined as expanding or moving from one place to another without changing direction or stopping. For example, Bata has no distribution channel; it sells its products directly to the end consumers.

- Indirect Distribution

It can be defined as means that are not directly caused by or resulting from something. For example, LG sells its product from the factory to the dealers, and it reaches the consumers through dealers.

Distribution Strategies

In an intensive distribution approach, the marketer relies on chain stores to reach broad markets in a cost efficient manner

Prior to designing a distribution system, the planner needs to determine what the distribution channel is to achieve in broad terms. The overall approach to distributing products or services depends on a number of factors including the type of product, especially perishability; the market served; the geographic scope of operations and the firm's overall mission and vision. The process of setting out a broad statement of the aims and objectives of a distribution channel is a strategic level decision.

Strategically, there are three approaches to distribution:

- *Mass distribution* (also known as *intensive distribution*): When products are destined for a mass market, the marketer will seek out intermediaries that appeal to a broad market base. For example, snack foods and drinks are sold via a wide variety of outlets including supermarkets, convenience stores, vending machines, cafeterias and others. The choice of distribution outlet is skewed towards those than can deliver mass markets in a cost efficient manner.

- *Selective distribution:* A manufacturer may choose to restrict the number of outlets handling a product. For example, a manufacturer of premium electrical goods may choose to deal with department stores and independent outlets that can provide added value service level required to support the product. Dr Scholl orthopedic sandals, for example, only sell their product through pharmacies because this type of intermediary supports the desired *therapeutic* positioning of the product. Some of the prestige brands of cosmetics and skincare, such as Estee Lauder, Jurlique and Clinique, insist that sales staff are trained to use the product range. The manufacturer will only allow trained clinicians to sell their products.

- *Exclusive distribution:* In an exclusive distribution approach, a manufacturer chooses to deal with one intermediary or one type of intermediary. The advantage of an exclusive approach is that the manufacturer retains greater control over the distribution process. In exclusive arrangements, the distributor is expected to work closely with the manufacturer and add value to the product through service level, after sales care or client support services. The most common type of exclusive arrangement an agreement between a supplier and a retailer granting the retailer exclusive rights within a specific geographic area to carry the supplier's product.

Summary of strategic approaches to distribution

Approach	Definition
Intensive distribution	The producer's products are stocked in the majority of outlets. This strategy is common for mass produced products such as basic supplies, snack foods, magazines and soft drink beverages.
Selective distribution	The producer relies on a few intermediaries to carry their product. This strategy is commonly observed for more specialised goods that are carried through specialist dealers, for example, brands of craft tools, or large appliances.
Exclusive distribution	The producer selects only very few intermediaries. Exclusive distribution occurs where the seller agrees to allow a single retailer the right to sell the manufacturer's products. This strategy is typical of luxury goods retailers such as Gucci.

Push vs Pull Strategy

In consumer markets, another key strategic level decision is whether to use a push or pull strategy. In a *push strategy*, the marketer uses intensive advertising and incentives aimed at distributors, especially retailers and wholesalers, with the expectation that they will stock the product or brand, and that consumers will purchase it when they see it in stores. In contrast, in a *pull strategy*, the marketer promotes the product directly to consumers hoping that they will pressure retailers to stock the product or brand, thereby pulling it through the distribution channel. The choice of a push or pull strategy has important implications for advertising and promotion. In a push strategy the promotional mix would consist of trade advertising and sales calls while the advertising media would normally be weighted towards trade magazines, exhibitions and trade shows while a pull strategy would make more extensive use consumer advertising and sales promotions while the media mix would be weighted towards mass-market media such as newspapers, magazines, television and radio.

Channels and Intermediaries

Distribution of products takes place by means of channels to become available on markets, in stores or in webshops. Channels are sets of interdependent organizers (called in-termediaries or distributors) involved in making the product available for consumption to end-user. This is mostly accomplished through merchant retailers or wholesalers, or in international context by importers. In certain specialist markets, agents or brokers may become involved in distribution channel.

A wholesale fish market at Haikou

Typical intermediaries involved in distribution include:

- Wholesaler: A merchant intermediary who sells chiefly to retailers, other merchants, or industrial, institutional, and commercial users mainly for resale or business use. Wholesalers typically sell in large quantities. (Wholesalers, by definition, do not deal directly with the public).

- Retailer: A merchant intermediary who sells direct to the public. There are many different types of retail outlet - from hypermarts and supermarkets to small, independent stores.

- Agent: An intermediary who is authorized to act for a principal in order to facilitate exchange. Unlike merchant wholesalers and retailers, agents do not take title to goods, but simply put buyers and sellers together. Agents are typically paid via commissions by the principal. For example, travel agents are paid a commission of around 15% for each booking made with an airline or hotel operator.

- Jobber: A special type of wholesaler, typically one who operates on a small scale and sells only to retailers or institutions. For example, rack jobbers are small independent wholesalers who operate from a truck, supplying convenience stores with snack foods and drinks on a regular basis.

Channel Design

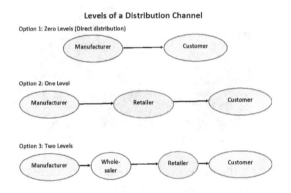

Types of distribution systems

A firm can design any number of channels they require to reach customers efficiently and effectively. Channels can be distinguished by the number of intermediaries between producer and consumer. If there are no intermediaries then this is known as a zero-level distribution system or direct marketing. A level one (sometimes called one-tier) channel has a single intermediary. A level two (alternatively a two-tier) channel has two intermediaries, and so on. This flow is typically represented as being manufacturer to retailer to consumer, but may involve other types of intermediaries. In practice, distribution systems for perishable goods tend to be shorter - direct or single intermediary, because of the need to reduce the time a product spends in transit or in storage. In other cases, distribution systems can become quite complex involving many levels and different types of intermediaries.

Channel Mix

In practice, many organizations use a mix of different channels; a direct sales force may call on larger customers may be complemented with agents to cover smaller customers and prospects. When a single organisation uses a variety of different channels to reach its markets, this is known as a multi-channel distribution network. In addition, online retailing or e-commerce is leading to disintermediation, the removal of intermediaries from a supply chain. Retailing via smartphone or m-commerce is also a growth area.

Managing Channels

The firm's marketing department needs to design the most suitable channels for the firm's products, then select appropriate channel members or intermediaries. An organisation may need to train staff of intermediaries and motivate the intermediary to sell the firm's products. The firm should monitor the channel's performance over time and modify the channel to enhance performance.

Channel Motivation

Harrod's food hall, a major retailer

To motivate intermediaries the firm can use positive actions, such as offering higher margins to the intermediary, special deals, premiums and allowances for advertising or display. On the other hand, negative actions may be necessary, such as threatening to cut back on margin, or hold back delivery of product. Care must be exercised when considering negative actions as these may fall foul of regulations and can contribute to a public backlash and a public relations disaster.

Channel Conflict

Channel conflict can arise when one intermediary's actions prevent another intermediary from achieving their objectives. Vertical channel conflict occurs between the levels within a channel, and horizontal channel conflict occurs between intermediaries at the same level within a channel. Channel conflict is a perennial problem. There are risks that a powerful channel member may coordinate the interests of the channel for personal gain.

Trends in Distribution

Channel Switching

Channel-switching is the action of consumers switching from one type of channel intermediary to a different type of intermediary for their purchases. Examples include switching from brick-and-mortar stores to online catalogues and e-commerce providers; switching from grocery stores to convenience stores or switching from top tier department stores to mass market discount outlets. A number of factors have led to an increase in channel switching behaviour; the growth of e-commerce, the globalization of markets, the advent of Category killers (such as Officeworks and Kids 'R Us) as well as changes in the legal or statutory environment. For instance, in Australia and New Zealand, following a relaxation of laws prohibiting supermarkets from selling therapeutic goods, consumers are gradually switching away from pharmacies and towards supermarkets for the purchase of minor analgesics, cough and cold preparations and complementary medicines such as vitamins and herbal remedies.

The advent of "category killers", such as Australia's Officeworks, has contributed to an increase in channel switching behaviour.

For the consumer, channel switching offers a more diverse shopping experience. However, marketers need to be alert to channel switching because of its potential to erode market share. Evidence of channel switching can suggest that disruptive forces are at play, and that consumer behaviour is undergoing fundamental changes. A consumer may be prompted to switch channels when the product or service can be found at cheaper prices, when superior models become available, when a wider range is offered, or simply because it is more convenient to shop through a different channel (e.g. online or one-stop shopping). As a hedge against market share losses due to switching behaviour, some retailers engage in multi-channel retailing.

Customer Value

The emergence of a service-dominant logic perspective has focussed scholarly attention on how distribution networks serve to create customer value and to consider how value is co-created by all the players within the distribution chain, including the value created by customers themselves. This emphasis on value-creation is contributing to a change in terminology surrounding distribution processes; "distribution networks" are often termed value-chains while distribution centres" are often termed customer fulfillment centres. For example, the retail giant Amazon, which utilises both direct online distribution alongside bricks and mortar stores, now calls its despatch centres "customer fulfillment centres". Although the term, "customer fulfillment centre" has been criticised on the grounds that it is a neologism, its use is becoming increasingly mainstream as it slowly makes its way into introductory marketing textbooks.

Disintermediation

Disintermediation occurs when manufacturers or service providers eliminate inter-mediaries from the distribution network and deal directly with purchasers. Disinter-mediation is found in industries where radically new types of channel intermediaries displace traditional distributors. The widespread public acceptance of online shopping has been a major trigger for disintermediation in some industries. Certain types of tra-ditional intermediaries are dropping by the wayside.

Advantages of a Distribution Channel

- Reduced costs

  Sure, you can do it yourself, but Including a new location to your distribution map involves a lot of resources - time, money, and human resources. Using an existing distribution network, however, extends your company's geographical reach much more easily and quickly than if you do everything on your own.

  And because retailers stock their shelves with your products and customers go to store locations to purchase them, you don't incur additional stocking and delivery expenses.

- A tighter focus on your core competencies

  To successfully expand in unfamiliar territory, you need local expertise - a deep understanding of what the people in the area need and want. If you're a small business, doing this may require that you hire new personnel so your existing workforce can focus on doing what they need to be doing.

  Wholesalers, retailers, and dealers take care of the nitty-gritty involved in the product distribution process: order and inventory management, management of retailer and customer relationships, customer service initiatives pre- and post-sale, and product shipment to various locations.

- More efficient marketing

  To maximize the value of your marketing dollars, you can collaborate with oth-er manufacturers and run joint marketing or promotional campaigns to drive more foot traffic to the retail outlets that sell your products. This way, you don't have to shoulder the full advertising costs.

- Wider customer reach

  Another advantage of distribution channels is the speed at which you can distribute your products in large geographic areas. Established distributors can readily tap a network of retailers and other distributors to help with market coverage.

As such, you don't have to deal with the time, cost, and effort it takes to build those relationships. Plus, you need not go through the difficulties of setting up your own direct distribution channel in the area you're expanding in.

- Logistic support

Distributors and retailers have to efficiently manage their stocks and are generally good at it. They can fulfill orders daily and know when to request large shipments from manufacturers. And in case a fulfillment error occurs, the distributor or retail chain takes care of resolving any issues.

- Easily available feedback

Retail chains know which products sell well in their specific areas of coverage. Their feedback can prove valuable in making a product that more customers need and want.

- Faster growth

If you plan to introduce your products to a global audience, international agents specialize in distributing products in various areas of the world. Particularly if you're a small manufacturing business, you can use their expertise to put your product in front of a customer base you would otherwise not reach on your own.

References

- Harrison, T.P., Lee, H.L. and Neale., J. J., The Practice of Supply Chain Management,Springer, 2003, ISBN 0-387-24099-3

- How-to-create-a-b2b-marketing-strategy: walkersands.com, Retrieved 08 July 2018

- Dholakia1, R.R., Zhao, M. and Dholakia, N., "Multichannel retailing: A case study of early experiences.," Journal of Interactive Marketing, vol. 19, March, 2009, pp 63–74, DOI: 10.1002/dir.20035

- Market-analysis-for-business-plan: thebusinessplanshop.com, Retrieved 28 June 2018

- "Volkswagen's New Guerrilla Campaign Encourages People To Try The ‹Fast Lane›". Creative Guerrilla Marketing. Retrieved 2016-04-01

- Identifying-target-market-important-company-76792: smallbusiness.chron.com, Retrieved 18 May 2018

- Eskilson, Stephen J. (2007). Graphic Design: A New History. New Haven, Connecticut: Yale University Press. p. 58. ISBN 978-0-300-12011-0

- Pricing-in-marketing: businessjargons.com, Retrieved 22 March 2018

- Kaplan, Andreas M.; Haenlein, Michael (2010-01-01). "Users of the world, unite! The challenges and opportunities of Social Media". Business Horizons. 53 (1): 59–68. doi:10.1016/j.bushor.2009.09.003

- Advantages-increase-promotion-advertising-23195: smallbusiness.chron.com, Retrieved 20 March 2018

- Tran, Mark (2009-07-23). "Singer gets his revenge on United Airlines and soars to fame". The Guardian. ISSN 0261-3077. Retrieved 2016-04-01

- What-is-marketing-communication-marcom: marsdd.com, Retrieved 28 April 2018

- Dhar, Vasant; Chang, Elaine A. (2009-11-01). "Does Chatter Matter? The Impact of User-Generated Content on Music Sales". Journal of Interactive Marketing. 23 (4): 300–307. doi:10.1016/j.intmar.2009.07.004

- The-advantages-of-a-distribution-channel-for-manufacturers: apruve.com, Retrieved 18 April 2018

- McChesney, Robert, Educators and the Battle for Control of U.S. Broadcasting, 1928–35, Rich Media, Poor Democracy, ISBN 0-252-02448-6 (1999)

Pricing in Business-to-Business (B2B) Marketing

An understanding of B2B marketing requires an understanding of pricing strategies and pricing mistakes that a business can make in B2B commerce. This chapter has been written so as to give a detailed explanation of the different aspects of B2B pricing and discusses the central concepts of market risk, market price, clean price, price ceiling, price floor and dirty price.

B2B Pricing Strategies

An efficient B2B pricing strategy is critical to staying competitive in today's business-to-business (B2B) markets, where you face low-cost competitors from all over the world. Inefficient pricing can compromise revenue, sales and customer satisfaction. Yet too many B2B companies get caught in the trap of reacting to cost and competition pressures instead of proactively facing negotiations with a compelling value-based B2B pricing strategy.

Value-based pricing creates higher profits compared to cost- or competition-based pricing, according to leading practitioners and researchers at top business schools. Done right, your value-based B2B pricing strategy can come close to the precise point of the customer's willingness to pay within the context of the competitive landscape and the financial consequences. On top of this, engaging with customers in this way can lead to breakthroughs in innovation that build stronger customer relationships. This integrates your longer-term marketing strategy as it can provide you with extra value needed to position your company at premium prices.

When your customer wants to know about the price, what they really want to know is the value – even if they don't know that yet. With an effective B2B pricing strategy you respond to this by understanding their need and communicating your value in meeting that need. This is a departure from old tricks of the B2B sales and marketing trade like calculating costs of production and adding markup (cost-based pricing) or setting your prices in relation to your competition's (competition-based pricing). Instead, with value-based pricing, you clichés are often true put yourself in the customer's shoes. Through business coaching and skills training including pricing psychology, value-based segmentation and pricing elasticity, you can learn to communicate the differentiating value of your offer.

When you transition to a B2B pricing strategy, your product or service is no longer interchangeable with those of your competitors because it meets the customer's specific needed value.

Pricing excellence cannot be achieved if you focus solely on costs or competition. It can be tempting, it must be admitted, to fall back on these sales and marketing methods because the data is easy to obtain and simple to calculate. Unfortunately, cost- and competition-based pricing are ultimately inefficient B2B pricing strategies.

Cost-based B2B pricing strategy offer simplicity since you already know how much your product or service costs you to create and how much you feel you should profit. However, you will either eventually turn customers off with prices that are too high, or you will find yourself frustrated with margins that are too low.

In competition-based B2B pricing strategies, you need to also account for the market competitiveness, but once again, the data is practically at your fingertips. Unfortunately, when you base your B2B marketing strategies on what the competition is doing, someone else will always come along with a lower price. Get caught in that, you'll get commoditized and ultimately undersold.

In both cases, your relationship with the customer is skin-deep at best. Your offer is a commodity, not particularly distinguishable from the competition. You are continually subject to competing objectives of different stakeholders – being pulled in multiple directions. Cost- and competition-only are not only weak B2B pricing strategies, they also impede the integration of relationship-building into your marketing-strategy plan, to enable deeper value creation and pricing excellence.

No one said it was easy to reach pricing excellence through value-based propositions. This process can involve additional costs to design and implement. An efficient B2B pricing strategy must, of course, be informed by business costs, competitors and value. However, it is by perfecting your value-based strategies that will help you create a sustainable B2B relationship enabling both you and your client to grow and adapt to market changes with consistent pricing excellence.

Effective pricing strategies require gathering deep insights into your customers and knowledge about the economics impacting your company. A good means of perfecting your B2B sales and marketing skills and strategy is through executive education. A top business school course in B2B pricing strategy can demystify pricing excellence, whether on-campus or through distance learning.

Studying B2B pricing strategy offers an opportunity to take stock of your business value, identify gaps in your B2B pricing strategy, and hone skills for aligning your value proposition. This includes training your skills in price management and pricing psychology and learning to better identify price elasticity and feasible value-based segmentation. Alternatively, you may consider improving your B2B strategy skills with a marketing management program, which will offer similar tools, with a particular focus on ensuring you are part of the solution in terms of the customer's perception of value. Either way, executive coaching can be leveraged to improve your communications and negotiations skills. When you develop the skills for pricing excellence, you'll be able to create an action plan to secure your company's profit margins through an improved B2B pricing strategy.

The optimal price for a product is influenced by many variables. Competition, the general economic environment, perceived value, and emotional factors are just a few to consider. In addition, the product, the customer, and the market all have unique price sensitivities to consider. Constructing an algorithm to accurately factor all variables is difficult, but by considering the heuristics for product, customer, and market price sensitivities, you can improve pricing performance for each transaction.

- Product: Different products have different price sensitivities. Within your own product line, you may have premium products, commodity-type products, and custom-type products. Margins on your commodity-type products are typically lower and they tend to be very price-sensitive. They should be priced differently than your premium or custom products, which are less price sensitive and have higher margins. Your pricing strategy should reflect these heuristics. Begin pricing by correctly identifying the product category based on price sensitivity.

- Customer: Every customer is unique and has their own price sensitivity. Large volume customers tend to be more price sensitive than smaller volume customers. Customers who purchase frequently are also more price sensitive than less frequent buyers. In addition, different customers have an individual perception of the value of support and brand relationship. Customers who place a high value on relationship and product support are less price sensitive than those who perceive these elements to be less significant. You should also know where your customers are in their own business cycle.

- Market: Each market has its own level of sensitivity. If your products serve multiple markets, you must consider the sensitivity of the market as well as the product. The pricing environment of your industry is a variable as well. In some markets, movement by an industry price leader can impact prices for all market players.

Align Economic and Emotional Value

Willingness-to-pay isn't just a factor in the B2C marketplace. B2B companies need to consider it as well. It's the sweet spot where economic and emotional value intersect to create perceived value. If you are targeting customers that are innovators and early adopters, they are less price conscious. This segment is driven by the high emotional value of gaining a competitive edge and supports a high economic value.

On the opposite end of the spectrum are buyers that place no emotional value on your product. The purchase has low to no emotional value and willingness-to-pay is low as well. You must carefully match their perceived economic value to your price.

But the vast majority of your market lays in the middle, meaning that buyers are rational overall, but can sometimes be subject to emotional surges. For these you must price according to the economic drivers specific to their niche. Your pricing must support their own pricing metrics and value models.

Pricing Strategies

Too often, cost plus pricing is the standard strategy. It's easy because it doesn't require market research or understanding the psychology of customers or competitors. It is also inefficient and does not maximize profits. Cost plus pricing assigns the same margin to every customer; but we know customers have different price sensitivities and emotional values. Cost plus pricing can be effectively used to set price and margin floors. These floors can be used as the starting point for developing a value-based pricing strategy.

- Competitive pricing is essentially price plagiarism. You look at what the competition is doing and price your products accordingly. Using this strategy places no more value on your products or brand than that of your competitors.

- Value based pricing takes time and data but it maximizes profit per customer. By pricing per customer, per product, and per market, you focus on the customer to set your price. For example, large customers with tremendous buying power are priced differently than small customers who make infrequent purchases. Unlike static cost plus or competitive pricing strategies, value based pricing is more dynamic and because it is more customer-based, it can improve marketing efforts as well. After all, once you understand your high value customers, you can grow by targeting leads that resemble these customers.

Market Risk

Market risk is the possibility of an investor experiencing losses due to factors that affect the overall performance of the financial markets in which he or she is involved. Market risk, also called "systematic risk," cannot be eliminated through diversification, though it can be hedged against.

Sources of market risk include recessions, political turmoil, changes in interest rates, natural disasters and terrorist attacks.

Market risk and specific risk make up the two major categories of investment risk. The most common types of market risks include interest rate risk, equity risk, currency risk and commodity risk.

Publicly traded companies in the United States are required by the Securities and Exchange Commission (SEC) to disclose how their productivity and results may be linked to the performance of the financial markets. This requirement is meant to detail a company's exposure to financial risk. For example, a company providing derivative investments or foreign exchange futures may be more exposed to financial risk than companies that do not provide these types of investments. This information helps investors and traders make decisions based on their own risk management rules.

In contrast to market risk, specific risk or "unsystematic risk" is tied directly to the performance of a particular security and can be protected against through investment diversification. One example of unsystematic risk is a company declaring bankruptcy, thereby making its stock worthless to investors.

Interest rate risk covers the volatility that may accompany interest rate fluctuations due to fundamental factors, such as central bank announcements related to changes in monetary policy. This risk is most relevant to investments in fixed-income securities, such as bonds.

Equity risk is the risk involved in the changing prices of stock investments, and commodity risk covers the changing prices of commodities such as crude oil and corn.

Currency risk, or exchange-rate risk, arises from the change in the price of one currency in relation to another; investors or firms holding assets in another country are subject to currency risk.

Market risk exists because of price changes. The standard deviation of changes in the prices of stocks, currencies or commodities is referred to as price volatility. Volatility is rated in annualized terms and may be expressed as an absolute number, such as $10, or a percentage of the initial value, such as 10%.

Investors can utilize hedging strategies to protect against volatility and market risk. Targeting specific securities, investors can buy put options to protect against a downside move, and investors who want to hedge a large portfolio of stocks can utilize index options.

To measure market risk, investors and analysts use the value-at-risk (VaR) method. VaR modeling is a statistical risk management method that quantifies a stock or portfolio's potential loss as well as the probability of that potential loss occurring. While well-known and widely utilized, the VaR method requires certain assumptions that limit its precision. For example, it assumes that the makeup and content of the portfolio being measured is unchanged over a specified period. Though this may be acceptable for short-term horizons, it may provide less accurate measurements for long-term investments.

Beta is another relevant risk metric, as it measures the volatility or market risk of a security or portfolio in comparison to the market as a whole; it is used in the capital asset pricing model (CAPM) to calculate the expected return of an asset.

There are several major types of market risk, which are mentioned below:

Equity Risk

The risk associated with stock prices. In many cases, stocks have higher associated risks than other investment classes such as government bonds. Some types of equities such as small cap stocks traded on emerging markets can be extremely volatile.

Equity risk premium refers to the excess return that investing in the stock market provides over a risk-free rate. This excess return compensates investors for taking on the relatively higher risk of equity investing. The size of the premium varies depending on the level of risk in a particular portfolio and also changes over time as market risk fluctuates. As a rule, high-risk investments are compensated with a higher premium.

The equity risk premium is based on the idea of the risk-reward tradeoff. As a forward-looking quantity, the equity-risk premium is theoretical and cannot be known precisely, since no one knows how a particular stock, a basket of stocks or the stock market as a whole will perform in the future. It can be estimated as a backward-looking quantity by observing stock market and government bond performance over a defined period of time, for example, from 1970 to the present. Estimates, however, vary wildly depending on the time frame and method of calculation.

Some economists argue that, although certain markets in certain time periods may display a considerable equity risk premium, it is not, in fact, a generalizable concept. They argue that too much focus on specific cases e.g., the U.S. stock market in the last century has made a statistical peculiarity seem like an economic law. Several stock exchanges have gone bust over the years, for example, so a focus on the historically exceptional U.S. market may distort the picture. This focus is known as survivorship bias.

The majority of economists agree that the concept of an equity risk premium is valid: over the long term, markets compensate investors more for taking on the greater risk of investing in stocks. How exactly to calculate this premium is disputed. A survey of academic economists gives an average range of 3–3.5% for a 1-year horizon, and 5–5.5% for a 30-year horizon. CFOs, meanwhile, estimate the premium to be 5.6% over T-bills (U.S. government debt obligations with maturities of less than one year) and 3.8% over T-bonds (maturities of greater than 10 years).

The second half of the 20th century saw a relatively high equity risk premium, over 8% by some calculations, versus just under 5% for the first half of the century. Given that the century ended at the height of the dot-com bubble, however, this arbitrary window may not be ideal.

To calculate the equity risk premium, we can begin with the capital asset pricing model (CAPM), which is usually written:

$$R_a = R_f + \beta_a (R_m - R_f)$$

where:

R_a = expected return on investment in "a"

R_f = risk-free rate of return

β_a = beta of "a"

R_m = expected return of market

In the context of the equity risk premium, a is an equity investment of some kind, such as 100 shares of a blue-chip stock, or a diversified stock portfolio. If we are simply talking about the stock market (a = m), then $R_a = R_m$. The beta coefficient is a measure of a stock's volatility, or risk, versus that of the market; the market's volatility is conventionally set to 1, so if a = m, then $\beta_a = \beta_m = 1$. $R_m - R_f$ is known as the market premium; $R_a - R_f$ is the risk premium. If a is an equity investment, then $R_a - R_f$ is the equity risk premium; if a = m, then the market premium and the equity risk premium are the same.

The equation for the equity risk premium, then, is a simple reworking of the CAPM:

Equity Risk Premium = $R_a - R_f = \beta_a (R_m - R_f)$

This summarizes the theory behind the equity risk premium, but questions arise in practice. If, instead of calculating expected rates of return, we want to plug in historical rates of return and use those to estimate future rates, the calculation is fairly straightforward. If, however, we are attempting a forward-looking calculation, the question is: how do you estimate the expected rate of return?

One method is to use dividends to estimate long-term growth, using a reworking of the Gordon Growth Model:

$$k = D / P + g$$

where:

k = expected return, expressed as a percentage (this value could be calculated for R_a or R_m)

D = dividends per share

P = price per share

g = annual growth in dividends, expressed as a percentage

Another is to use growth in earnings, rather than growth in dividends. In this model, expected return is equal to the earnings yield, the reciprocal of the P/E ratio.

$$k = E / P$$

where:

k = expected return

E = trailing twelve-month earnings per share

P = price per share.

Interest Rate Risk

The risk of unpredictable interest rate changes. The prices of most assets are sensitive to changes in interest rates. For example, the price of fixed interest rate bonds typically declines as interest rates rise.

The interest rate risk is the risk that an investment's value will change due to a change in the absolute level of interest rates, in the spread between two rates, in the shape of the yield curve, or in any other interest rate relationship. Such changes usually affect securities inversely and can be reduced by diversifying (investing in fixed-income securities with different durations) or hedging (such as through an interest rate swap).

Interest rate risk affects the value of bonds more directly than stocks, and it is a major risk to all bondholders. As interest rates rise, bond prices fall, and vice versa. The rationale is that as interest rates increase, the opportunity cost of holding a bond decreases, since investors are able to realize greater yields by switching to other investments that reflect the higher interest rate. For example, a 5% bond is worth more if interest rates decrease, since the bondholder receives a fixed rate of return relative to the market, which is offering a lower rate of return as a result of the decrease in rates.

Interest rate risk is most relevant to fixed-income securities whereby a potential increase in market interest rates is a risk to the value of fixed-income securities. When market interest rates increase, prices on previously issued fixed-income securities as traded in the market decline, since potential investors are now more inclined to buy new securities that offer higher rates. Only by having lower selling prices can past securities with lower rates become competitive with securities issued after market interest rates have turned higher.

For example, if an investor buys a five-year bond that costs $500 with a 3 percent coupon, interest rates may rise to 4%. In that case, the investor may have difficulty selling the bond when others enter the market with more attractive rates. Older bonds look less attractive as newly issued bonds carry higher coupon rates as well. Further, lower demand may cause lower prices on the secondary market, and the investor is likely to get less for the bond on the market than he paid for it.

The value of existing fixed-income securities with different maturities declines by various degrees when market interest rates rise. This is referred to as price sensitivity, meaning that prices on securities of certain maturity lengths are more sensitive to increases in market interest rates, resulting in sharper declines in their security values.

For example, suppose there are two fixed-income securities, one maturing in one year and the other in 10 years. When market interest rates rise, holders of the one-year security could quickly reinvest in a higher-rate security after having a lower return for only one year. Holders of the 10-year security would be stuck with a lower rate for 9 more years, justifying a comparably lower security value than shorter-term securities to attract willing buyers. The longer a security's maturity, the more its price declines to a given increase in interest rates.

The greater price sensibility of longer-term securities leads to higher interest rate risk for those securities. To compensate investors for taking on more risk, the expected rates of return on longer-term securities are normally higher than on shorter-term securities. This extra rate of return is called maturity risk premium, which is higher with longer years to maturity. Along with other risk premiums, such as default risk premiums and liquidity risk premiums, maturity risk premiums help determine rates offered on securities of different maturities beyond varied credit and liquidity conditions.

Exchange Rate Risk

Exchange rates can change rapidly as they are affected by a wide range of political and economic conditions. Many businesses have exposure to interest rates both in terms of costs and revenue sources. As a result, changes in exchange rates can lead to volatility in a company's margins and profitability. Exchange rates also directly impact the value of foreign assets such as property.

Types of Exposure

Transaction Risk

A firm has *transaction risk* whenever it has contractual cash flows (receivables and payables) whose values are subject to unanticipated changes in exchange rates due to a contract being denominated in a foreign currency. To realize the domestic value of its foreign-denominated cash flows, the firm must exchange foreign currency for domestic currency. As firms negotiate contracts with set prices and delivery dates in the face of a volatile foreign exchange market with exchange rates constantly fluctuating, the firms face a risk of changes in the exchange rate between the foreign and domestic currency. It refers to the risk associated with the change in the exchange rate between the time an enterprise initiates a transaction and settles it.

Applying public accounting rules causes firms with transnational risks to be impacted by a process known as "re-measurement". The current value of contractual cash flows are remeasured at each balance sheet.

Economic Risk

A firm has *economic risk* (also known as *forecast risk*) to the degree that its market value is influenced by unexpected exchange rate fluctuations. Such exchange rate adjustments can severely affect the firm's market share position with regards to its competitors, the firm's future cash flows, and ultimately the firm's value. Economic risk can affect the present value of future cash flows. Any transaction that exposes the firm to foreign exchange risk also exposes the firm economically, but economic risks can be caused by other business activities and investments which may not be mere international transactions, such as future cash flows from fixed assets. A shift in exchange rates that influences the demand for a good in some country would also be an economic risk for a firm that sells that good.

Translation Risk

A firm's *translation risk* is the extent to which its financial reporting is affected by exchange rate movements. As all firms generally must prepare consolidated financial statements for reporting purposes, the consolidation process for multinationals entails translating foreign assets and liabilities or the financial statements of foreign subsidiaries from foreign to domestic currency. While translation risk may not affect a firm's cash flows, it could have a significant impact on a firm's reported earnings and therefore its stock price.

Contingent Risk

A firm has *contingent risk* when bidding for foreign projects or negotiating other contracts or foreign direct investments. Such a risk arises from the potential of a firm to suddenly face a transnational or economic foreign exchange risk, contingent on the outcome of some contract or negotiation. For example, a firm could be waiting for a project bid to be accepted by a foreign business or government that if accepted would result in an immediate receivable. While waiting, the firm faces a contingent risk from the uncertainty as to whether or not that receivable will happen.

Measurement

If foreign exchanges market are efficient such that purchasing power parity, interest rate parity, and the international Fisher effect hold true, a firm or investor needn't protect against foreign exchange risk due to an indifference toward international investment decisions. A deviation from one or more of the three international parity conditions generally needs to occur for an exposure to foreign exchange risk.

Financial risk is most commonly measured in terms of the variance or standard deviation of a variable such as percentage returns or rates of change. In foreign exchange, a relevant factor would be the rate of change of the spot exchange rate between currencies. Variance represents exchange rate risk by the spread of exchange rates, whereas standard deviation represents exchange rate risk by the amount exchange rates deviate, on average, from the mean exchange rate in a probability distribution. A higher standard deviation would signal a greater currency risk. Economists have criticized the accuracy of standard deviation as a risk indicator for its uniform treatment of deviations, be they positive or negative, and for automatically squaring deviation values. Alternatives such as average absolute deviationand semivariance have been advanced for measuring financial risk.

Value at Risk

Practitioners have advanced and regulators have accepted a financial risk management technique called value at risk (VaR), which examines the tail end of a distribution of returns for changes in exchange rates to highlight the outcomes with the worst returns. Banks in Europe have been authorized by the Bank for International Settlements to employ VaR models of their own design in establishing capital requirements for given levels of market risk. Using the VaR model helps risk managers determine the amount that could be lost on an investment portfolio over a certain period of time with a given probability of changes in exchange rate.

Management

Firms with exposure to foreign exchange risk may use a number of foreign exchange hedging strategies to reduce the exchange rate risk. Transaction exposure can be reduced either with the use of the money markets, foreign exchange derivatives such as forward contracts, futures contracts, options, and swaps, or with operational techniques such as currency invoicing, leading and lagging of receipts and payments, and exposure netting.

Firms may adopt alternative strategies to financial hedging for managing their economic or operating exposure, by carefully selecting production sites with a mind for lowering costs, using a policy of flexible sourcing in its supply chain management, diversifying its export market across a greater number of countries, or by implementing strong research and development activities and differentiating its products in pursuit of greater inelasticity and less foreign exchange risk exposure.

Translation exposure is largely dependent on the accounting standards of the home country and the translation methods required by those standards. For example, the United States Federal Accounting Standards Board specifies when and where to use certain methods such as the temporal method and current rate method. Firms can manage translation exposure by performing a balance sheet hedge. Since translation exposure arises from discrepancies between net assets and net liabilities on a balance sheet solely from exchange rate differences. Following this logic, a firm could acquire an appropriate amount of exposed assets or liabilities to balance any outstanding discrepancy. Foreign exchange derivatives may also be used to hedge against translation exposure.

Commodity Risk

The prices of commodities such as grains or fuels can be volatile in the short term. Commodity prices can also follow long cycles meaning that prices can remain elevated or depressed for extended periods of time. As a result, commodity price volatility is a key risk to industries that directly produce commodities or that use them as an input.

Commodity production inputs include raw materials like cotton, corn, wheat, oil, sugar, soybeans, copper, aluminum and steel. Factors that can affect commodity prices include political and regulatory changes, seasonal variations, weather, technology and market conditions. Commodity price risk is often hedged by major consumers. One way to implement these hedges is with commodity futures and options contracts traded on major exchanges like the Chicago Mercantile Exchange (CME). These contracts are equally beneficial to commodity users and producers by reducing price uncertainty.

Commodity price risk stems from unexpected changes in commodity prices that can reduce a producer's profit margin and make budgeting difficult. For example, in the first half of 2016, steel prices jumped 36% while natural rubber, which declined for more than three years, rebounded by 25%. This led many Wall Street financial analysts to conclude that major auto manufactures, as well as major parts makers, could see a materially negative impact on their profit margins for the full financial year.

Major crude oil producing companies are especially aware of commodity price risk. As oil prices fluctuate, the potential profit these companies can make also fluctuates. Some companies publish sensitivity tables to help financial analysts quantify the exact level of commodity price risk facing the company. For example, the French oil major Total SA says that, for every $10 per barrel change in the price of oil, their net operating income fluctuates by $2 billion and their operating cash flow by $2.5 billion. From June 2014 to January 2016, oil prices fell by over $70 per barrel. The magnitude of this price move reduced Total's operating cash flow by $17.5 billion in the period.

Fortunately, producers can protect themselves from fluctuations in commodity prices by implementing financial strategies that will guarantee a commodity's price (to minimize uncertainty) or lock in a worst-case-scenario price (to minimize potential losses). Futures and options are two financial instruments commonly used to hedge against commodity price risk.

Market Price

The market price is the current price at which an asset or service can be bought or sold. The economic theory contends that the market price converges at a point where the forces of supply and demand meet. Shocks to either the supply side or demand side can cause the market price for a good or service to be re-evaluated.

The market price of a security is the most recent price at which the security was traded. It is the result of traders, investor and dealers interacting with each other in a market.

To comprehend how a market price is derived, it is important to understand some basic trading concepts. There are two sides to every trade; when a trader buys or sells a security, a dealer takes the other side of the trade. When a trader buys a stock, dealers sell the stock. In most cases, the dealer is an intermediary representing other traders. When traders place a limit or stop orders away from the market price, the dealer holds the orders in its order book until the market price approaches the order price and the orders are executed.

Dealers, or market makers, quote market prices using a bid and an ask price. The bid is always lower than the ask, and the difference is the spread. From the dealer's perspective, the bid represents the price at which the dealer will buy. The ask price represents the price at which the dealer will sell. Dealers adjust these prices at their discretion. From the trader's perspective, a trader wanting to execute a trade at the market price must buy at the ask and sell at the bid.

The interaction between dealers and traders is what manipulates the market price. For example, assume the market price for XYZ stock is $50/51. There are eight traders wanting to buy XYZ stock; this represents demand. Five buy 100 shares at $50, three at $49 and one at $48. These orders are listed on the bid. There are also eight traders wanting to sell XYZ stock; this represents supply. Five sell 100 shares at $51, three at

$52 and one at $53. These orders are listed on offer. At this point, supply and demand are balanced, and traders do not want to cross the spread to execute their trade.

Say a new trader comes in and wants to buy 800 shares at the market price, which is the shock. This trader has to buy at the offer: 500 shares at $51, and 300 at $52. Now the spread widens, and the market price is $50/53. Dealers immediately take action to close the range. Since there are more buyers, the spread is closed by the bid adjusting upward. The result is a new market price of $52/53. This interaction is continually taking place in both directions.

In securities trading, the market price is the current price as dictated by the latest recorded trade. In accounting, the market price is the transfer price of a good or service at which the entire profit will be maximized. Meanwhile, the market price in the bond market is the last reported price excluding accrued interest; this is also called the clean price.

Clean Price

Clean price is the price of a coupon bond not including any accrued interest. A clean price is the discounted future cash flows, not including any interest accruing on the next coupon payment date, and immediately following each coupon payment, the clean price will equal the dirty price. The clean price is calculated by subtracting the accrued interest from the dirty price.

Clean Price = Dirty Price - Accrued Interest

The country in which the coupon-paying bond is traded will influence how the bond is quoted. In the United States, it is the market convention to quote a bond in terms of its clean price; in other markets, bonds are more commonly quoted in terms of their dirty price.

Bonds are quoted as either a percentage of their par value, or face value, or in dollar terms. For example, if a bond is quoted at 98, this indicates that it is 98% of the bond's par value. Therefore, if the bond's par value is $1,000, the bond price is $980. This is the clean price of the bond since it does not reflect the accrued interest on the bond. Although bonds are typically quoted in terms of the clean price, investors pay the dirty price unless the bond is purchased on the coupon payment date.

On a bond's interest payment date, the accrued interest is reset to zero. If the next coupon payment is not due or the bond has not expired, the accrued interest is added to sale price of the bond. For example, assume a $1,000 par value bond has a coupon rate of 5%, which is paid quarterly, and 30 days have passed since the last coupon date. Therefore, the accrued interest is calculated to be 0.42, or (5% x (30/90) x (1/4)). 90 days represents the average number of days in a quarter.

For example, assume a corporate bond has a par value of $1,000 and has a coupon rate of 6%, which is paid on a semi-annual basis on Jan. 1 and July 1. The bond is sold for a dirty price of 93, or 93% of par value, on March 2. To calculate the clean price, the number of days between the coupon dates is calculated to be 60 days, excluding the day that the bond was sold. Therefore, the accrued interest is calculated to be 1.00, or (6% x (1/2) x (60/180)). Therefore, the clean price of the bond is calculated to be 92.00, or 93 - 1.00, which is equivalent to $920.

Dirty Price

The price of a bond is the present value of its future cash-flows. To avoid the impact of the next coupon payment on the price of a bond, this cash flow is excluded from the price of the bond and is called the accrued interest. In finance, the dirty price is the price of a bond including any interest that has accrued since issue of the most recent coupon payment. This is to be compared with the clean price, which is the price of a bond excluding the accrued interest.

Dirty Price = Clean Price + Accrued Interest

When bond prices are quoted on a Bloomberg Terminal, Reuters or FactSet they are quoted using the clean price.

Bond Pricing

Bonds, as well as a variety of other fixed income securities, provide for coupon payments to be made to bond holders on a fixed schedule. The dirty price of a bond will decrease on the days coupons are paid, resulting in a saw-tooth pattern for the bond value. This is because there will be one fewer future cash flow (i.e., the coupon payment just received) at that point.

To separate out the effect of the coupon payments, the accrued interest between coupon dates is subtracted from the value determined by the dirty price to arrive at the clean price. The accrued interest is based on the day count convention, coupon rate, and number of days from the preceding coupon payment date.

The clean price more closely reflects changes in value due to issuer risk and changes in the structure of interest rates. Its graph is smoother than that of the dirty price. Use of the clean price also serves to differentiate interest income (based on the coupon rate) from trading profit and loss.

It is market practice in US to quote bonds on a clean-price basis. When a bond settles the accrued interest is added to the value based on the clean price to reflect the full market value.

Example

A corporate bond has a coupon rate of 7.2% and pays 4 times a year, on the 15th of January, April, July, and October. It uses the 30/360 US day count convention.

A trade for 1,000 par value of the bond settles on January 25. The prior coupon date was January 15. The accrued interest reflects ten days' interest, or $2.00 = (7.2% of $1,000 * (10 days/360 days)). Thus $2.00 is being paid to the seller as compensation for his or her share of the upcoming interest payment on April 15th.

The bonds are purchased from the market at $985.50. Given that $2.00 pays the accrued interest, the remainder ($983.50) represents the underlying value of the bonds. The following table illustrates the values of these terms.

The market convention for corporate bond prices assigns a quoted (clean price) of 98.35. This is sometimes referred to as the price per 100 par value. The standard broker valuation formula (incorporated in the Price function in Excel or any financial calculator, such as the HP10bII) confirms this; the main term calculates the actual (dirty price), which is the total cash exchanged, less a second term which represents the amount of accrued interest. The result, the actual price less accrued interest is referred to as the quoted price. The actual price is a present value amount determined by applying the market rate of interest to the bond's remaining cash flows. Accrued interest is simply a fractional (last interest date to the settlement date of the entire interest period) portion of an interest payment. Thus, the quoted price cannot be determined independently. Many people are confused by the fact that bonds are sold for "price plus accrued interest". However, "price" here refers to the quoted (clean) price. Thus it is more precise to say that bonds sell for "quoted price plus accrued interest", not because the quoted price is calculated and then accrued interest is added, but because the quoted price is determined by deducting accrued interest from the calculated actual (dirty) price.

Price Ceiling

A price ceiling occurs when the government puts a legal limit on how high the price of a product can be. In order for a price ceiling to be effective, it must be set below the natural market equilibrium.

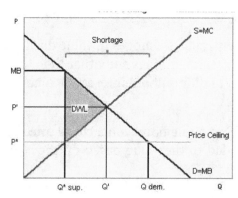

Figure: Price ceiling

When a price ceiling is set, a shortage occurs. For the price that the ceiling is set at, there is more demand than there is at the equilibrium price. There is also less supply than there is at the equilibrium price, thus there is more quantity demanded than quantity supplied. An inefficiency occurs since at the price ceiling quantity supplied the marginal benefit exceeds the marginal cost. This inefficiency is equal to the deadweight welfare loss.

This graph shows a price ceiling. P* shows the legal price the government has set, but MB shows the price the marginal consumer is willing to pay at Q*, which is the quantity that the industry is willing to supply. Since MB > P* (MC), a deadweight welfare loss results. P' and Q' show the equilibrium price. At P* the quantity demanded is greater than the quantity supplied.

Recent increases in the price of gas have left many individuals asking for a price ceiling on gas. You now see why this is a bad idea. If the government sets a price ceiling on gas, there will be a shortage. Remember the long gas lines in the 1970's? This is exactly what happened.

If a price ceiling is set, then there must be a way to assign who gets the low supply of the product. Of course, since there is a legal limit on the price, the price can't simply be raised. There are several ways this is done without raising the price:

- Lottery: One way to distribute a product for which there is a shortage is to draw names out of a hat. In some states there is a high demand to be able to hunt for moose, but the government has a limit on the amount of permits it gives out. Often these states have a lottery and if you are lucky enough to get drawn, you can try your luck at finding and shooting a moose during the season.

- Black Market: For those lucky enough to get some of the short supply, they are often better off selling what they have obtained to the demanders that will get more benefit out of it. In some cities there have been ceilings put on the apartment rent. While the demand for apartments increases, the rent remains the same. When some renters are ready to move, they sublease their apartment instead of ending their contract. If they were renting for $500, but someone is willing to pay $1000, then the subleaser can continue paying $500 and pocket the extra $500 he gets from the subleasee.

- Queue/First Come First Serve: Had they raised the price of tickets to $100 the opening night of Star Wars: Episode I, I wouldn't have been willing to camp out two nights to get a ticket. Since they didn't let the market determine the price, however, there was a huge line and those that were there first got to buy tickets. Of course, in this case they may have wanted the "buzz" that would come from having people camp out a week early just to get tickets, but there are other cases where a buzz isn't useful.

- Historical Use: Sometimes the government will allow the consumers that were already consuming to continue consuming. This would be hard to do since after the price ceiling there will be many more people claiming they have consumed in the past. Also, the quantity supplied is decreased which will even leave some of the historical consumers wanting.

Real-world Examples

Rent Control in New York City

"Pay no more than Ceiling Price," US poster during World War II

Rent control is a price ceiling on rent. When soldiers returned from World War II and started families, which increased demand for apartments, but stopped receiving military pay, many of them could not deal with higher rents. The government put in price controls so that soldiers and their families could pay their rents and keep their homes. However, it increased the quantity demand for apartments and lowered the quantity supplied, and so the number of available apartments rapidly decreased until none were available for latecomers. Price ceilings create shortages when producers may to abdicate market share or go unsubsidized.

"New ceiling price lists are here," US Office of Price Administration during World War II

Apartment Price Control in Finland

According to professors Niko Määttänen and Ari Hyytinen, price ceilings on Helsinki City Hitas apartments are highly inefficient economically. They cause queuing and discriminate against the handicapped, single parents, elderly, and others who are not able to queue for days. They cause inefficient allocation, as apartments are not bought by those willing to pay the most for them. Also, those who get an apartment are unwilling to leave it, even when their family or work situation changes, as they may not sell it at what they feel the market price should be. The inefficiencies increase apartment shortage and raise the market price of other apartments.

The Coulter Law in Australian Rules Football

Uniform wage ceilings were introduced in Australian rules football to address uneven competition. In the Victorian Football League (VFL) a declining competitive balance followed a 1925 expansion that had admitted Footscray, Hawthorn and North Melbourne. The effects on financially-weaker clubs were exacerbated in 1929 by the beginning of the Great Depression. In 1930, a new ceiling system, formulated by VFL administrator George Coulter, stipulated that individual players were to be paid no more than A£3 (approximately A$243 in 2017) for a regular home-and-away match, that they must also be paid if they were injured, that they could be paid no more than A£12 (approximately A$975 in 2017) for a finals match, and that the wages could not be augmented with other bonuses or lump-sum payments. The "Coulter law", as it became known, remained a strictly-binding price ceiling through its history.

During its early years, the Coulter law adversely affected only a minority of players, such as stars and players at wealthier clubs. Those individuals experienced, in effect, a drastic cut in wages. For instance, from 1931 the ceiling payment of £3 per game fell below the legal minimum award wage. While players at the more successful clubs of the day, such as Richmond, had previously paid significantly higher average wages, clubs that were struggling financially often could not meet the ceiling under the Coulter law. Clubs with a longstanding amateur ethos became significantly more competitive under the Coulter law, such as Melbourne, which had long attracted and retained players by indirect or non-financial incentives (such as finding players employment not related to football). The Coulter law led to at least one VFL star of the 1930s, Ron Todd, moving to the rival VFA, because he was dissatisfied with the maximum pay that he could receive at Collingwood.

As a result of World War II, the wage for a regular game was halved (to £1 and 10 shillings) for the 1942–45 seasons. After the war, the ceilings were modified several times in line with inflation. During the 1950s, the "Coulter law" was also blamed for shortening the careers of star players such as John Coleman and Brian Gleeson, as they and their clubs could not pay for the private surgery that the players required to continue their careers.

The Coulter law was abolished in 1968. However, in 1987 a club-level salary cap was introduced by the VFL and has been retained by its successor, the Australian Football League (AFL).

State Farm Insurance

On February 4, 2009, a Wall Street Journal article stated, "Last month State Farm pulled the plug on its 1.2 million homeowner policies in Florida, citing the state's punishing price controls. State Farm's local subsidiary recently requested an increase of 47%, but state regulators refused. State Farm says that since 2000, it has paid $1.21 in claims and expenses for every $1 of premium income received."

Venezuela

On January 10, 2006, a BBC article reported that since 2003, Venezuela President Hugo Chávez had been setting price ceilings on food and that the price ceilings had caused shortages and hoarding. A January 22, 2008, article from Associated Press stated, "Venezuelan troops are cracking down on the smuggling of food the National Guard has seized about 750 tons of food. Hugo Chavez ordered the military to keep people from smuggling scarce items like milk. He's also threatened to seize farms and milk plants." On February 28, 2009, Chávez ordered the military to seize control of all the rice processing plants in the country temporarily and to force them to produce at full capacity. He alleged they had been avoiding doing so in response to the price caps.

On January 3, 2007, an International Herald Tribune article reported that Chávez's price ceilings were causing shortages of materials used in the construction industry. According to an April 4, 2008, article from CBS News, Chávez ordered the nationalization of the cement industry, which had been exporting its products to receive higher prices outside the country.

Price Ceilings that Lead to Higher Prices

There is a substantial body of research showing that under some circumstances price ceilings can, paradoxically, lead to higher prices. The leading explanation is that price ceilings serve to coordinate collusion among suppliers who would otherwise compete on price.

More precisely, forming a cartel becomes profitable by enabling nominally-competing firms to act like a monopoly, limiting quantities and raising prices. However, forming a cartel is difficult because it is necessary to agree on quantities and prices, and because each firm will have an incentive to "cheat" by lowering prices to sell more than it agreed to. Antitrust laws make collusion even more difficult because of legal sanctions.

Having a third party, such as a regulator announce and enforce a maximum price level, can make it easier for the firms to agree on a price and to monitor pricing. The regulatory price can be viewed as a focal point, which is natural for both parties to charge.

One research paper documenting the phenomenon is Knittel and Stangel, which found that in the 1980s United States, states that fixed an interest rate ceiling of 18 percent had firms charging a rate only slightly below the ceiling. However states without an interest rate ceiling had interest rates that were significantly lower.

Another example is a paper by Sen et al. that found that gasoline prices were higher in states that instituted price ceilings. Another example is the Supreme Court of Pakistan's decision regarding fixing a ceiling price for sugar at 45 Pakistani rupees per kilogram. Sugar disappeared from the market because of a cartel of sugar producers and the failure of the Pakistani government to maintain supply even in the stores that it owned. The imported sugar required time to reach the country, and it could be sold at the rate fixed by the Supreme Court of Pakistan. Eventually, the government went for a review petition in the Supreme Court and obtained the withdrawal of the earlier decision of the apex court. Eventually, the market equilibrium was achieved at 55 to 60 rupees per kilogram.

Disadvantage of Price Ceiling

The disadvantage is that it will lead to lower supply. There will also be a shortage, demand will exceed supply; this leads to waiting lists and the emergence of black markets as people try to overcome the shortage of the good and pay well above market price.

For examples,

1) During the second world war, price of goods was fixed and good rationed. However, this encouraged people to sell on the black market through inflated prices.

2) Tickets for football prices and concerts are often set at a maximum price. (e.g. if left to the market, equilibrium prices would be much higher). e.g. at current prices F.A. Cup final could sell many more tickets than 80,000.

The advantage of setting this maximum prices is that it keeps football affordable for the average football supporter. It is argue if prices were set solely by market forces, it would be just the wealthy who could afford to go to games.

The disadvantage is that it means some who want to go to the game can't because there is a shortage of tickets. The government may set a maximum price for renting to keep housing affordable.

This may reduce supply of housing leading to homelessness.

However, it may be that landlords have monopoly power and supply is very inelastic. In this case a maximum price may make renting cheaper without reducing supply.

Price Floor

A price floor is the lowest legal price a commodity can be sold at. Price floors are used by the government to prevent prices from being too low. The most common price floor is the minimum wage the minimum price that can be payed for labor. Price floors are also used often in agriculture to try to protect farmers.

For a price floor to be effective, it must be set above the equilibrium price. If it's not above equilibrium, then the market won't sell below equilibrium and the price floor will be irrelevant.

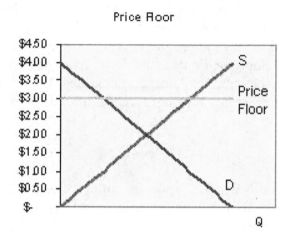

Drawing a price floor is simple. Simply draw a straight, horizontal line at the price floor level. This graph shows a price floor at $3.00. You'll notice that the price floor is above the equilibrium price, which is $2.00 in this example.

A few crazy things start to happen when a price floor is set. First of all, the price floor has raised the price above what it was at equilibrium, so the demanders (consumers) aren't willing to buy as much quantity. The demanders will purchase the quantity where the quantity demanded is equal to the price floor, or where the demand curve intersects the price floor line. On the other hand, since the price is higher than what it would be at equilibrium, the suppliers (producers) are willing to supply more than the equilibrium quantity. They will supply where their marginal cost is equal to the price floor, or where the supply curve intersects the price floor line.

As you might have guessed, this creates a problem. There is less quantity demanded (consumed) than quantity supplied (produced). This is called a surplus. If the surplus is allowed to be in the market then the price would actually drop below the equilibrium. In order to prevent this the government must step in. The government has a few options:

- They can buy up all the surplus. For a while the US government bought grain surpluses in the US and then gave all the grain to Africa. This might have been nice for African consumers, but it destroyed African farmers.

- They can strictly enforce the price floor and let the surplus go to waste. This means that the suppliers that are able to sell their goods are better off while those who can't sell theirs (because of lack of demand) will be worse off. Minimum wage laws, for example, mean that some workers who are willing to work at a lower wage don't get to work at all. Such workers make up a portion of the unemployed (this is called "structural unemployment").

- The government can control how much is produced. To prevent too many suppliers from producing, the government can give out production rights or pay people not to produce. Giving out production rights will lead to lobbying for the lucrative rights or even bribery. If the government pays people not to produce, then suddenly more producers will show up and ask to be payed.

- They can also subsidize consumption. To get demanders to purchase more of the surplus, the government can pay part of the costs. This would obviously get expensive really fast.

Although some of those ideas may sound stupid, the US government has done them. In the end, a price floor hurts society more than it helps. It may help farmers or the few workers that get to work for minimum wage, but it only helps those people by hurting everyone else. Price floors cause a deadweight welfare loss.

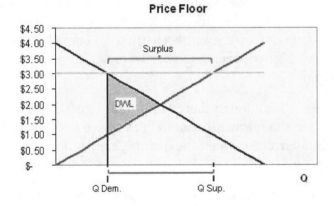

A deadweight welfare loss occurs whenever there is a difference between the price the marginal demander is willing to pay and the equilibrium price. The deadweight welfare loss is the loss of consumer and producer surplus. In other words, any time a regulation is put into place that moves the market away from equilibrium, beneficial transactions that would have occured can no longer take place. In the case of a price floor, the deadweight welfare loss is shown by a triangle on the left side of the equilibrium point, like in the graph. The area of the triangle is the amount of money that society loses.

A price floor can be set below the free-market equilibrium price. In the first graph at right, the dashed green line represents a price floor set below the free-market price. In this case, the floor has no practical effect. The government has mandated a minimum price, but the market already bears a higher price.

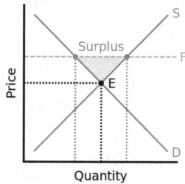

An effective, *binding* price floor, causing a surplus (supply exceeds demand).

By contrast, in the second graph, the dashed green line represents a price floor set above the free-market price. In this case, the price floor has a measurable impact on the market. It ensures prices stay high so that product can continue to be made.

Effect on the Market

A price floor set above the market equilibrium price has several side-effects. Consumers find they must now pay a higher price for the same product. As a result, they reduce their purchases or drop out of the market entirely. Meanwhile, suppliers find they are guaranteed a new, higher price than they were charging before. As a result, they increase production.

Taken together, these effects mean there is now an excess supply (known as a "surplus") of the product in the market to maintain the price floor over the long term. The equilibrium price is determined when the quantity demanded is equal to the quantity supplied.

Further, the effect of mandating a higher price transfers some of the consumer surplus to producer surplus, while creating a deadweight loss as the price moves upward from the equilibrium price.

Minimum Wage

An example of a price floor is minimum wage laws; in this case, employees are the suppliers of labor and the company is the consumer. When the minimum wage is set above the equilibrium market price for unskilled labor, unemployment is created (more people are looking for jobs than there are jobs available). A minimum wage above the equilibrium wage would induce employers to hire fewer workers as well as allow (or entice) more people to enter the labor market; the result is a surplus in the amount of labor available. However, workers would have higher wages. The equilibrium wage for workers would be dependent upon their skill sets along with market conditions.

This model makes several assumptions which may not hold true in reality, however. It assumes the costs of providing labor (food, commuting costs) are below the minimum wage, and that employment status and wages are not sticky. Unemployment in the United States, however, only includes participants of the labor force, which excludes 37.2 percent of Americans as of June 2016.

Previously, price floors in agriculture have been common in Europe. Today the EU uses a "softer" method: if the price falls below an intervention price, the EU buys enough of the product that the decrease in supply raises the price to the intervention price level. As a result of this, "butter mountains" in EU warehouses have sometimes resulted.

Difference between Price Floor and Price Ceiling

Price floor, is the setting of minimum price for a good or service. price floor can result in a surplus because the price may be artificially high. Market demand is about volume and price.

Price floors are common in agricultural commodities such as milk or corn, where the controls are designed to protect farmers' income.

A price ceiling is the opposite of a price floor: It's the maximum price for a good or service. Rent-control law in major cities is an example of price ceilings. Market demand is the overall demand for a product or service. It doesn't really change in terms of volume but it will if the price is too low or too high.

The four basic laws of supply and demand are:

1. If demand increases (demand curve shifts to the right) and supply remains unchanged, a shortage occurs, leading to a higher equilibrium price.

2. If demand decreases (demand curve shifts to the left) and supply remains unchanged, a surplus occurs, leading to a lower equilibrium price.

3. If demand remains unchanged and supply increases (supply curve shifts to the right), a surplus occurs, leading to a lower equilibrium price.

4. If demand remains unchanged and supply decreases (supply curve shifts to the left), a shortage occurs, leading to a higher equilibrium price.

B2B Pricing Mistakes

The following is a list of the most common mistakes companies make when pricing their products and services.

- Companies base their prices on their costs, not their customers' perceptions of value.

  Prices based on costs invariably lead to one of the following two scenarios:

  ◦ If the price is higher than the customers' perceived value the cost of sales goes up, discounting increases, sales cycles are prolonged and profits suffer;

  ◦ If the price is lower than the customers' perceived value, sales are brisk, but companies are leaving money on the table, and therefore are not maximizing their profit.

Costs are only relevant in the pricing process because they establish a lower boundary for the price. In certain circumstances, there are strategic reasons a company may decide to sell a product below its cost for a period of time, or to a certain market segment as a "loss leader." However, when a price is set according to the perceived value of the product or service, sales are brisk, and profits are maximized.

For example, a client manufactures audio components. Across their product line, they set prices according to a multiple of the parts cost. When the market for high-end audio components boomed, the company did well enough. But as competition began to increase, sales stagnated and profits evaporated. Our research showed that particular products were perceived by certain segments of the marketplace as "priced too low." Repricing of those products created enough additional revenue to pay for the launch and marketing of a new line of products and restored the company's leadership position in its niche of the industry.

- Companies base their prices on "the marketplace."

The marketplace is often cited as the "wisdom of the crowds," the collective judgment of the value of a product. But by resorting to "marketplace pricing," companies accept the commoditization of their product or service. Marketplace pricing is a resting place for companies that have given up, where profits end up being thin. Instead of giving up, these management teams must find ways to differentiate their products or services so as to create additional value for specific market segments. The marketplace is full of companies that have managed to drag themselves out of commoditization and establish a unique value proposition. They have then gone on to capture that unique value at prices higher than those of "the marketplace."

The best-known case of reverse commoditization is Starbucks in its early days. By rethinking the entire experience consumers engage when they consume a cup, the company has produced prodigious growth and outsized profits. A Starbucks cup of coffee delivers a unique value proposition that engages millions of consumers daily (including this author!), and they happily pay $3.00 to $4.95 for what used to be a ninety-nine cent cup of coffee. More recently, Starbucks has surrendered its vision of innovation supporting premium prices. It has allowed other companies to encroach on its claim of superior taste and a better experience. It has begun to count on price cutting as its primary mechanism for creating customer value. In March of 2009, we predict a rapid decline in the company's stature, fortunes and profits.

- Companies attempt to achieve the same profit margin across different product lines.

Some financial strategies support a drive for uniformity, and companies try to achieve identical profit margins for disparate product lines. The iron law of pricing is that different customers will assign different values to identical products. For any single product, profit is optimized when the price reflects the customer's willingness to pay. This willingness to pay is a reflection of his or her perception of value of that product, and the profit margin in another product line is completely irrelevant.

The Wall Street Journal reported on March 27 of last year how the industrial behemoth Parker had a uniform 35% gross profit objective across its 800,000 products. They were stuck in a "profit-margin rut." A new CEO in 2002 determined to change this. The change was championed in the face of determined opposition from the division managers. "There was so much pushback," according to the Journal, "the CEO eventually assembled a list of the 50 most commonly given reasons why the new pricing scheme would fail. If a manager came up with an argument not already on the list, then Mr. Washkewicz agreed to hear it out. Otherwise, he told them, get on board." The company credits the new pricing program with adding $200 million to their bottom line, improving return-on-invested capital from 7% to 21% and its shares have gained nearly 88%. By 2009, the company was able to point to over $800 million in profits earned by its singular focus on pricing.

- Companies fail to segment their customers.

Customer segments are differentiated by the customers' different requirements for your product. The value proposition for any product or service is different in different market segments, and the price strategy must reflect that difference. Your price realization strategy should include options that tailor your product, packaging, delivery options, marketing message and your pricing structure to particular customer segments, in order to capture the additional value created for these segments.

For example a client developed an innovative software product. They priced the desktop version at $79.00 per seat, a figure that "felt right" for the executive team. Sales stagnated. Atenga research showed that there were two distinct market segments: consumers and professionals. The $79.00 price was too high for the consumers who were interested in purchasing the product, and too low for the professionals. It communicated "not a serious tool" for the professionals who were interested in its value proposition. As a result of this research, the company decided to focus on the professional marketplace, and raised the price to $129.00. Sales soared.

- Companies hold prices at the same level for too long, ignoring changes in costs, competitive environment and in customers' preferences.

While we don't advocate changing prices every day, the fact is that most companies fear the uproar of a price change and put it off as long as possible. Savvy companies accustom their customers and their sales forces to frequent price changes. The process of keeping customers informed of price changes can, in reality, be a component of good customer service. Marketplaces change radically in a short period of time. It is important to recognize that the value proposition of your products changes along with changes in the marketplace, and you must adjust your pricing to reflect these changes.

For example, a customer sells services to the biopharmaceutical marketplace. Over the past few years, demands for its services have increased dramatically, and the entire industry has run into limitations in the number of trained personnel to do the work, and restricted capacity in terms of the required facilities and equipment. The company has held prices constant for the past seven years, even in the face of rising costs for capable staff. Atenga research found that customers believed the company was the best "value for money" in the industry, and they could raise prices about 12% without impacting sales. The additional 12%, however, more than doubled the company's profits in the second quarter after it was initiated.

- Companies often incentivize their salespeople on unis sold or revenue generated, rather than on profits.

    Volume-based sales incentives create a drain on profits when salespeople are compensated to push volume, even at the lowest possible price. This mistake is especially costly when salespeople have the authority to negotiate discounts. They will almost always leave money on the table by:

    ○ Selling lower-priced products,

    ○ Dropping prices to "clinch the deal."

When their "job" is to get the deal, regardless of profitability, salespeople will do exactly that. And, as a result, your profitability will diminish. Companies need to redefine the salesperson's "job" as maximizing profitability, and incentivize profitability, while also providing the salespeople the necessary "tools" to do so. These tools include information on profitability on each of the products your company sells, strict control of the awarding of discounts, and alternative choices and configurations to enable the salesperson to manage the inevitable negotiation about price.

For example, a client was persuaded by its sales staff to reduce the price of its keynote component from $2,400 to $1,800. The staff believed and persuaded management that lowering the price would drive proportionately higher sales volumes. The result was catastrophic. Sales volume over the following year declined almost 40%, as customers and channel partners perceived that the lower price signaled a lower quality. That lower-quality perception prevented the company from reversing the price increase, and it was not until a new product was designed 18 months later and released that the company began to recapture its former price point, and sales volume.

- Companies change prices without forecasting competitors' reactions.

Any change in your prices will cause a reaction by your competitors. Smart companies know enough about their competitors to forecast their reactions, and prepare for them. This avoids costly price wars that can destroy the profitability of an entire industry. Savvy companies understand that any significant lowering of your price which may drive increases in volume will provoke a reaction from your competitors.

For example, a client dominates its marketplace for a specific type of internet web services. As they prepared to move into a new market for the services, smaller competitors were already selling into it with a different form factor. Atenga research showed that the new form factor would be preferred by the entire market including the client's existing customers. The new entrants were financially weak, however and a low price point by the client would put pressure on the competitors that they would not be able to stand. At the end of the Atenga engagement, the client purchased one of the competitors, and went on to dominate the market in the new form factor, as well.

- Companies spend insufficient resources managing their pricing practices.

There are three basic variables in a company's profit calculation: cost, sales volume and price. Most management teams are comfortable working on cost reduction initiatives, and they have some level of confidence in growing their sales volume. But good price setting practices is seen as a "black art." Consequently, many companies resort to simplistic price procedures, while the same companies use highly sophisticated procedures and technologies to track and control their costs in minute detail and in real time. Likewise, companies may confidently forecast what effect marketing campaigns and "the number of feet on the street" have on sales volume. Managers feel comfortable with these two hard data sets. Therefore, they spend nearly all their time on the issues of sales volume growth and cost control, overlooking the vital role of pricing strategy. They erroneously believe that pricing is not important, or that hard data and rigorous methods are not available to enable them to control pricing. In fact pricing is of outmost importance, and a key element of the marketing mix. Good pricing strategies use hard data generated by modern methods such as Value Attribute Positioning, Conjoint Analysis or Van Westendorp's Price Sensitivity Meter, to generate accurate hard data on the perceived value of a product or service, thereby enabling mangers to maximize their profits by optimizing their prices.

For example a client managed prices by reviewing the prices of their competitors and making adjustments to their own accordingly. The primary data input to the pricing decision was the stories customers and salespeople told them about how competitors were offering lower prices. Atenga research showed that a significant segment of the customers desired a particular set of services along with the product, and that if our client, as opposed to its competition, offered those services, customers would be willing to pay significantly higher prices, as their overall costs would decline. Setting price levels and strategies based on competitive information was missing important growth and profit opportunities.

- Companies fail to establish internal procedures to optimize prices.

In some companies, the hastily-called "price meeting" has become a regular occurrence – a last-minute meeting to set the final price for a new product or service, or a semi-regular review of the company's price list. The attendees are often unprepared, and research is limited to a few salespeople's anecdotes, perhaps a competitor's last year's price list, and a financial officer's careful calculation of the product's cost structure across a variety of assumptions.

A more productive approach to price optimization requires data, analysis and discipline. These are the same ingredients that drove the cost-cutting success of the 1980s and 1990s, when companies systematically studied, reviewed and re-engineered their processes to eliminate redundancy and to reduce costs and cycle times. Price optimization requires, and deserves, the same level of attention and support.

Price optimization data comes from focused research. The research comes from surveys constructed and conducted by professionals who know what to ask for and how to extract the information that is important to the pricing project. They have experience structuring the questions, questionnaires and data to uncover the most important points, inconsistencies, and above all, the values perceived by the interviewees.

- Companies spend most of their time serving their least profitable customers.

Most companies do not even know who their most profitable customers are. While 80% of a company's profits generally come from 20% of its customers, a careful review of the data often will show surprises, since a company's largest customers are often only marginally profitable. Failure to identify and focus on their most profitable customers leaves companies undefended against wlier competitors. Such failure also deprives the company of the loyalty that more attention and better service would provide. It can also mean that the company cannot actively seek out more profitable customers because they identified or profiled them. These companies base their decisions on anecdotes, stories, whispers and hearsay rather than hard data about customers and competitors.

- Bonus entry

Companies rely on salespeople and other customer-facing staff for intelligence about the value perceptions of their customers. Such people are an uncertain source, because their information gathering methodology is often haphazard, and the information obtained thereby can be purely anecdotal. Such information is neither precise nor quantifiable. A customer will rarely tell the "complete truth" to a salesperson, so any information the customer may volunteer will be biased in many ways. Salespeople can readily identify those anecdotes that advance their interests (e.g., lower prices means higher revenues, regardless of profitability), and those that operate against them. Savvy companies employ trained professionals to collect and analyze the data to identify and evaluate the value perceptions of their marketplace. Large companies have entire departments doing this fulltime; smaller companies may outsource it to a specialist like Atenga.

- Failing to identify the value metric

Knowing how to identify your value metric, and adjust your pricing strategy accordingly can help to move your business out of the realm of "surviving" and onto the track for success. Simplistically put, a value metric is what you're charging for and how you're charging. In the B2B world, determining the most effective value metrics can help to ensure that your customers are buying your services because they think the pricing of the service is equal to the value they are receiving from it. In order to use a value metric properly, it's important for businesses to adjust their pricing strategy to reflect the things that their customers feel are beneficial and important in your services. In other words, your value metric should align with your customer's needs and outcomes.

- Using one-size-fits-all pricing

By using a "One-size-fits-all" pricing strategy, companies risk sending customers who are willing to pay more for better services to competitors, while scaring away customers who want fewer services for a lower price. Some businesses have avoided this trap—which can make them less appealing to sub-segments of their target market—by using adaptive pricing. With adaptive pricing, companies have the opportunity to reach out to different sub-segments of customers that define value differently. In our work, we describe this as customers having different value drivers. Here is a sample list of value drivers that lay the foundation for adaptive pricing:

- Uptime;
- Workflow productivity;
- Brand experience;
- Enterprise integration;
- Technical capabilities.

The driving force behind this concept is the idea that price, just like size, color, or material, is just another of a product's attributes. Just as a company may make a product with high-end materials, or in a smaller size to appeal to different types of clients, pricing can change when products and services sell to customers with different business models or sell through different channels. With adaptive pricing, companies can alter the attributes of product to appeal to their clients' sense of value – without reducing profits.

- Offering too many options

Most of the time, B2B pricing strategies work better when they are simple and easy to understand. A company should display their pricing strategy in a way that is transparent, clear, and easy for clients to match to their own perception of value for the product or service. Some businesses, when employing concepts like adaptive pricing, take the model too far, and offer excessive options. Unfortunately, too many choices can lead to decision fatigue, and stop possible customers in their tracks. In these circumstances, clients end up walking away because it's too difficult for them to figure out the best next step.

- Resorting to discounts

When stuck in a particularly competitive industry and failing to make the right number of sales, many B2B companies turn to discounts as a way of attracting and maintaining customers. Unfortunately, discounting products without careful consideration is a risky business, which may devalue your brand, and set a poor precedent for your customers. Offering discounts can lead customers to expect lower prices from you in the future. If people get used to paying a certain price for a particular product when discounted, it's much harder to restore value to that item back to its original price when demand picks up again.

References

- Moosa, Imad A. (2003). International Financial Operations: Arbitrage, Hedging, Speculation, Financing and Investment. New York, NY: Palgrave Macmillan. ISBN 0-333-99859-6

- Basic-pricing-strategies-b2b-commerce, b2b-ecommerce: oroinc.com, Retrieved 15 May 2018

- 10-common-pricing-mistakes-companies-make: reliableplant.com, Retrieved 19 May 2018

- Florida's Unnatural Disaster Archived 2017-08-12 at the Wayback Machine., Wall St. Journal, February 4, 2009

- Price-floor-price-ceiling-concepts-pros-4176: ukessays.com, Retrieved 31 March 2018

- Common-b2b-pricing-mistakes-businesses-make: valueandpricing.com, Retrieved 10 July 2018

- Wang, Peijie (2005). The Economics of Foreign Exchange and Global Finance. Berlin, Germany: Springer. ISBN 978-3-540-21237-9

- What-is-the-difference-between-a-price-floor-and-price-ceiling?-1094303: studypool.com, Retrieved 29 June 2018

- Eun, Cheol S.; Resnick, Bruce G. (2011). International Financial Management, 6th Edition. New York, NY: McGraw-Hill/Irwin. ISBN 978-0-07-803465-7

Business-to-Business (B2B) Sales and Distribution

The aim of this chapter is to provide a basic understanding of the different facets of B2B sales and distribution. It includes topics such as solution selling, selective distribution, exclusive distribution, inclusive distribution, push strategy, pull strategy, etc. for an extensive understanding.

Characteristics of B2B Sales

B2B sales is short for business-to-business sales. It refers to an activity where a business is selling its products or services (=*creating value*) to another business. It is distinct from B2C or business-to-consumer sales, which mean sales to individuals rather than businesses.

The key features in B2B sales are the following:

- Larger average transactions than in B2C: Business-to-business transactions are often thousands of dollars and can reach millions or even billions. A shop that sells shoes, for example, buys the shoes from a wholesaler 1000 pieces a time but sell them one by one (or rather two by one).

- Professional decision-making: The average shoe shopper buys maybe two pairs of shoes a year and has a million other things to do with their life as well. They are happy to find a fitting shoe and go on with their lives (well, some people might disagree on their level of professionalism when it comes to buying shoes but you get the point). But when a B2B sales person goes to meet a shoe shop owner to sell them some shoes, they are expected to face a lot more knowledgeable team of people who'll ask tough questions on the materials, supply chains and corporate responsibility. B2B buyers are experts so a B2B sales person has to be an expert, too. In B2B sales you have to find the right arguments to convince your counterpart.

- More stakeholders: Especially in the case of bigger deals a business-to-business sales person has to convince not only one but many different stakeholders. Often these stakeholders even have contradicting priorities. Someone working in marketing wants the shoes to be from a well-known brand and someone in the purchasing wants to make sure they are as cheap as possible. In B2B sales you are most often dealing with more than one buyer from the same account. Charming one person is not enough to close your deal.

- Longer time-to-purchase: On average business-to-business sales take longer to close. When you are buying new shoes, you just go in the nearest shop and buy them. On the other hand, when the shoe shop bought their last batch of shoes, selecting which shoes, which colors and how many they would buy involved decisions from the CEO, marketing manager, store manager and a consultant, and litres of coffee and dozens of Powerpoint presentations and Excel sheets. Don't expect to get big deals from your new B2B customers. Building trust takes time and you'll probably be handling smaller things until your new customer trusts you.

- Fewer prospects and customers: B2B customers usually have a lot higher LTV (life-time-value) than B2C customers. The pool from where a B2B business can draw new customers is also smaller. When an underserved shoe shopper gets tired of waiting and leaves angrily, another comes in (at least up to a point). This means that B2B customers must be well taken care of. You don't want to burn bridges with any of your prospects and especially you don't want to lose your current customers. Getting more customers is usually a lot more cumbersome and expensive than in B2C sales.

Steps to a more Successful B2B Sales Approach

- Research: Every lead that comes in or that you generate needs to be researched. Things like company size, how many of your website pages they have visited, etc. Even if a lead calls you out of the blue, start researching them while they are on the phone. And while reaching prospects has never been more difficult, the ability to research them has never been easier.

- Ask: The more information you get, the more you can help, add value, differentiate yourself from your competition and close sales. Questions are the most important sales tool. Ask open ended questions that begin with words like what, how, why, where, when and who. Try to avoid yes or no questions. One of the biggest mistakes a sale person makes is to assume something about the buyer. Asking questions minimizes the perils of assuming.

- Listen: Once you ask, listen Don't think about what your next question will be. Instead, repeat back what they buyer has said. This will make the buyer feel understood and will force you to focus on what the buyer is really saying. Strive to do only 30% of the talking. This may feel awkward at first, but you'll be amazed at how well it works.

- Teach: Teaching is the new pitching. In the course of actively listening to the buyer, look for teaching opportunities that can help educate them. Teaching helps the buyer discover that what they want might not be what they need. When a customer learns something new that will help them, the psychological power of reciprocity helps build preference and loyalty. When teaching, avoid talking about your own product or services.

- Qualify: "Always be closing" was a mantra from the old days of selling. If you're still using that approach, stop. Now, the mantra should be "always be qualifying." This tells you what your next steps should be. When qualifying, follow the popular GPCT and BANT approaches:

  o Goals: Try to get quantitative goals. What do they need to achieve?

  o Plans: What are their strategies and tactics to achieve those goals?

  o Challenges: What is standing in their way?

  o Timing: When are they supposed to achieve their goals?

  o Budget: Do they have a means of funding a solution to their problem?

  o Authority: Determine what person has influence within the company to authorize the purchasing decision.

  o Need: Is there a specific pain point the buyer has that you can solve?

  o Timeline: Is there a specific time frame for when the prospect needs your solution?

Most failed sales opportunities don't have good answers for GPCT and BANT:

- Close: If you've done the first five steps correctly, closing will feel more like an agreement than an arm-twisting manipulation (which doesn't work anyway). The buyer will feel comfortable and will know what they need to do next and have fewer questions and less buyer's remorse.

- Know the company before you reach out.

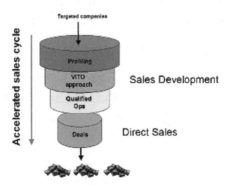

Do your research and understand everything you can about your prospect prior to that initial outreach. Pay particular attention to challenges and potential pain points the prospect may have so that you can position your product or service as a solution to those challenges.

- Subscribe to your prospects' newsletters or marketing campaigns

This will help you understand how they operate and sell their own product or service so that you can tailor your conversation with them to be relevant to their context or use case.

- Read your prospects' blog,

You'll be able to better understand what the company values, and how it thinks and operates as a whole. Take note if C-level executives (i.e. the ultimate decision makers) are drafting blog posts, as this will provide you with insight into what's important to them.

- Don't stop cold calling, just do it intelligently

When you conduct deep research into a prospect before making a call, you'll ensure that you bring relevant and helpful information to the conversation. If you know their challenges before they share them with you, you'll be able to present solutions to them off the top of your head, right in the moment.

- Collaborate with prospects through the buying process

Allow the flow of information to be two-way. Listen to what they have to say so you can work together to help them find the solution that best meets their needs. You'll not only increase conversions but also gain valuable anecdotal insight that you'll continue to build upon and use throughout your career in sales.

- Don't communicate with prospects through generic email blasts

That's the job of marketing. Instead, write personal emails to your prospects.

It takes more time but the personal approach will pay off dividends in the long run.

- Be diplomatic

As they say: diplomacy is the art of letting someone else have your way. Get them to tell you your own idea, while thinking it's theirs. Always look for common ground. Be empathetic. It's not about what you say, but how you say it.

- Address difficult questions up front

If there are sensitive issues that could potentially derail the sale down the line, it's better to ask those when you first begin a dialogue. It's much better to scrap a deal in the early stages than to invest loads of time into moving a deal along, only to find out later that the answers to those difficult questions killed the deal.

- Share customer success stories

Get referrals from clients that you supported through to success and share them with prospects. People will always be more likely to believe great things about you if they come from someone else.

- Share case studies

Good case studies help a prospect visualize a real-world application of your product or service. It lets them see how your solution solved a real problem for a real company or organization. This helps prospects think about how they would apply your solution to their own challenges.

- Don't be nearsighted

Nobody likes a pushy salesperson. The temptation to close a sale as quickly as possible is strong, but that's not a sustainable game plan. Recurring revenue is important to B2Bs, so focus on closing a sale with a happy customer, rather than rushing through the deal and closing it as quickly as possible, only to find them cancelling after a few months.

- Become a product expert

Know your product inside and out. Be able to demo it like a pro, and adapt your demo to fit the exact use case of your prospect. This will generate significant credibility for you, which will help you close deals effectively and grow your reputation through word of mouth.

- Focus less on price and more on ROI

Move the focus of your prospect conversations away from the price point. Instead, lead with the benefits they will receive from your product or service. How much time and resources will it save them? Convince them they can't live without it and price will be a non-issue. This is among the most effective B2B selling strategies that you could adopt.

- Create ideal customer profiles (ICPs)

Define everything about your ideal (hypothetical) customer, from demography to personality types and they type of language they use. Use this to guide you in targeting leads who are the best fit for your product. This will maximize the results of your outreach as you won't waste time on dead-end leads.

- Sell solutions rather than products

Help your prospect clearly see that they have a need, pain-point or challenge that needs to be solved. Next, present them with your solution to their problem by explaining how your product or service will fulfill their need. Products can be abstract. Solutions, if positioned properly, resonate with prospects by letting them envision how it would help them in their actual, real-world context.

- Write articles and publish them on social media

Show prospects that you're a thought leader by sharing insights that help them in their day-to-day. If you haven't done so before, start out with an article about the five best practices of X, Y or Z. Nothing is going to build your credibility quite like establishing yourself as someone the market looks to for education and insights.

- Join relevant LinkedIn groups and actively participate

You don't want to be pitching your product to the group, but rather providing helpful and relevant insights that are beneficial to the members of that group. If you're seen as an active member of the community, you'll further establish credibility that will help you build trust among prospects.

- Monitor prospects on social media

This will let you see what they are talking about and give you a window into their thought process. If you know how they are thinking, you can touch on the right points when you finally do reach out and have a conversation.

- Reply to prospects' comments, answer questions, and like their social media posts

It's a great way to illustrate that you're knowledgeable about the subject matter and that you are genuinely invested and participating in the community.

- Be timely in your responses to customer issues or concerns

Even if you have to acknowledge an error of your own of your company's, it's much better to be available and respond than to appear unengaged. Otherwise, you won't be seen as authentic. And although it's with customers, not prospects, rest assured that prospects are watching.

- Follow your competitors on social media

It's incredibly helpful and advantageous to understand common issues that your competitors' customers are facing and to see how they are being handled. This will provide actionable insight that will help you differentiate yourself from the competition.

- Use a customer relationship management (CRM) tool

This should be table stakes at this point in the game, but you'd be surprised by how many companies still have not adopted a CRM to manage sales. A powerful CRM streamlines your management of prospects, outreach, deals pending, sales meetings, and essentially the entire sales cycle, from start to finish—leaving you more time to focus on one-on-one interactions with prospects and customers.

- Leverage marketing automation

Again, this should be par for the course. A great marketing automation solution provides you quick insight into every interaction your prospects have had with your marketing efforts—such as emails opened, emails clicked, websites visited, content consumed, and more. Imagine how effective you'll be if you have so much insight into the prospect's interests.

- Sit down with marketing often

Try to meet with your marketing team at least once a month, if not more. Ask to help them analyze the sales funnel, lead scoring, lead qualification criteria, etc. Close alignment between marketing and sales helps ensure that marketing's efforts are effectively supporting your sales objectives. This one is particularly important—consider it your B2B sales tip of the week.

- Talk to everyone, not just the decision makers

You may have heard that you should bypass influencers and skip straight to the decision makers. In fact, that's not the case. If you transform power users and other internal influencers into advocates of your solution, you'll find it much easier to get an audience with the C-level decision maker.

- Plan to have important meetings in person

Tell them that you'd love to stop by for a face-to-face visit and discuss how your solution can solve their challenges. Illustrating to them that you'll be invested in their success by actually showing up in person will go a long way towards building mutual trust.

- Use confident body language

When you arrive for an onsite meeting, shake peoples' hands. Be sure to look them in the eye. And practice power poses (learn more about power poses here). This helps you appear more confident and knowledgeable, which will ease prospects' concerns and make them more confident in your ability to solve their problems.

- Uses live chat software to communicate with leads on your website

  There are many options these days for live chat solutions. Prospects are more likely to open up and engage with you in this way than if you were to cold call them.

- Put a calendar link in your email signature

  Use an appointment scheduling solution that gives prospects the freedom to schedule meetings with you at their convenience. Then include the link to your interactive calendar in your email signature. If you pressure someone on the phone for a meeting, they are likely to hang up. If, on the other hand, you put the ball in their court and give them time to think and check their schedules, they are more likely to come back and book a time to meet with you.

- Follow up with old leads

  The B2B sales cycle takes much longer than B2C. It's common that a lead you speak to today won't be ready to make a buy decision until next year. Don't toss cold leads out the window in frustration. Rather, hang onto them and circle back periodically to check in and see how their situation has evolved since you last spoke.

Some Examples of B2B Sales

B2B sales often take the form of one company selling supplies or components to another. For example, a tire manufacturer might sell merchandise to a car manufacturer.

Another example would be wholesalers that sell their products to retailers who then turn around and sell them to consumers. Supermarkets are a classic example of this activity. They buy food from wholesalers then sell it at a slightly higher price to individual consumers.

Business-to-business sales can also include services. Attorneys who take cases for business clients, accounting firms that help companies do their taxes, and technical consultants who set up networks and email accounts are all examples of B2B service providers.

B2B vs. B2C Sales

Selling B2B is different from selling B2C in a number of ways. The greatest difference is that you'll typically be dealing with either professional buyers or high-level executives when you attempt to make B2B sales. Buyers make their livings getting the best deals possible out of salespeople and they're good at it. Executives might include the CEOs of major corporations.

In either case, B2B sales often call for a somewhat higher level of professionalism than B2C sales. You'll have to dress and behave more formally to succeed.

B2B sales also require that you know how to effectively deal with gatekeepers such as receptionists and assistants. You have to get past them to get to your target—the individual who has the ultimate authority to commit to the sale.

Dealing with Buyers

Keep in mind that most professional buyers have received extensive training in how to work with—and see through—salespeople. Selling tactics that might work well with uninitiated consumers often fail with buyers. They'll see you coming a mile away.

Buyers also know exactly how to manipulate salespeople, often employing tricks like stalling to try to wrangle a better price from you on the product.

Dealing with Executives

Dealing with executives is a whole different ball game. C-suite decision makers can be very intimidating. They're often extremely busy people who don't appreciate others wasting their time.

You should be well versed in all aspects of your product so that you can promptly and easily answer any questions posed to you. You can't say, "Let me get back to you on that," because the executive might not take your call or open the door to you a second time. You could lose the sale just like that.

Do your research on the prospect ahead of time. Understand what he does for the company and how he does it. Get a firm grasp on the company's products or services as well. You'll want to be completely prepared to wow executives with your knowledge of their operations during your sales presentations.

Similarity between B2C and B2B Sales

1. B2B and B2C sales both require a unique sales process with a well-defined strategy, regardless of their length.

2. B2B and B2C sales both require a strong alignment with marketing. If marketing communications are weak, sales will suffer on both sides.

3. Customer service is vital regardless of the type of selling in question. It is important that the customer or organization consuming your products and services have the ability to reach the service team and are attended at the top level.

Solution Selling

Also referred to as Consultative Selling, back in the mid-1970's, Frank Watts, who at the time was an employee of Wang Laboratories, spent an awful lot of time developing a new, and rather an unusual approach to selling. This new sales technique, which would become known as solution selling, had a radically different sales process than the most popular sales methodology of the time which was called product selling.

Product selling involves merely trying to persuade a customer that the product you sell is a better version than the similar products each of your competitors is selling. However, salespeople using the product selling method of sales spend much of their time with potential buyers going over feature lists and pricing options.

Successful solution selling requires an alternative way of making a sale. Salespeople utilizing Watts' approach to sales don't concentrate on showing potential customers everything a product is capable of doing. Instead, they pinpoint the real-world problem the customer is currently facing and explain how their product can solve the problem in the best way possible.

So, it sounds simple enough: Solution selling is finding ways you can make your customers' lives better with your product. However, to begin to profit from solution selling, you need to master these Four Steps to Solution Selling.

Four Steps to Solution Selling

Here is the secret process of getting the most from solution selling. Following these steps can help supercharge your sales team.

Know what you have to Offer

Without the knowledge about the products or services your company offers, it is almost impossible for your sales team to solve the problems for prospective customers. Make sure each salesperson knows precisely what he is selling, and keep your staff up-to-date by using frequent e-learning and live training sessions to go over new releases and to review the capability of older products.

Have a Game Plan Ready

Before any member of your sales team approaches a potential customer, make sure he does his homework first. The seller needs to have a clear understanding of the customers' needs, what potential problems the customer may be experiencing, and several arguments prepared beforehand to prove your company's products or services can solve these issues.

Ask the Right Questions

When meeting with a prospect for the first time, it is critical to ask the right questions to uncover any problems and the degree of their seriousness. Although you should already be aware of most of the existing issues a potential customer is facing, having him state a problem aloud often makes the need to resolve the issue more immediate and can help close sales.

Suggest a Solution

Once a potential customer admits he has a problem, it is the perfect time to offer a solution using one of your products or services. Instead of focusing on the features of the product or service, talk about how your company can make the customer's problem disappear. Convince the customer that if he chooses to use your the product or service, it is a win-win situation.

Origins of Solution Selling

Frank Watts developed the sales process dubbed "solution selling" in 1975. Watts perfected his method at Wang Laboratories. He began teaching solution selling as an independent consultant in 1982. He presented his sales process as a one-day workshop to Xerox Corporation in 1982. By 1983 *Electronics* magazine would portray solution selling as "an unmistakable trend in the distribution of systems-related products". In a 1984 account Dick Heiser could look back to IBM's pre-1975 "solution sale" methodology.

Mike Bosworth founded a sales training organization named Solution Selling in 1983, based on his experiences at Xerox Corporation (the Huthwaite International SPIN (Situation, Problem, Implication, Need-payoff) selling pilot project) and began licensing affiliates in 1988. With intellectual-property contributions from his affiliate network, Bosworth's methodology continued to evolve through the years. He sold the intellectual property in 1999 to one of his original affiliates, Keith M. Eades.

While the term "solution selling" has become somewhat generic in the marketplace, the core brand of solution selling still carries distinct characteristics. Followers of "solution-selling" generally apply a consultative sales approach to all aspects of their sales process (or cycle) including:

- Prospecting;
- Diagnosing customer needs;
- Crafting a potential solution;
- Establishing value;
- Understanding the buying center/decision making unit (DMU);

- Bargaining for access to decision-makers;

- Positioning proof, ROI and the total solution;

- Negotiating a win-win solution;

- Following up to ensure customer success.

The solution selling methodology has evolved as key components of professional selling evolve. As a result, solution selling has become more broadly defined—to include dimensions of "sales process", "competitive selling", "value selling" as well as "consultative selling" or "complex selling" which set the focus on the team's aspects of the sales.

Solution Selling in Management Contexts

The advent of solution selling may impact on business models and on organization practices. Eades and Kear discuss solution-centric organizations and the focal role of solution sales in such environments. Robert J Calvin compares some of the financial implications of various type of sales: transactional sales, value-added sales, solution sales, and feature/benefit sales. Robert L Jolles proposed that, among managers and salespeople, a chosen solution is not always the best solution.

Solution selling is ideal for industries with highly customized products and/or packages. For example, a company who offers a cloud storage platform along with maintenance and security services will probably create a unique bundle for each of its customers. The salesperson will figure out how much data her prospect needs to store, how many devices he'll be accessing his files on, what kind of extra features and support he'll need, and so forth.

Get Started With Solution Selling

Use this three-step plan to begin solution selling:

- Identify Common Pain Points

   Figuring out your customers' most common pain points might be the most important part of the process without this information, you can't effectively target prospects or present your solution.

   Analyze your won deals to see which problems prompted prospects to buy your product. Ask them, *"What factored into your decision to work with us?"* and *"When did you decide to solve [problem], and why?"*

- Develop Your Questions

   Once you've figured out the most pressing problems your product solves for buyers, develop a set of questions that'll help you diagnose prospects.

Having the right questions prepared means you'll spend the majority of the sales conversation focused on the buyer and their company, rather than your product and its features.

Start with broad, open-ended questions that probe into the relevant aspects of your prospect's business. Then get more narrow -- you're looking for specific facts and figures that will help you build a case for your solution.

- Practice Selling Value

Solution selling is effective because it focuses on the ROI of a product, not its feature set or sticker price. Whether you're a sales manager or individual salesperson, make sure you understand and can demonstrate your product's value. It might be helpful to consider these questions:

- o How is life easier with your product? Which challenges or tasks are eliminated or reduced?

- o Does your product save the buyer time? If so, how much? What could they accomplish in those minutes, hours, or days?

- o Does your product save the buyer money? If so, how much? What could they accomplish with that amount?

- o How does your product influence others' perception of your prospect? Do they look more credible, important, effective, or successful?

- o What's the impact on your prospect's bottom line one month after buying your product? Six months? A year?

Practice highlighting the answers to these questions to your prospects.

Solution Selling Sales Process

"Solution selling" is used pretty broadly these days, but salespeople using this methodology typically follow this sales process:

1. Prospect: Look for a buyer with a problem their product solves;

2. Qualify: Understand the decision-making unit (DMU);

3. Discovery: Diagnose the buyer's needs;

4. Add value: Develop a customer champion; gain access to key decision makers;

5. Present: Share a custom solution; demonstrate its ROI;

6. Close: Come to a mutually beneficial agreement.

Solution Selling Questions

To accurately diagnose your prospect's pain points, you need the right questions. There are three main goals of this stage (typically the discovery call):

- Identify the causes: Which factors are responsible for the buyer's pain? How are they ranked in terms of importance and impact?

- Calculate the magnitude: How is this pain affecting your prospect, their team, other departments, and the entire company? How many people will benefit from solving the problem?

- Get buy-in: Gauge the buyer's interest in life with your product. Are they excited about the solution you can provide?

To give you an idea, here are sample questions for each objective.

Identify the Causes

- How has [problem] gotten to [current state]?

- How significant is [factor]?

- Have you seen [factor they haven't considered] making any impact on [problem]?

Calculate the Magnitude

- How has this problem changed your [daily, weekly] workload and focus?

- How has this problem affected your [coworkers, boss, direct reports]?

- What does [job title] think about this problem?

Get Buy-in

- In a world where [problem] doesn't exist, what's different about [your results, your priorities, the company's success]?

- We can solve [problem] with [X solution]. What do you think?

Selective Distribution

Selective distribution is the most effective distribution strategy for high-end brands that want to set up a limited number of outlets in a particular geographical location. This is quite different from exclusive distribution (which can be a little too extreme) and is considered as a middle path approach to distribution.

This type of strategy works best when dealing with consumers that like to "shop around". Or simply put, it's ideal for customers who may have special brand preferences when they are purchasing a specific product.

For better clarity, selective distribution occurs when a company resorts to opening up a limited number of outlets in a specific geographical location.

Sure, this may sound restrictive at best but it actually helps the producer filter out the best-performing outlets. This yields better results and allows the company to put in all their focus effort (training facilities and resource) to better use.

It functions as a favorable alternative for manufacturing firms that would rather focus on a few outlets instead of dissipating their energies and resources on countless marginal ones.

Need for Companies to Opt for Selection Distribution Strategies

A selection distribution strategy allows companies to select appropriate outlets according to different locations.

Additionally, it's highly beneficial for manufacturers since they're able to choose price points based on their consumers. This eventually leads to a more personalized shopping experience that encourages consumers to come back again and again.

Examples

Since this form of distribution caters to the needs of consumers of a specific geographical area, its best suited for companies that want to maintain quality. This is why it's no surprise that luxury goods manufacturers often opt for selective distribution.

High-end companies that produce exceptional quality clothing and accessories are likely to use selective distribution. For example, you may find Dolce & Gabbana products in stores like Neiman Marcus but not at JC Penneys or Wal-Mart. This is done set standards and keep a close eye on distributors.

Exclusive distribution is a more extreme type of selection distribution. It usually involves just one or two distributors in a specific area.

Television, home appliances, and furniture brands are also popularly distributed using this method.

Advantages of Selective Distribution

The nature of the advantages obtained by the manufacturer or distributor from qualitative criteria depend on the terms of the criteria applied or the obligations imposed.

Where the dealer is expected to have technical qualifications or to maintain technically qualified staff, the manufacturer may benefit from the assurance that the dealer will be able to provide advice and after sales service to his customers. Even where no such advice or service is required or even possible, the manufacturer, particularly of luxury or prestige products, may for presentational reasons wish his products to be sold only by sales representatives with a certain training and perhaps appearance. Similarly the manufacturer may wish his products to be sold only from trading premises at which certain technical equipment or facilities are available, or where the surroundings have the atmosphere that he thinks best for selling his product, without involving the manufacturer in vertical integration.

Such requirements may be called technical or presentational criteria or qualifications. What are called "commercial qualifications" are often expressed in quantitative terms, and are really obligations imposed on the dealer, e.g., to maintain a stock of a certain size or variety, to achieve a minimum turnover, to engage in a certain amount of advertising or other promotional activity, and to keep certain records. The advantages of such commercial qualifications for the manufacturer are that he is assured a certain minimum demand for the products in question through a limited number of outlets, and that customers may have a larger selection of his products available to them on the dealer's premises than the dealer might otherwise think it worthwhile to maintain. The manufacturer, therefore, may get certain modest benefits in planning his production and the marketing of his products at the point of sale, the maintenance of the reputation of his brand and, in the case of technical qualifications, an assurance of adequate services to the users of his products.

In the case of a product of which supplies are limited, the dealer may perhaps get an assurance of rather more secure supplies than would be the case without a selective distribution system. More important, he is likely to benefit, in practice, from a rather higher profit margin than he would have otherwise. Specialized dealers may benefit from being free from competition from large scale non-specialized outlets which, if the distribution system were nonselective, could often sell the goods more cheaply, perhaps without providing services. The consumer or user may benefit from the availability of technically qualified advice and after-sales service where these are necessary, and sometimes the convenience of having a nearby outlet in an area where an outlet would be uneconomical if the number of outlets in neighboring areas was unlimited.

Whether and to what extent any of these advantages are realized in fact in any given selective distribution system will depend entirely on the circumstances. How far factor allocation and economic efficiency is optimized by limiting outlets and thereby tending to increase the return on the dealers' capital will also depend entirely on the circumstances. Of course selective distribution agreements may also contain a wide variety of other clauses which may restrict intrabrand or interbrand competition but which are not caused by or directly related to the selective nature of the distribution system in which they occur. Except in the case of presentational requirements for luxury products, the essence of the argument for selective distribution is that the dealers are asked to make an investment, in specialized knowledge or in staff, premises, or equipment, to sell the goods, and selectivity is intended to give them an assurance that their investment will be profitable.

However, selectivity is not a sufficient condition for profitability because it does not in itself give the dealer immunity from parallel imports or from interbrand competition. Nor is it a necessary condition for profitability; low prices to dealers, or resale price maintenance, if it were lawful, would provide much the same assurance. Nor is selectivity in itself sufficient to ensure that dealers make the investment desired: specific obligations must be imposed. In practice, even quantitative criteria are often not related, except in the most vague and general way, to the cost of the investment that the dealer is required to make.

The best course of action is for the manufacturer to specify in detail what he requires the dealers to provide, and to oblige himself to apply these requirements in a nondiscriminatory way, which it is in any case normally required to do. The cost of providing whatever is necessary can be estimated, and dealers who do not think it is profitable to provide it will not enter the system. The dealers may then be entitled to an assurance that the calculations they have made will not be upset by the appointment of additional dealers unless this is justified by an expansion of the market. However, the calculations must in any case be liable to be upset by parallel imports and interbrand competition, and to be valid may often assume a certain degree of stability both of buying and of resale prices.

The economic effects of selective distribution and of resale price maintenance are often similar. Sometimes resale price maintenance is defended on the grounds that it is a substitute for, or a necessary supplement to, specific obligations imposed on dealers. The argument is that unless dealers are assured substantial profits they will not make, or will not accept the obligation to make, the investment which the manufacturer wishes them to make. This may be the real purpose of many selective distribution systems. However, if manufacturers disguise resale price maintenance measures as selective distribution, they will confuse the arguments for what they are doing, and they will cause their agreements to become void, and make themselves liable for fines, as soon as they try to use their selective distribution agreements for, or to supplement them with, resale price maintenance measures.

It follows that it may often be necessary to look at the real aims and needs behind a selective distribution agreement, not at the reasons put forward for it. This must be done in the context of the Common Market as a whole, and the parties must be able to explain how parallel imports from other member states fit into what they are trying to do.

There are various kinds of products for which before-sales or after-sales services may be thought advantageous. If these services are provided by dealers, there may be nonprice competition in respect of those services. It is, however, hard to see any justification for the suggestion that intrabrand nonprice competition in respect of these services is, or could be, more important than intrabrand price competition. The services may be necessary in order to enable the dealers to compete. But they are not the main way, and they should not become the only way, in which they do compete. In any case, if the number of dealers is limited, it is unlikely that intrabrand competition between them in services will be very vigorous.

Disadvantages of Selective Distribution

By definition a selective distribution system involves fewer outlets than would exist if the system was nonselective. Whether the number of approved dealers is only marginally less than, or is a tiny proportion of, the number of dealers who otherwise would exist depends on all the circumstances. A substantially reduced number of outlets in a given region may undesirably restrict the choice conveniently available to consumers, and reduce intrabrand price and other competition. Quantitative criteria necessarily impede market entry by new dealers and by new types of retail outlets such as supermarkets.

Selective distribution systems greatly facilitate pressure both on manufacturers and approved dealers to act, or not to act, in certain ways. In particular, these systems put pressure on dealers and manufacturers not to reduce their resale prices, not to buy parallel imports, not to sell outside their territories, or not to sell competing brands. Pressure can be imposed by reducing supplies, restricting credit, or threatening to refuse supplies or actually doing so, or in other ways. At Community level a series of national selective distribution systems may maintain prices at significantly different levels in different member states, because they greatly inhibit sales between dealers in different member states.

The disadvantages of selective distribution systems are of two kinds: those that result inevitably from the reduced number of outlets, and those which result from the incentives and opportunities given by a selective system. It may be argued that selective distribution normally restricts only intrabrand competition, and that vertical restrictions on intrabrand competition are less serious than horizontal restrictions and restrictions on interbrand competition.

Nevertheless, there are a number of other issues to consider. First, selective distribution inhibits price competition, which is, or ought to be, the most important kind of competition in most consumer markets. Second, a series of vertical restrictions may have the same economic effects as a horizontal restriction between dealers. Third, insofar as selective distribution inhibits price competition, it necessarily reduces interbrand competition. Fourth, if all or most of the manufacturers in a given sector operate selective distribution systems, they will tend substantially to reduce interbrand competition and they will facilitate horizontal restrictions on price competition between dealers, or between manufacturers, or both. Fifth, selective distribution systems have the effect of confining dealers to their own member states and preventing sales of trade quantities across intra-Community frontiers which alone could reduce differences in price levels between member states. These price differences are often much greater than the differences in price within any one member state, and therefore it is particularly important in the interests of Community users and consumers, that competition should be free to reduce or eliminate them.

Clearly, while selective distribution systems may have worthwhile effects, few generalizations can be made about them: their effects depend on the circumstances, and cannot be deduced merely from the terms of the agreements themselves.

Selective distribution systems limit market entry by manufacturers of competing products, if each distributor is free to sell only one manufacturer's products. If all existing suitable dealers are bound by exclusive arrangements, a new manufacturer may be unable to enter the market without setting up his own dealers. Sometimes, even if the existing dealerships are not formally exclusive the dealers are reluctant to sell competing products, especially imported products, and it may be uneconomic for a dealer to sell only the imported products and not domestic ones; for example, newspapers, as in Salonia v. Poidomani.6 The extent of the effects on intrabrand and interbrand competition resulting from a selective distribution system varies greatly. Partitioning of the Common Market almost always has a substantial effect on competition. Resale price maintenance usually does so. On the other hand, whether quantitative criteria significantly affect consumer choice, intrabrand competition or market entry by dealers depends on the circumstances. It is possible to imagine circumstances in which a relatively small number of large dealers could provide more effective intrabrand competition than a large number of small outlets, although it is doubtful whether this often occurs in practice.

Exclusive Distribution

Exclusive distribution is an agreement between a distributor and a manufacturer that the manufacturer will not sell the product to anyone else and will sell it only to the exclusive distributor. At the same time, even the exclusive distributor has to enter the agreement that he will only sell the products of the manufacturers exclusively and will not sell those of the competition. This ways, the market is an open ground for the manufacturer and the distributor and they have complete control on the distribution of the product.

Example of Exclusive Distribution

Rolex watches wants a distributor in region A. Now, Rolex knows that it cannot have showrooms everywhere in Region A because it will dilute the brand equity. So ROLEX appoints an exclusive distributor for Region A. This exclusive distributor starts his own exclusive ROLEX shops and also sells the brand through only the cream outlets of Region A.

Now, Rolex is satisfied with this concept of exclusive distribution and repeats it when it wants to enter Region B. Rolex might use the same distributor as Region A or it might give the exclusive distribution to another dealer. However, because Rolex does not want to dilute the brand equity, it will not enter in the region directly and won't hire too many distributors so that it has "premium" and "exclusive" positioning of the brand.

A similar model is observed in many different industries. Even in the industrial machinery segment, many a times exclusive distribution is given to distributors who are good at selling and have good relations in the local market and who can focus on selling the brand more than the competitors.

Such exclusive distributors might cover a large region or a small region. Nonetheless, within their appointed territory, no one else but them can distribute the product for the brand they have tied up with. These distributors can in turn bill the product to other smaller distributors, wholesalers and retail shops.

Advantages

Focus

Exclusive distribution helps in keeping the focus simple for the firm. The brand need not worry of losing its own distributor to the competitor. The brand has a trustworthy alliance and hence it is more focused on winning over competition rather than deciding on its distribution base.

Control

Because the exclusive distributor is himself dependent on the company, the company is very much in control. Besides distribution, the company can concentrate on marketing and advertising activities to increase the pull of the brand.

Availability

A key characteristic of Exclusive distributors is that they are financially capable of stocking huge amount of inventory. As a result, material is easily reachable to retailers and wholesalers and thereby distribution is increased.

Financial Advantages for Company

The brand's cash crunch is averted as distributor is expected to have good cash in hand and is expected to carry the inventory and provide payments. As a result, the risk is mainly on distributor rather than the company and company's finances are safe. This is off course if the distributor they have chosen is ethical and financially stable.

Penetration becomes Easier for the Company

Because the company does not need to cover its own back and does not need to spend manpower in finding, convincing and maintaining the distribution channel, the company can completely concentrate on building the brand and doing promotional activities so that its penetration in the market becomes much better.

Localisation

One of the major advantages of exclusive distribution is localization. If a company is entering a foreign country, there are many things which the company won't know. At such time, entering a exclusivity agreement with a local distributor who is trustworthy is excellent for the firm because the local distributor will have relations with existing retailers and wholesalers. As a result, he can cement the brand in his market.

Disadvantages of Exclusive Distribution

Trust

As can be seen in the advantages above, we mentioned the word "Trust" several times. There is a reason for this. Your business will be successful in distribution only if the exclusive distributor is trustworthy. Otherwise, he might take marketing and advertising budgets from use and use it to fill his own pockets rather than helping the brand rise.

Dependency

If your brand is new or is not as popular as a Rolex or a BMW, then you will find that there is a dependency created on the exclusive distributor. Brands like Rolex and BMW can sell regardless of what type of distributor is selling them. Besides that, known brands have a line of distributors ready to tie up with the company. However, unknown brands becomes highly dependent on their exclusive distributors and will have to do as the distributor advices.

Disputes Cause Huge Losses

When considering regular distribution, a dispute with one distributor means that the single distributor wont perform but the distribution will go one through some other distributor.

However, if there is a dispute with your exclusive distributor then you might lose the whole market. This exclusive distributor might have very good relations in local market so it becomes difficult for another distributor to create the same relations. Thus, in exclusive distribution, if there is a major dispute then it means huge losses might be incurred, not only in terms of money but in terms of time lost too.

Choosing the Right Exclusive Distributor

It is very important that you choose the right distributor who is well aligned with your brand and is aggressive with regards to the sale and marketing of your brand. Otherwise, you might miss chance of tying up with even better distributors because your exclusive ones are not ready to budge.

Inclusive Distribution

Intensive distribution mainly means distribution on a large-scale and displaying the product in as many ways and places as possible so that the customer sells in high volume due to large scale distribution. The chosen level of distribution generally depends on different factors such as the production capacity, the size of the target market, pricing and promotion policies as well as the seasonal requirement of the product by the end user.

Objective of Intensive Distribution

The objective of intensive distribution is providing a vast coverage of the existing market by using all available outlets. Intensive distribution is most commonly used when the product is a very common product in the market and there are many different alternatives available. So, if the customer does not buy your brand, he will buy someone else's. Hence the complete push is towards vast distribution of the product due to which the intensive distribution strategy is used.

As total sales are directly linked to the number of outlets displaying the products (example – cigarettes, alcoholic products, soft drinks, soaps etc), intensive distribution is heavily applied in product driven companies like FMCG as well as consumer durable.

This strategy covers all the possible outlets and display points that can distribute and sell the products. Hence, for this kind of products, the key to success relies on the distribution strategy. The easier it is to find the product for the customer, the more profit the company will get in the long run.

Any possible outlet where the customer is expected to visit is also an outlet for the distribution of the respective product. For example – it is not necessary that outlets be strictly physical showrooms. Even E-commerce is an outlet because end customers can buy products online as well.

Likewise, these products are available in the restaurants or in five star hotels as well as being available on countless kiosks, sweet shops, tea shops and so on.

In other terms, an intensive distribution strategy is a plan that places products in many different locations for distribution. Products that are used every day and replaced often may be found in dozens of different retail outlets in any given area.

A customer seldom has to go out of his or her own way to find her favorite brand of toothpaste because of the intensive distribution that is in place by companies like HUL, P&G, Colgate and others. Other common products that benefit from intensive distribution include soap, deodorant, laundry, detergent, feminine hygiene products, soft drinks and cigarettes.

The company that produces the product on the first place benefits greatly from intensive distribution. This is because they get the first mover advantage and can place the product before anyone else. It can easily become the recipient of brand loyalty.

For the retailers, the benefit of keeping more brands is because they get the reputation of carrying more items in their display and hence, more customers are bound to visit the retailers. It increases customer satisfaction and allows the retailer to establish a positive reputation with producers and customers alike.

Advantages

The advantage of applying an intensive distribution strategy is in generating revenue, product awareness and pushing for impulse buying.

- As more products are sold, more money is earned.

- As more locations carry the products, the more opportunities there are for manufacturers to make profit.

- As the product is in as many locations as possible, it will raise awareness concerning the product. Thus, customers begin to associate commercials and print ads with products regularly seen in stores.

- Lastly, when one of the products is not available on the shelves of a store, customers will usually select another brand rather than going to another store. This benefits the retailers also.

Challenges of Adopting Inclusive Distribution

Like other types of distribution, inclusive distribution offers its own unique set of advantages and disadvantages. For maximum results, companies should carefully evaluate the products they are offering and should conduct a thorough market research.

Conducting a detailed market research will also help companies determine whether their product is ready for the new market or not. Some major challenges of adopting inclusive distribution include.

Limited Funding Opportunities

One of the major challenges of implementing inclusive distribution is the limited funding opportunities amidst public finance and donors. For optimum results, companies must work hard to identify the most suitable technological solution to obtain favorable outcomes.

Readapting Business Model

Since most initiatives target areas with low population density, companies may have to readapt their business model to suit social differences and cultural values of the specific area. This can be an extensive process, often involving a plethora of resources.

Technology's Aid to Inclusive Distribution

Technology can greatly aid inclusive distribution models by reducing costs, improving communication and standardization in target areas. This is all made possible due to the incredibly high mobile penetration rate in developing countries.

In fact, companies are now shifting towards geo-mapping software and other popular mobile-based software to aid entrepreneurs and distributors.

Push Strategy

Push marketing focuses on taking the product to the customer, and putting the product in front of the customer at the point of purchase. This type of marketing strategy hopes to minimize the amount of time between a customer discovering a product and buying that product. To accomplish this, companies use aggressive and wide-reaching ads to make the biggest and most immediate impact they can on customers.

Examples:

- Trade show promotions;
- Direct selling to customers in showrooms;
- Negotiating with retailers to stock a product;
- Maintaining an efficient supply chain;
- Appealing looking packaging;
- Point of sale displays;
- Radio ads;
- TV ads;
- Email ads;
- Direct mail ads;
- Pay per click ads.

Traditional marketing is often synonymous with push marketing. Classic marketing strategies like primetime television advertisements, buy one get one free coupons, and direct mail catalogs are all examples of push marketing. This marketing strategy casts a wide net in the hopes of grabbing as many potential customers as possible. It does not try to build relationships with customers but focuses only on pushing products towards them. Statements about value, quality, and innovativeness are emphasized to try and create immediate customer demand.

The greatest advantage of push marketing is that it produces quick results and makes clear statements to customers. It is less concerned with branding, and more concerned with creating an instant demand for a new product.

The major disadvantage of push marketing is that it can be expensive and only produce temporary effects. Since the goal is not to create long-term customer relationships, push marketing strategies have to constantly make new pitches about the value of products. It keeps the customer at a distance, meaning they must constantly be reengaged.

Companies which Employs Push Marketing

Push marketing is a strategy that is used most frequently by start-ups and companies introducing new products into the market. Since the focus is on taking the product to the consumer, it is particularly suited to products that the consumer is not yet aware of.

This style of marketing can be used by companies large and small. A new shoe store might send out mailers to all the residents in the area, while an established pharmaceutical company might blanket the airwaves with TV ads for a new drug.

Most companies will employ a push strategy in conjunction with other marketing techniques. For instance, companies will often run TV ads and also maintain an official company website. The TV ads push customers towards the products, while the website pulls them deeper into the company's offerings.

Push Marketing in Action

- Nintendo: The video game industry's largest trade convention, Nintendo hired 250 brand ambassadors to work at their booth. The ambassadors were there to show attendees new games, answer their questions, and introduce them to a new gaming system. Nintendo hired this army of short term staff to aggressively push their games towards consumers with a helpful, human face.

- Dunkin Donuts: The doughnut maker distributed coupons to mobile phone users in the Boston area. They sent the coupons to people who had opted into a program after responding to ads run on radio stations and online. The company saw a huge number of people redeem the coupon and try one of their new products because they provided an easy incentive.

- Clorox: The maker of over 60 consumer brands including Hidden Valley, noticed that sales of ranch dressing went up 10% after they started marketing it as a dip for frozen foods like pizza. The company began looking for other ways to market nontraditional uses for classic products. If they could push new uses on consumers, they could increase demand.

- Saks Fifth Avenue: Any time a user downloads the luxury retailers mobile app, they are enrolled into a program to begin receiving mobile notifications about sales, new products, and in-store events. The retailer used the power of mobile technology to keep interested customers informed on all the latest news about the store.

Developing and Implementing Push Marketing Plan

The first step in developing a push marketing plan is to research the location, age, race, sex, socioeconomic status, and other demographic details about customers that will be targeted. Different marketing strategies work better for different audiences. For instance, push marketing is often targets the young and the elderly because they are less likely to form long-term relationships with companies.

Companies must determine the specific marketing mix after they have settled on a push marketing strategy. This industry term refers to the mix of different advertising channels a company might use. It is rare that a company advertises in only one place, and they usually mix print, TV, online, and trade show ads to make a stronger impact on customers.

Once the media platform of the campaign has been decided, it is necessary to design ads. Teams of graphic designers, copywriters, technology professionals, and managers will work collaboratively to define a message and find the most efficient way to present that message. Advertisements should ask customers to act quickly to purchase products.

For example, imagine a new cell phone company that wants to introduce themselves to the market. Since they are new and unknown, they elect to use push marketing in order to familiarize customers with what makes them different and valuable. They decide on a marketing mix that includes TV, radio, and billboard advertisements because these forms of ads reach the largest number of customers and make clear, direct statements. They set a goal for themselves of increasing sales by 15% and track their growth in every month of the campaign. By the time the campaign is complete; customers recognize the brand and are familiar with their products.

Push Marketing Interrupts your Potential Customers

Push marketing is defined as a promotional strategy in which a business attempts to get their message in front of their potential customers without them having a desire or interest to buy the product or learn more about it. Push marketing requires a lot of reach and can be considered to be 'interruptive'. Just think of radio and TV advertising and how they interrupt your favorite Katy Perry song, or the latest Fox Life TV show. Unless you're passionate about advertising, then you probably don't find these ads to be entertaining or informational.

Of course, there are many different marketing channels defined as push marketing, and not all are as interruptive as others. For instance coupon sites, such as Groupon, are great examples of push marketing performed with finesse to minimize the interrupting element.

It is not said that push marketing should be immediately considered as negative, since it can be very efficient if executed properly. For the majority of businesses with an average marketing budget, it's simply not the most cost-efficient distribution of ad spend.

Push Marketing Excels in Raising Awareness for Lesser-known Products

If many consumers don't know your product, or if consumers simply aren't actively looking for your product because of lack of need, then push marketing is your best friend.

It's almost impossible to build awareness with pull marketing as it is about attracting consumers already interested in your product or service. If your product isn't even known, then nobody will be looking for it.

Advertising on relevant industry websites with big banner ads, sponsored blogging, Social Media ads, Display Marketing and TV advertising are all great channels for you if you want to get your product known. Be aware though, that it's not for the small or medium sized marketing budget. If you want to change the mind of consumers, then you better be great at producing viral content, have an amazing product or a lot of budget to spend on push marketing.

Pull Strategy

Pull marketing is any method a company uses to generate demand for a product. This is contrasted with "push" marketing, which is a strategy intended to sell out an existing supply of a product.

Modern pull marketing uses various media channels to generate interest about a product or company, encouraging customers to seek out the product or company on their own. This is especially popular and effective within Internet marketing, because pull marketing benefits greatly from independent social behavior like word-of-mouth and the "viral" content effect.

With Tickle Me Elmo, Tyco Toys created demand for their product by making sure customers saw it in prominent places, like toy magazines and on TV shows, prior to actually placing the toy in stores. By targeting the right media outlets, Tyco created demand that let them manufacture as many Tickle Me Elmo dolls as their clients (toy retailers) needed, rather than manufacturing the dolls first and trying to convince their clients to stock them.

Methods of Pull Marketing

There are many different ways to reach customers using pull marketing techniques. Any of the following can build excitement for a product or trust in a company:

- Social networking for the word-of-mouth effect;

- Media coverage to reach a wider audience;

- Strategic placement of a product or store;

- Informational content like blogs to attract people who are interested in similar products or services.

Companies which uses Pull Marketing

Companies that produce or sells goods can use pull marketing to raise awareness about a product before it becomes available for purchase. Though the results of the marketing campaign are not certain until the product is made available, the manufacturer can save money on production costs by producing fewer units of the product prior to launch, and using the money they save to invest in pull advertising.

Ideally, the demand will exceed the supply, and the company will be able to set a higher price because of this. This is exactly what happened with Tickle Me Elmo. Tyco produced only a small number of dolls to start, but spent more time and money on market research and advertising. The demand for the toy resulting from this advertising allowed Tyco to set higher prices for their product simply because people were willing to pay more to acquire the limited number of dolls available.

Service industry companies use pull marketing to generate interest in new services or to create positive feedback about the company. If a massage clinic, for example, wanted to increase its business, it could use social media sites to encourage their customers to share information about the clinic with their friends. People are much more likely to buy a product or visit a business on the recommendation of a friend. Through social networking, the massage clinic can rely on some of its existing customers to "advertise" for the clinic through recommendations.

Social Media: The Biggest Demographic

The number of people who use major social media networks like Facebook and Twitter is staggering, while the cost of maintaining a social media presence is minimal. For the cost of a computer and one hour a day of employee time, any company can have a strong social media presence that reaches thousands of potential customers or more every day.

- Number of people who use Facebook: 500 million;

- Number of Twitter users who follow eight or more other Twitter accounts: 56 million;

- Number of registered Foursquare users: 7.5 million;

- Number of unique visitors to Yelp per year: 78 million.

Using Pull Marketing

A pull marketing campaign is customer-focused, but should still start with the analysis of the product the company wants to sell. The company needs to determine what the product's key features are and who is most likely to demand it through extensive market research.

If, for instance, a company wanted to open an ice skating rink during the winter, the company should start researching several months before the season to learn the who, what, where, when, and how of creating an ice skating rink in the area. This research could consist of analyzing demographic data about surrounding neighborhoods, and surveying people in a high-traffic area like a shopping mall to find out who is most interested in ice skating.

Using the market research data to tailor their message, the company might develop an advertising plan to generate interest in the new ice skating rink before it opens. Because the purpose of pull marketing is to convince customers to seek out a product on their own, using direct methods of advertising like mail fliers and TV commercials may not be effective.

Instead, the rink-building company could develop a blog about winter activities, using keywords that relate to the geographic area of the ice skating rink to be a source of information local people would seek out for themselves. The blog would be especially effective if it linked to a social networking page about the rink itself so readers could receive periodic reminders about the business and share that information with others.

If the pull marketing plan is successful, interest in the new ice skating rink will exist before it even opens. Customers will be curious and excited to visit the rink and are very likely to tell other people about their experience once the rink actually opens, generating a powerful word-of-mouth effect.

Advantages of using Pull Strategy

There are many advantages to using pull strategy besides using a push strategy.

- Value creation: Because the company wants to use pull marketing instead of push, the company focuses more on creating value for the brand rather then just pushing a sub standard product.

- Brand equity creation: With use of ATL and BTL techniques, the company can create a high brand equity for itself thereby winning over competition repeatedly.

- Customer life time value: The customer lifetime value rises for brands which focus on pull strategy. Example – I have always been a lover of Hush puppies and I don't remember any other formal shoe brand which I have worn. I have always worn Hush puppies.

- Sustainable competitive advantage: The use of pull strategy provides a competitive advantage to all firms which have created amazing value over the years. HUL and P&G are companies known to use pull strategy effectively and many of their brands like Dove and others are closely connected to their consumers. As a result, any new entrant in the market finds it very tough to compete with these brands.

There are hardly any disadvantages of using Pull strategy but one of the major hurdles while using pull marketing is the cost involved in it. If we are talking of buying prime time advertising in ATL, then we are talking of lakhs of rupees and dollars. Similarly, while doing BTL, much of the money is invested in giving product trials and samples. Pull strategy involves huge expenditures but the benefits are huge in return mainly because of its contribution to brand building.

Lately, the applications of holistic marketing and customer concept have increased in the market. The customer is at the pinnacle for any organization and the organization wants to focus what customers want. As a result, pull strategy becomes more important then push because you want to create enough value so that the customer comes to you.

Another example of pull strategy being important is E-commerce. Till date, in retail, you had ground people to push a product to customers. However, in E-commerce the customer already knows most of the products and brands and buys only those products which it trusts. As a result, it is imperative that companies start building brands so that their products get liquidated in an online economy.

Pull Marketing as Often Way more Cost-efficient

Pull marketing takes the opposite approach. Consumers actively seeking out a product define it and the retailer presents his ads, or products, in the path of the consumer.

In order to use pull marketing it requires an interest for the product you're selling. Back in the day, pull marketing was associated with big brands because you first needed to use push marketing to get a message out and then attracting the consumers using pull marketing.

Today, it's a completely different story though. Today's pull marketing can happen on so many different free platforms that have wielded unlimited possibilities for marketers.

Stories of small business owners making it big with pull marketing are growing all the time. Pull marketing stars like Marcus Sheridan from "The Sales Lion" and Gary Vaynerchuk from "WineLibrary.com" are some of the best examples of how successful pull marketing can be these days if you just have the right product.

With Gary selling wine and Marcus selling pools, it wasn't needed for them to create a big push for their products. Their products were already in demand. They simply succeeded by putting their solutions in front of consumers.

Supply Chain Management

- Push: As stated by Bonney et al. control information flow is in the same direction of goods flow.

- Semi push or Push-pull: Succeeding node makes order request for preceding node. Preceding node reacts by replenishing from stock that is rebuilt every fixed period.

- Pull: Succeeding node makes order request for preceding node. Preceding node reacts by producing the order, which involves all internal operations, and replenishes when finished.

- Semi-pull or pull-push: Succeeding node makes order request for preceding node. Preceding node reacts by replenishing from stock that is rebuilt immediately. There are several levels of semi-pull systems as a node can have stock at several layers in an organization.

Information Flow

With a push-based supply chain, products are pushed through the channel, from the production side up to the retailer. The manufacturer sets production at a level in accord with historical ordering patterns from retailers. It takes longer for a push-based supply chain to respond to changes in demand, which can result in overstocking or bottlenecks and delays (the bullwhip effect), unacceptable service levels and product obsolescence.

In a pull-based supply chain, procurement, production and distribution are demand-driven rather than to forecast. However, a pull strategy does not always require make-to-order production. Toyota Motors Manufacturing is frequently used as an example of pull production, yet do not typically produce to order. They follow the "supermarket model" where limited inventory is kept on hand and is replenished as it is consumed. In Toyota's case, Kanban cards are used to signal the need to replenish inventory.

A supply chain is almost always a combination of both push and pull, where the interface between the push-based stages and the pull-based stages is sometimes known as the *push–pull boundary*. However, because of the subtle difference between pull production and make-to-order production, a more accurate name for this may be the *decoupling point*. An example of this is Dell's build to order supply chain. Inventory levels of individual components are determined by forecasting general demand, but final assembly is in response to a specific customer request. The decoupling point would then be at the beginning of the assembly line:

- Applied to that portion of the supply chain where demand uncertainty is relatively small;

- Production and distribution decisions are based on long term forecasts;

- Based on past orders received from retailer's warehouse (may lead to bullwhip effect);

- Inability to meet changing demand patterns;

- Large and variable production batches;

- Unacceptable service levels;

- Excessive inventories due to the need for large safety stocks;

- Less expenditure on advertising than pull strategy.

In a marketing *pull* system, the consumer requests the product and "pulls" it through the delivery channel. An example of this is the car manufacturing company Ford Australia. Ford Australia only produces cars when they have been ordered by customers:

- Applied to that portion of the supply chain where demand uncertainty is high;

- Production and distribution are demand driven;

- No inventory, response to specific orders;

- Point of sale (POS) data comes is helpful when shared with supply chain partners;

- Decrease in lead time;

- Difficult to implement.

Use of Pull, Push, and Hybrid Push-pull Strategy

Harrison summarized when to use each one of the three supply chain strategies:

- A push based supply chain strategy is usually suggested for products with low demand uncertainty, as the forecast will provide a good indication of what to produce and keep in inventory, and also for products with high importance of economies of scale in reducing costs.

- A pull based supply chain strategy, usually suggested for products with high demand uncertainty and with low importance of economies of scales, which means, aggregation does not reduce cost, and hence, the firm would be willing to manage the supply chain based on realized demand.

- A hybrid push–pull strategy, usually suggested for products which uncertainty in demand is high, while economies of scale are important in reducing production and delivery costs. An example of this strategy is the furniture industry, where production strategy has to follow a pull-based strategy, since it is impossible to make production decisions based on long-term forecasts. However, the distribution strategy needs to take advantage of economies of scale in order to reduce transportation cost, using a push-based strategy.

Examples in Push and Pull

Hopp and Spearman consider some of the most common systems found in industry and the literature and classify them as either push or pull:

- *Material requirements planning* (MRP) is a push system because releases are made according to a master production schedule without regard to system status. Hence, no a priori WIP limit exists.

- *Classic kanban* is a pull system, the number of *kanban* cards establishes a fixed limit on WIP.

- The *classic base stock system* is a push system because there is no limit on the amount of work in process in the system. This is because backorders can increase beyond the basestock level.

- *Installation stock* is also a push system as are echelon stock systems because neither imposes a limit on the number of orders in the system.

- *CONWIP* is a pull system because it limits WIP via cards similar to *kanban*. An important difference from *kanban* from an implementation standpoint is that the cards are line specific rather than part number specific. However, from a push-pull perspective, CONWIP cards limit WIP in the same manner as *kanban* cards.

- (K, S) systems (proposed by Liberopoulos and Dallery) are pull systems if $K < \infty$ and are push systems otherwise.

- POLCA systems proposed by Suri are pull systems because, like *kanban* and CONWIP, WIP is limited by cards.

- PAC systems proposed by Buzacott and Shanthikumar are pull systems when the number of process tags (which serve to limit WIP) is less than infinity.

- MRP with a WIP constraint (as suggested by Axsäter and Rosling) is a pull system.

Marketing

An advertising push strategy refers to a situation when a vendor advertises its product to gain audience awareness, while the pull strategy implies the aims to reach audiences which have shown existing interest in the product or information about it. The difference between "push" and "pull" marketing can also be identified by the manner in which the company approaches the lead. If, for example, the company were to send a sales brochure, that would be considered pushing the opportunity toward the lead. If, instead, the company provided a subject matter expert as a speaker for an industry event attended by targeted leads, that could be one tactic used as part of a strategy to pull in a lead by encouraging that lead to seek out the expert in a moment of need for that expertise.

Push strategy tactics:

- Trade show promotions to encourage retailer demand;
- Direct selling to customers in showrooms or face to face;
- Negotiation with retailers to stock your product;
- Efficient supply chain allowing retailers an efficient supply;
- Packaging design to encourage purchase;
- Point of sale displays.

Pull strategy tactics:

- Advertising and mass media promotion;
- Word of mouth referrals;
- Customer relationship management;
- Sales promotions and discounts.

Hotel Distribution

The online world has brought this pull push decision to the hotel distribution business:

- *Push strategies* in the hotel distribution business imply that hotel inventory is placed for the distributors or resellers outside the hotel system in one or several extranets that belong to these distributors (online travel agencies, tour operators, and bed banks). The inventory must be therefore updated in these extranets. The hotel servers receive less traffic preventing server crashes but booking must be transferred to the hotel system.

- *Pull strategies* are based on distributors interfacing with the hotel property management system. In this case the inventory is "pulled" from the hotel (or hotel chain) system. This method provides a much more precise picture of the real availability and saves time loading the bookings but, requires more IT development and a bigger server.

Basis for Comparison	Push Strategy	Pull Strategy
Meaning	Push strategy is a strategy that involves direction of marketing efforts to channel partners.	Pull strategy is a strategy that involves promotion of marketing efforts to the final consumer.

Basis for Comparison	Push Strategy	Pull Strategy
What is it?	A strategy in which third party stocks company's product.	A strategy in which customers demand company's product from sellers.
Objective	To make customer aware of the product or brand.	To encourage customer to seek the product or brand.
Uses	Sales force, Trade promotion, money etc.	Advertising, Promotion and other forms of communication.
Emphasis on	Resource Allocation	Responsiveness
Suitability	When the brand loyalty is low.	When the brand loyalty is high.
Lead Time	Long	Short

Key Differences between Push and Pull Strategy

The differences between push and pull strategy, is provided in the points given below:

1. The type of marketing strategy which involves direction of marketing efforts to intermediaries is called push strategy. On the other hand, the marketing strategy involving the promotion of marketing efforts to the end user is called pull strategy.

2. In pull strategy, communication of products or information is demanded by the buyer, while in push strategy, no such communication is demanded.

3. Push strategy aims at making customer aware of the product or brand. As against this, pull strategy encourages the customer to seek the product or brand.

4. Push strategy uses sales force, trade promotion, money, etc. to induce channel partners, to promote and distribute the product to the final customer. Conversely, pull strategy uses advertising, promotion and any other form of communication to instigate customer to demand product from channel partners.

5. Push strategy focuses on resource allocation whereas pull strategy is concerned with responsiveness.

6. There is a long lead time in push strategy. However, it is just opposite in the case of pull strategy.

7. Push strategy is best suited when there is low brand loyalty in a category. Unlike pull strategy, is appropriate for the products with high brand loyalty, where the consumers are well known about the differences in various brands, and they opt for a particular brand before they go shopping.

Channels and Intermediaries

Marketing Intermediaries: The Distribution Channel

Many producers do not sell products or services directly to consumers and instead use marketing intermediaries to execute an assortment of necessary functions to get the product to the final user. These intermediaries, such as middlemen (wholesalers, retailers, agents, and brokers), distributors, or financial intermediaries, typically enter into longer-term commitments with the producer and make up what is known as the marketing channel, or the channel of distribution. Manufacturers use raw materials to produce finished products, which in turn may be sent directly to the retailer, or, less often, to the consumer. However, as a general rule, finished goods flow from the manufacturer to one or more wholesalers before they reach the retailer and, finally, the consumer. Each party in the distribution channel usually acquires legal possession of goods during their physical transfer, but this is not always the case. For instance, in consignment selling, the producer retains full legal ownership even though the goods may be in the hands of the wholesaler or retailer—that is, until the merchandise reaches the final user or consumer.

Channels of distribution tend to be more direct—that is, shorter and simpler—in the less industrialized nations. There are notable exceptions, however. For instance, the GhanaCocoa Marketing Board collects cacao beans in Ghana and licenses trading firms to process the commodity. Similar marketing processes are used in other West African nations. Because of the vast number of small-scale producers, these agents operate through middlemen who, in turn, enlist sub-buyers to find runners to transport the products from remote areas. Japan's marketing organization was, until the late 20th century, characterized by long and complex channels of distribution and a variety of wholesalers. It was possible for a product to pass through a minimum of five separate wholesalers before it reached a retailer.

Companies have a wide range of distribution channels available to them, and structuring the right channel may be one of the company's most critical marketing decisions. Businesses may sell products directly to the final customer, as is the case with most industrial capital goods. Or they may use one or more intermediaries to move their goods to the final user. The design and structure of consumer marketing channels and industrial marketing channels can be quite similar or vary widely.

The channel design is based on the level of service desired by the target consumer. There are five primary service components that facilitate the marketer's understanding of what, where, why, when, and how target customers buy certain products. The service variables are quantity or lot size (the number of units a customer purchases on any given purchase occasion), waiting time (the amount of time customers are willing to wait for receipt of goods), proximity or spatial convenience (accessibility of the product),

product variety (the breadth of assortment of the product offering), and service backup (add-on services such as delivery or installation provided by the channel). It is essential for the designer of the marketing channel—typically the manufacturer—to recognize the level of each service point that the target customer desires. A single manufacturer may service several target customer groups through separate channels, and therefore each set of service outputs for these groups could vary. One group of target customers may want elevated levels of service (that is, fast delivery, high product availability, large product assortment, and installation). Their demand for such increased service translates into higher costs for the channel and higher prices for customers.

Channel Functions and Flows

In order to deliver the optimal level of service outputs to their target consumers, manufacturers are willing to allocate some of their tasks, or marketing flows, to intermediaries. As any marketing channel moves goods from producers to consumers, the marketing intermediaries perform, or participate in, a number of marketing flows, or activities. The typical marketing flows, listed in the usual sequence in which they arise, are collection and distribution of marketing research information (information), development and dissemination of persuasive communications (promotion), agreement on terms for transfer of ownership or possession (negotiation), intentions to buy (ordering), acquisition and allocation of funds (financing), assumption of risks (risk taking), storage and movement of product (physical possession), buyers paying sellers (payment), and transfer of ownership (title).

Each of these flows must be performed by a marketing intermediary for any channel to deliver the goods to the final consumer. Thus, each producer must decide who will perform which of these functions in order to deliver the service output levels that the target consumers desire. Producers delegate these flows for a variety of reasons. First, they may lack the financial resources to carry out the intermediary activities themselves. Second, many producers can earn a superior return on their capital by investing profits back into their core business rather than into the distribution of their products. Finally, intermediaries, or middlemen, offer superior efficiency in making goods and services widely available and accessible to final users. For instance, in overseas markets it may be difficult for an exporter to establish contact with end users, and various kinds of agents must therefore be employed. Because an intermediary typically focuses on only a small handful of specialized tasks within the marketing channel, each intermediary, through specialization, experience, or scale of operation, can offer a producer greater distribution benefits.

Management of Channel Systems

Although middlemen can offer greater distribution economy to producers, gaining cooperation from these middlemen can be problematic. Middlemen must continuously be motivated and stimulated to perform at the highest level. In order to gain such a high level of performance, manufacturers need some sort of leverage. Researchers have distinguished five bases of power: coercive (threats if the middlemen do not comply), reward (extra benefits for compliance), legitimate (power by position—rank or contract), expert (special knowledge), and referent (manufacturer is highly respected by the middlemen).

As new institutions emerge or products enter different life-cycle phases, distribution channels change and evolve. With these types of changes, no matter how well the channel is designed and managed, conflict is inevitable. Often this conflict develops because the interests of the independent businesses do not coincide. For example, franchisers, because they receive a percentage of sales, typically want their franchisees to maximize sales, while the franchisees want to maximize their profits, not sales. The conflict that arises may be vertical, horizontal, or multichannel in nature. When the Ford Motor Company comes into conflict with its dealers, this is a vertical channel conflict. Horizontal channel conflict arises when a franchisee in a neighboring town feels a fellow franchisee has infringed on its territory. Finally, multichannel conflict occurs when a manufacturer has established two or more channels that compete against each other in selling to the same market. For example, a major tire manufacturer may begin selling its tires through mass merchandisers, much to the dismay of its independent tire dealers.

Importance of Intermediaries

In an age where it is easy for any company to set up shop with an e-commerce website, it may be tempting for a small business to eliminate intermediaries to maximize profit. For a scaling business, however, this can create a lot of work in logistics and customer support.

For example, if 1,000 customers were to buy a product directly from the producer in a single month, this would entail 1,000 separate shipments to 1,000 locations, and with a minimum of 1,000 customer interactions. If you added customer inquiries about the product, returns and after-sale support and all the customers who initiate a purchase without following through you would have several thousand interactions with customers for every 1,000 sales. Selling through three or four intermediaries with a weekly shipping schedule, the manufacturer would have only a dozen shipments to schedule each month with a fraction of the interactions.

Wholesalers

A distributor that sells products to a retailer. A wholesaler will sell his product in bulk quantities to retailers, allowing the retailer to take advantage of a lower price than if he were to buy single items. The wholesaler will typically buy goods direct from the manufacturer, but could also buy from a reseller. In either case, the wholesaler gets large discounts for buying large quantities of goods. The wholesaler is rarely involved in the actual manufacture of a product, focusing instead on distribution.

A wholesaler requires a license to sell his product to the retailer, and his product will generally not be available to the customer at the same price as to the retailer. This is because the retailer makes their profits by marking up the price they pay to the whole-saler. In the case that a customer wishes to purchase a product from the wholesaler he will be charged for a drop shipment, this charge being charged to the customer as well as the wholesaler by a drop shipping merchant.

Often a wholesaler is a specialist in one specific product, or in a category of products. Other wholesalers will offer a wide variety of products. In addition, the wholesaler can focus on one type of business for their products, or they can offer items for sale to anyone.

Wholesalers also differ from distributors in that they are typically not associated with a particular good, and therefore they are not likely to offer the higher service level or support often offered by official product distributors. This is because the wholesaler is rarely directly affiliated with the manufacturer they buy from and are unfamiliar with the specifics and intricacies of the products they sell. Wholesalers can also offer com-peting products, which is not the case for distributors.

- Merchant Wholesalers

These are the most common type of wholesalers used in the FMCG industry, agricul-ture industry or Private label industry. Quite simply, Merchant wholesalers are the ones who buy directly from the manufacturer, store the product and then sell it to the customer. They might sell in any channel and they are not restricted to selling to retail only or to online only.

If there is any loss between the buying and selling of the product, it must be borne by the merchant wholesaler.

Example – A vegetable wholesaler buys produce directly from the farm and stocks it at his own warehouse. He then sells these products to the local retail outlets or even to end customers. He may also sell to restaurants. However, any loss of the produce due to spillage or any other reason is a cost to the merchant wholesalers.

Even in FMCG, companies like Britannia or P&G use merchant wholesalers. These wholesalers have a greater control in the region they operate. They benefit because they buy in bulk from the company and take charge of the risk they are facing. Plus, they are responsible for the sales targets, however, they achieve it.

- Full-service Wholesalers – Retail Wholesalers

They are most commonly observed in Consumer Durables or Engineering products. The full-service type of wholesalers is, as the name suggests, giving full service to the end retailer. These wholesalers mainly operate in the retail market and sell products to a reseller (a retailer in this case) Everything except service of the product is the respon-sibility of the full-service wholesaler.

Example – Samsung wants to expand its operation in region A but it does not have a sales office in that region. So it appoints a distributor in region A. This distributor is solely responsible for order picking, delivery, training sales associates, promotions and everything for the Samsung brand. He is now a full-service wholesaler. However, for service of the product, there is a different service franchise opened in the same region.

In real life scenario, Many full-service wholesalers also start a second services related business and start giving services for the products they are wholesaling. Example – A Samsung wholesaler also starting a service center of Samsung.

As a result, they might get both – sales and service orders. However, for theoretical purposes, Servicing and maintenance of the product is not a part of a full-service wholesaler. He is mainly for sales, deliveries, and financing. These are the second most common types of wholesalers in the market.

- Limited Service Wholesalers

A limited service wholesaler is someone who stocks the products of the company and sells it in a limited channel. He does not have a large turnover or does not cover all channels of the company.

Example – Company X wants to sell its products online but it knows that if it allows local distributors to sell online, there will be a huge price war. As a result, Company X appoints an exclusive online wholesaler. This online wholesaler has only one job – To purchase the product and stock it and sell it online. So whenever an order comes from Amazon or eBay, this wholesaler gives the machine to Amazon or eBay. That's his only job.

The same way – there are other limited-service wholesalers, two are mentioned below:

- ◦ Cash and Carry wholesalers: Strong FMCG products are sold as cash and carry. Immediate payment is demanded on a delivery of material.

- ◦ Logistics wholesalers: A milk wholesaler who delivers whole trucks of milk across the market. His only work is to deliver the milk and not to get orders for the company.

- Brokers and Agents

Most commonly observed in the real estate industry or in the chemical markets. A broker assumes no risk. He has the producer or the manufacturer on one side and he has the buyer on the other side. The work of the broker is to get the deal done and he gets a commission on the deal.

Example – A small lab has regular requirement of litmus paper. There is a litmus paper wholesaler in their area who is a broker for several companies and who arranges any lab material in bulk. The lab approaches the broker and wants to purchase huge quantity. The broker then talks to multiple manufacturers and finally, a deal is struck with one manufacturer. The manufacturer pays 2% commission to the broker for his work and for bringing the enquiry. Similarly, this broker can pick an order of Beakers, Petri dishes or any other equipment. He will keep arranging meetings with the right supplier and keep earning commissions.

A similar example like above is also observed in the retail industry wherein the broker earns a commission to sell an apartment.

The difference between a broker and agent is that a Broker is short-term and he will be there for a couple of orders. However, an Agent is long-term and specialized in repeated purchase so that he stays for a longer time with the company and specifically works for the betterment of the company. Example – Insurance has Agents (repeated buying) whereas real estate has brokers (single buying).

- Branches and mini offices

Although branches and mini offices do not come in the various types of wholesalers, these are common ways for companies to start selling their products in a region they are targeting. A branch can also be called a type of wholesaling wherein the branch directly picks the orders from the end customers in bulk and ensures the supply and reorders from the customer.

Example – Paper company like B2B or 3M knows that large companies require a lot of print paper across the month. These companies then establish branch offices which also act as the sales office. They pick a bulk order of paper and the company might transport the complete order from their warehouse to the company.

- Specialized wholesalers

These are wholesalers who do wholesale of specialized items only. Example – A used car wholesaler who sells directly to customers or to other used car dealers. He is specialized in used cars and knows the ins and outs of selling a used car to consumers or refurbishing the used cars.

Agents

Agents and brokers sell products or product services for a commission, or a percentage of the sales price or product revenue. These intermediaries have legal authority to act on behalf of the manufacturer or producer. Agents and brokers never take title to the products they handle and perform fewer services than wholesalers and distributors. Their primary function is to bring buyers and sellers together. For example, real estate agents and insurance agents don't own the items that are sold, but they receive a commission for putting buyers and sellers together. Manufacturers' representatives that sell several non-competing products and arrange for their delivery to customers in a certain geographic region also are agent intermediaries.

Types of Agents

An "agent" is a person employed to do any act for another, or to represent another in dealing with third persons. The person for whom such act is done, or who is so represented, is called the "principal".

As between the principal and third persons, any person may become an agent, but no person who is not of the age of majority and sound mind can become an agent, so as to be responsible to the principal according to the provisions in that behalf herein contained. No consideration is necessary to create an agency.

The authority of an agent may be express or implied. An authority is said to be express when it is given by words spoken or written. An authority is said to be implied when it is to be inferred from the circumstances of the case; and things spoken or written, or the ordinary course of dealing, may be accounted circumstances of the case.

Agents can be classified in various ways:

- Special Agents: Agent appointed for a particular task only. The agency in such cases lasts for a specific period of for a particular type of job or work. For example, a property dealer appointed as an agent for a sale of a property is authorize his rights in regards to that property only and that too till its sale or revocation of agency by the principal.

- General Agents: As the name suggests, the agent has a general authority in such a case. To elaborate, we could say a general agent is one who has authority to do all the acts (usually related to business or Trade) in the interest of his principal. A general agent has a implied authority to bind his principal by doing various acts necessary for carrying on the business of his principal.

- Universal Agents: Universal agent is practically a general agent with very extensive rights. We can say that an universal agent is a substitute of principal for all those transactions where in principal cannot participate. We rarely find universal agents in business world today, however in personal life, a wife, son or a very close friend or relative could become a universal agent. For example: when a person leaves his country for a long time, he may appoint his son as his universal agent to act on his behalf in his absence.

- Co-Agents: This happens when a principal appoints two or more person as agents jointly. Their authority is joint when nothing is mentioned. It implies that all co-agents concur in the exercise of their authority unless their authority is fixed or unless circumstances reveal any intention to the contrary. But when their authority is several, any other of the co-agents can act without the concurrence of the other.

- Sub-Agents: In the language of law, a sub-agent would be "a person employed and acting under the control of the original agent in the business of the agency ". In simple words, sub-agent is an agent of the original agent. As far as third party is concerned, principal can be held liable for the acts of sub-agent in certain cases like fraud etc. however in general, agent is responsible to the principal for the acts of sub-agent.

- Substituted Agents: Substituted agent is almost same as a co-agent or sub-agent. Sections 194 and 195 deals with substituted agents. It states "when an agent holding on express or implied authority to name another person to act for and on behalf of his principal in his business, such agent is know as substituted agent. There are certain differences between the two, which could be better understood by the way of following illustration: Mr. RR authorizes Mr. YY, who is a businessman in Pune, to recover the money due to RR from ABC Company. YY, in turn, instructs NN, a solicitor, to take necessary legal actions and recover the dues. Here, NN is not a sub-agent but a solicitor for R.

To elaborate more on points of distinction between sub-agents and co-agents we can have following arguments:

- A substituted agent acts under the direct control his principal where as sub-agent works under the original agent.

- An agent does not delegate any part of his tasks or duties to a substituted agent, whereas as he does that to a sub-agent.

- In case of a substituted agent, there is always a privacy of contract between the principal and the substituted agent, both can sue each other, however a sub-agent is not directly answerable to the principal, they can't sue each other, however both can sue the agent.

Distributors

A distributor is an intermediary entity between a the producer of a product and another entity in the distribution channel or supply chain, such as a retailer, a value-added reseller (VAR) or a system integrator (SI). The distributor performs some of the same functions that a wholesaler does but generally takes a more active role.

At a minimum, distributors handle payment and procurement but, unlike wholesalers, their roles can be much more complex. For example, vendors that lack the means to build out a channel program by themselves often outsource that work to distributors. Distributors also frequently take a more proactive approach in educating resellers about new products, through such activities as presales training, road shows, and demos on behalf of vendors. Distributors may provide services around the procurement process, such as contract negotiation, marketing for resellers and SIs, and warrantees. Increasingly, distributors also host network operations centers (NOCs).

Exclusive Distributors

Some distributors will ask you to sign an agreement stating they will be the only distributor to work with your product within a certain geographic region. These exclusive distributors may be the right fit for your business if you are worried about maintaining your brand's image. When you work with multiple distributors, they become the face of your brand, so you have to trust that they will represent you well. However, if you work exclusively with one distributor, you have more control over how they present the products and who they are selling to, so you can protect your brand a little bit more.

Intensive Distributors

If you're aiming to enter the market and cover a wide range of territory quickly, you will need the help of a distributor who is skilled in intensive distribution. This type of distributor works best within industries where customers switch back and forth between brands when their first choice is not available. For example, if a customer prefers energy drink brand A, but it's not in stock, the customer will buy energy drink brand B instead. In this situation, energy brand A lost out on a sale because the energy drink distributor did not succeed in stocking that specific store's shelves, so the customer was forced to switch to a competitor. Brands often measure the success of an intensive distributor based on the number of retailers he has been able to secure.

Direct Distributors

Direct store distributors skip the middle man by selling products directly to the store instead of taking them to the retailer's distribution center. This type of distributor has quicker turnaround times, so he can easily restock items that are selling faster than the store anticipated. Retailers usually love working with direct distributors because of their fast service and ability to meet demand.

Selective Distributors

The companies who hire intensive distributors want their products in as many places as possible, but the companies who work with selective distributors do not. These brands pick and choose the retailers they would like to carry their products, and then hire a distributor to deliver products and provide high quality customer service to them. This type of distributor usually works in niche industries where the retail outlets are limited. For example, a car parts manufacturer would not be able to sell to grocery outlets, so they may work with a selective distributor who can sell and service the niche retailers that do sell their products.

Channel Mix

A channel mix plan for a social and behavior change communication (SBCC) program is a strategic document that identifies the types of communication channels that best reach the priority audience to deliver the messages and the optimal blend of channels that maximizes reach and effectiveness of the messages.

A channel mix plan includes:

- Information on what channels are most effective for the priority audience, based on past impact, audience needs and preferences, and channel availability.

- Recommendations for how the program should combine different channels based on the advantages and disadvantages of each, the fit between the message and the channel, as well as the appropriate timing and scheduling of the messages.

- Information on resources available and how they will be allocated to different channels.

Ultimately, the channel mix selected for the program depends on the communication landscape, audience characteristics, the program's objectives and messages, reach and intensity, and budget.

Need to Create a Channel Mix Plan

Without a well-developed channel mix plan, messages may not reach the priority audience, resulting in wasted resources. Even if the communication messages and materials are wonderfully and cleverly designed, if they do not reach the intended audience.

Steps

Step 1: Assess Available Channels

Assess what channels are available to the priority audience(s) and how effective they will be in reaching them. To locate this information for media channels, the team can consult local television, radio stations and press offices. Typically, local advertising agencies also compile latest versions of this information. Additional information may be found in published media analysis studies. For community and interpersonal channels, it can be helpful to look at partner organizations' reports, clinic-based data and local government statistics. Access to the Internet, social media and mobile phones is on the increase globally. These need to be considered as part of the media mix, as well.

At this stage, also determine the costs associated with each of the available channels, as well as how many people they reach on average with a single exposure. Keep this information for inclusion in the Channel Strategy Chart.

After reviewing these resources, make a list of all the channels that are available to the priority audiences.

Step 2: Determine the Priority Audience's Habits and Channel Preferences

It is critical to understand which channels the priority audience prefers and uses regularly so that the team can reach them with the messages. Start by reviewing the audience analysis and situation analysis to understand audience habits and channel preferences. Keeping in mind the available channels, look for the following information:

Step 3: Consider the Strengths and Limitations of Channels

There is no one perfect channel. Each channel has inherent strengths and limitations due to its nature. A blend of channels can be used to capitalize on inherent strengths, allowing for greater impact. Using multiple channels can also have a cumulative and reinforcing effect, increasing the effectiveness of the messages communicated.

For each channel available to the audience, make a list of its unique strengths and limitations. The table below provides examples of general strengths and limitations. The team should supplement this with relevant local information.

Channel	Strengths	Limitations
Interpersonal Communication Community dialogue, peer-to-peer, health provider-client, inter-spousal and parent-child communication	• Tailored and personalized • Interactive • Able to explain complex information • Can build behavioral skills • Can increase intention to act • Familiar context - enhances trust and influence	• Lower reach • Relatively costly • Time-consuming
Community/Folk Media Community drama, interactive story telling, music, community events, video group discussion, mobile video units, talks and workshops, door-to-door visits, demonstrations and community radio	• Stimulates community dialogue • Motivates collective solutions • Provides social support for change • Can increase intention to act • Reaches larger groups of people	• Less personalized than IPC • Time-consuming to establish relationships • Relatively costly • May have less control over content
Mass Media and Mid-Media Radio, TV, print, film, outdoor – posters, billboards	• Extensive reach • Efficient and consistent repetition of message • Capacity to model positive behaviors • Sets the agenda-- what is important and how to think about it • Legitimizes norms and behaviors	• Limited two-way interaction • Available only at certain times • Relatively impersonal

Digital and Social Media Mobile phones, SMS, Facebook, Internet, twitter, eToolkits, web sites, eForums, blogs, YouTube, Chat rooms	• Fastest growing and evolving • Potential to mobilize youth • Highly tailored • Interactive • Quickly shares relevant information in a personalized manner • Flexibility to change and adapt as needed	• Program may have less control over content • Requires literacy • Limited reach and accessibility • Can lack credibility

Step 4: Determine what Channels Best Fit the Program's Objectives

Channel selection depends on what the program is trying to accomplish.

Review program objectives from the creative brief or communication strategy. Ask what is the purpose of the SBCC intervention. It may be to:

- Inform and educate.
- Persuade and promote.
- Increase intention to act.
- Impart skills.
- Encourage behavior change.
- Reinforce behavior change.
- Nurture advocacy.

If the objective is to impart skills, for example, an interpersonal Channel that allows for interactivity and feedback would be an appropriate choice. If the objective is to inform, a mass media channel combined with social media may be the best option.

Determine which channels best fit the program's objectives and make a list of those channels.

Step 5: Establish a Preference for Reach or Intensity

Based on the program's objectives, determine the balance between reach – the number of individuals or households exposed to the program's messages – and intensity – the average number of times individuals or households are exposed to the program's messages. Due to resource constraints, there is a trade-off between the two. Typically, when reach is high, intensity will be low. If intensity is high, then reach will be low.

For example, a program may choose to broadcast a message on all radio stations (high reach) or concentrate on a few stations with more messages that reach a particular segment (high intensity).

In an epidemic, it is important to reach a large number of people with time-sensitive messages. In that case, the team might decide that reach is more important and select a mass-media channel that extends to a wide audience. If, instead, a health problem is concentrated in a certain area or among a specific population, the team might decide that intensity is more important and select channels that allow multiple contact points with the audience, such as peer education sessions.

Step 6: Consider the Fit between Messages and Channels

Certain channels lend themselves to certain messages. If a message is long or detailed, for example, print (in connectivity-challenged areas) or the Internet (where people search or browse) would be more appropriate than a 30-second TV spot. If a message must include images, certain channels, like radio, would not convey the whole message. Messages that are complex and may require clarification would be best suited to interpersonal or digital channels.

Take, for example, a message to youth about sexual behavior:

- What are the media policy and rules in the audience's environment? How much detail about sexual behavior can be depicted on television or on radio? Perhaps interpersonal or digital media are better platforms?

- What are the social values and culture? What would audiences find appropriate? Determining the most appropriate channel for sensitive topics will help avoid turning off the audience, offending them or making them uncomfortable.

Review the messages already designed for the intervention. Consider the characteristics and content of the messages to determine which channels are most appropriate.

Step 7: Select the Channel Mix

Review the lists and tables the team compiled in Steps 1-6. Based on those considerations, make a decision about what channels the program will use. Write down which channels will be used and how they complement each other. Also include how each channel is expected to contribute to the achievement of program objectives.

Step 8: Establish the Timing and Frequency

For each channel listed in Step 7, decide when and how frequently to use it. In establishing the timing, reflect back to the tables developed in Steps 1-6 to make sure the timing makes sense with how the channels complement and build on one another, and what the potential costs may be. For example, the team may start with a TV campaign to raise awareness, followed by a big community event and home visits to impact local norms and clarify the message.

Decisions about when to use a channel can depend on the following factors, among others:

- Health events;
- Festivals or established events;
- Elections;
- Weather/seasons;
- Agricultural and manufacturing cycles;
- Fiscal year;
- Holidays;
- Media costs at specific times (of day or in a season).

Decisions about how frequently to use a channel will depend partially on both cost considerations and desired impact. The team may choose, for example, to hold weekly community discussion groups because it is critical to get community members discussing a health topic regularly.

Step 9: Think about Budget

Think about what resources are available to the program and the cost for using each channel. Ask if the program has sufficient resources to utilize the channel mix and frequency selected. If not, determine how the program can generate additional resources. It may be that the team can negotiate costs with media sources (value added time given when some is paid for) or combine efforts and resources with a local partner. The team can also look for existing events and activities funded by other sources that they can take advantage of. There may be others already holding mothers' groups and the program could integrate messages into the existing activities. If sufficient resources still are not available, the program may need to modify the planned channel mix to fit the available budget.

Channel Profiling

In order to understand the potential product markets we have to understand the solutions. One of our consultants will be tasked with gaining a deep understanding of the solutions and how they fit into the competitive marketplace. Our aim is to fully understand how the maturity of the products and their unique position in the market space will affect the choice of and access to particular product markets.

We will evaluate the complexity of the solution and provide a clear understanding of what skills each channel type will need to ensure a superior customer experience. We will assess channel readiness, giving clear guidance on localization, local market technical requirements and any issues that relate to local solution specific differences. We will also gain a clear understanding of customer support issues and assess the most efficient model for local and regional technical support.

We will use insights from the customer buying behaviors of the current channels and markets to assist in understanding how International customers may want to buy from you. Our approach is to understand the buying motivation in each market place and to assess how value added services, price, local support and speed of delivery influence you customers buying behaviors.

Channel Economics

Another consideration in developing channel mix is to create a model that satisfies the specific transaction economics of the products and solutions. Understanding transaction costs between complex and high value solutions against simpler but high volume products will help develop an efficient channel mix.

Channel Conflict

Our approach ensures that channel conflict is minimized. Conflict is an inevitable consequence of a multiple channel strategy but with clear understanding of the needs of the customers we build in the means to manage channel conflict effectively and early.

Channel Strategy Project Plan

ProSecta will ensure that the channel strategy develops from careful analysis of the customers needs and by understanding how the complexity of the products will influence the type and costs of the sales channels selected. We will build this information into a project plan to assist in future enhancements to the channels.

Evolving the Channel Strategy

Finally, a channel strategy cannot remain static for long. Organizations are dynamic and are constantly changing in order to provide new products and services to their customers in increasingly diverse markets. Add to this the impact of mergers and acquisitions and you need to be continually evolving the channel strategy, to ensure that customer and corporate needs are satisfied.

References

- Martin, Michael J.C. (1994). Managing Innovation and Entrepreneurship in Technology-based Firms. Wiley-IEEE. p. 44. ISBN 0-471-57219-5

- What-is-b2b-sales-2917368: thebalancecareers.com, Retrieved 29 March 2018

- Jolles, Robert L (2005). The Way of the Road Warrior: Lessons in Business and Life from the Road Most Traveled (1 ed.). John Wiley & Sons. p. 112. ISBN 978-0787980627. Retrieved 2014-11-23

- What-is-the-difference-between-b2b-and-b2c-sales: cpsa.com, Retrieved 22 June 2018

- Marketing-intermediaries-the-distribution-channel: britannica.com, Retrieved 11 March 2018

- Edward G. Hinkelman & Sibylla Putzi (2005). Dictionary of International Trade – Handbook of the Global Trade Community. World Trade Press. ISBN 1-885073-72-0

- Selective-distribution-examples-strategy-explanation: advergize.com, Retrieved 12 July 2018

- Hopp, Wallace J.; Spearman, Mark L. "To pull or not to pull: what is the question?". Manuf Serv Oper Manage. Retrieved 13 June 2014

- Inclusive-distribution-examples-strategy-explanation: advergize.com, Retrieved 29 March 2018

- Peter, J. Paul; James H. Donnelly (2002). A Preface to Marketing Management. McGraw-Hill Professional. p. 132. ISBN 0-07-246658-8

- Difference-between-push-and-pull-strategy: keydifferences.com, Retrieved 11 April 2018

Business-to-Business (B2B) E-commerce

When products and services are sold between businesses via a sales portal through the Internet, such commerce is called B2B e-commerce. This chapter discusses in detail the important aspects of e-commerce and its significance in the context of the modern economy as well as current e-commerce trends, business models and mobile commerce.

Business-to-business, or B2B, describes companies doing business with each other such as manufacturers selling to distributors and wholesalers selling to retailers. This business model differs from B2C, often offering negotiated pricing for different businesses for example, e-Commerce or electronic commerce is the purchasing, selling, and exchanging of goods and services over computer networks (such as the Internet) through which transactions or terms of sale are performed electronically.

Example of B2B eCommerce

The 2016 edition of B2B e-Commerce World's B2B eCommerce 300 report lists some of the world's biggest companies as users of B2B eCommerce, and a growing number of small companies are benefiting from it too. The 300 companies featured in the report are projected to grow web sales by 13.3% this year to $547.1 billion (from $482.79 billion in 2014)—figures that easily eclipse the U.S. B2C e-commerce market.

Companies included in the report include manufacturers and distributors such as 3M, Boeing, Coca-Cola, ConAgra, Microsoft, Nike and many other of the world's biggest companies, as well as smaller companies like Four Seasons General Merchandise, Fox Outdoor and Augusta Sportswear.

Some companies are using large marketplaces either targeted at a specific market vertical or one with a broader appeal, like Alibaba or Amazon Business, to reach their customers.

Other companies are setting up their own eCommerce websites, which can range from simple to complex. This option allows businesses to customize their site for their exact needs. For instance, Augusta Sportswear – a sportswear manufacturer and distributor – has developed a website that allows it to sell sports uniforms and corporate apparel directly to schools, teams and businesses. On Augusta's site, customers can research and select fabric options and customize the apparel they select with team names, mascots, colors, and team member names.

B2B eCommerce is a very broad business concept that can be defined in a number of ways. The possibilities for companies to benefit from B2B eCommerce are equally broad, allowing companies to choose from a wide range of options to support their business objectives.

The Differences between B2B e-commerce and EDI

B2B transactions can be processed online in various ways, of which Electronic Data Interchange (EDI) and B2B e-commerce are most often used. Although EDI and B2B e-commerce both have their own, distinctive features, they are frequently mixed up.

EDI is built for placing large, recurring orders in a standardized process of supplying raw materials to manufacturers. For instance, in accordance with the example set before, an automobile manufacturer regularly needs to order a specific brand of tires for a certain type of car. When manufacturing a certain number of that type of car, EDI can automatically place an order for the number of tires needed. So, no product information – like a description, images or pricing – is provided, or needed.

Although, like EDI, sales orders are processed online, with B2B e-commerce it is possible for customers to order occasionally and in irregular order quantities. Also, B2B e-commerce enables the display of many different types of detailed figures and images. It is possible to exhibit a full range of products or parts. Therefore, a web store provides the opportunity to cross- and upsell.

Market Development and Trends

The B2B e-commerce market is changing fast. There is an increasing number of companies adding an online sales channel to their business. In 2014, 63% of industrial supplies buyers purchased their products online (UPC, 2014). It is expected that the USA B2B e-commerce market will even grow from $780B in 2015 to $1.1T in 2020.

Integrated B2B e-commerce Versus Interfaced e-commerce

With integrated e-commerce, part of the software solution is installed inside the ERP back-end system. This means that the connection between the business logic and database of a back-end system is configured automatically. Information that is available in the back-end system, for example article numbers, prices and current stock availability of products, is leveraged, without being copied to another system, and displayed in the front/back end of the e-commerce system. An integrated e-commerce software solution thus does not require investments in recreating and maintaining a separate database or business logic. Instead, it re-uses those of the back-end system, so all data are stored in one, single place. This can prevent input redundancy, errors and synchronization time.

In most cases, integrated e-commerce is in one way or another acknowledged by the supplier of the back-end system, such as SAP ERP or Microsoft Dynamics. Although many B2B e-commerce suppliers claim to be integrated, most web stores are interfaced. With integrated e-commerce, the software solution is installed on top of the back-end system. This means that the connection between the business logic and database of a back-end system is set up manually. Information that is available in the back-end system is being duplicated into the e-commerce software. An interfaced e-commerce software product thus has their own database and business logic that are being synchronized constantly through a connection to a certain back-end system.

Mobile

The phrase mobile commerce was originally coined in 1997 by Kevin Duffey at the launch of the Global Mobile Commerce Forum, to mean "the delivery of electronic commerce capabilities directly into the consumer's hand, anywhere, via wireless technology." Mobile e-commerce for B2B is becoming increasingly popular. B2B has features different from mobile e-commerce for B2C. Whereas B2C is mostly classic catalogue browsing, mobile e-commerce for B2B requires specific features, which include:

- Displayed prices that are customer specific;

- Stock indication that is always up-to-date;

- Discounts that are calculated real-time;

- Orders can be placed quickly, for example with order histories or lists based on filtered product sets;

- Sales agents should be able to represent their customers.

Role of B2B E-commerce

In this day and age, customers are attached to everything via the internet. Consumers generally prefer to make their purchases digitally, via a phone, tablet or computer, rather than in a brick and mortar store. This saves them the hassle of having to deal with lines and pushy sales people. Consumers prefer to make their purchases from the comforts of their own home, in a super easy process that is as simple as a few clicks of a button, so that they can move on and save time for other tasks.

The digitization of consumers' purchasing habits is a reason, now more than ever, for manufacturers and business owners to further connect and build direct relationships with the end users and consumers of their goods or services via B2C and B2B commerce platforms.

B2B commerce platforms and ecommerce for manufacturers are unique opportunities for manufacturers and suppliers to meet their customers' constantly changing goals and needs. Not only are they able to meet customer demands, but they are able to exceed them by providing a seamless and easy-to-use ordering experience for their customers, no matter what stage of the business-manufacturer relationship. Distributors and manufacturers are realizing the importance of adopting a B2B commerce platform to help improve their revenue stream and set them apart from their competition in order to build long term profitable relationships.

Manufacturers are able to make more revenue, because of more sales from their direct customer relationships. In addition to this increased revenue, manufacturers are able to cut certain costs, including some of the costs associated with serving customers and providing good customer service.

Instead of having to hire order-takers and people to sort through and manage the incoming orders to be filled and processed, manufacturers are able to automate the process and offer their customers self service options such as automatic re-stocks and low inventory notifications. These self service options make fulfilling customer orders seamless and more efficient for both parties. It also adds to the customer service experience. allowing them to place orders and check the status of orders, and even research future items, any time of day that they want, from anywhere that they want.

Additionally, B2B commerce platforms eliminate the need for manufacturers to hire costly multiple staff loads for order fulfillment and customer service salespeople, because all orders will be processed online and a few customer service representatives can be available via a computer for their customers, day or night.

B2B ecommerce for manufacturers is an integral part of the industry and is a necessity for success. Tech savvy customers have paved the way for digital purchasing power and the demand to complete purchases easy and seamlessly. Customers now prefer to have the entire process streamlined and automated, so they can see what's happening and the status of their order or service in real time. This all means manufacturers, distributors and businesses alike need commerce sites with functionalities that support and exceed the customer demand, providing a seamless and customer-oriented purchasing experience.

B2B E-commerce Trends

The following are the top B2B eCommerce trends:

Artificial Intelligence

Nowadays, more and more online stores integrate the so-called conversational commerce. They integrate AI chatbots and text-to-speech recognition technologies to help customers make purchasing decisions.

However, in 2018 the conversational commerce trends are also expanding to B2B markets, and it goes much deeper than chatbots. eCommerce strategists use AI as a part of B2B sales strategy because of its ability to predict sales, optimize prices, and calculate discounts based on similar customer profiles.

Modern technologies such as cloud computing and the availability of software APIs have made AI more accessible to all types of businesses, including B2B eCommerce companies.

Dynamic Pricing

In 2016, Gartner predicted that by 2018 nearly a half of all existing B2B eCommerce websites will be using Configure Price Quote (CPQ) tools.

These tools use special algorithms to adjust product prices based on several factors, such as sales volumes and order history. As a result, such trends in eCommerce help businesses configure prices to the unique needs of customers. This helps them provide a personalized experience. Besides, the prices will be transparent, without any hidden extra fees.

B2C-like Experience

The B2C expectation of instant service, such as those of Amazon or AliExpress customers, are now also in effect for eCommerce B2B businesses. As B2B customers come to expect the same quality of service, today's B2B eCommerce products and software are finally able to provide the same smooth user experience.

Moreover, according to the same research from Gartner, 70% of eCommerce businesses will be focusing on delivering individual customer experience by 2018. The researchers emphasize that such experience will be something else than that of "traditional" B2B and B2C models.

Synchronized Order Management

Modern cloud-based B2B eCommerce solutions provide integration with order management systems, which makes them able to sync order processing across all channels and ensure great customer experiences.

Other features and trends in the eCommerce industry include Just-in-Time (JIT) availability with customizable purchasing workflows, automatic replenishment, multi-warehouse shipping, and returns management.

Mobile Commerce Trends

According to recent Google statistics, half of modern B2B search queries originate from smartphones. The same statistics report that 80% of B2B buyers are using mobile technologies at work.

In other words, mobile search is growing. Most B2B eCommerce sites are optimized for mobile, and if they're not, they soon will be. More and more companies will be developing mobile-first websites as well as apps to support their offerings.

Social Selling

Instead of just being "salesy," B2B salespeople should be active on social media, where they can provide insights on their business, connect directly with leads in the process, focus on problem solving, ask questions, and form personal relationships.

This is called social selling, which isn't necessarily one of the new eCommerce trends, but rather, one that is just now being emphasized over other tactics. Unlike social media marketing, social selling involves building personal relationships with prospects rather than increasing brand awareness. Just be closer to people, and you will be surprised by rapidly growing conversion.

Explainer Videos on Landing Pages

Short videos that illustrate only the most important functionality of your product are also among the latest B2B eCommerce trends. Such videos increase brand awareness and build trust, ensuring some kind of personal connection between a business and its potential customers.

There can be different kinds of explainer videos depending on where prospects are located in your sales funnel. For example, introductory, overview videos are intended for prospects, whereas more detailed videos or demos are intended for existing customers.

Order Status Updates

Detailed insights on order status belong to those B2B trends that have been borrowed from B2C model. In B2B transactions, the timeliness of shipment and delivery influences the customer experience.

Detailed order statuses and frequent updates will keep your B2B customers coming back. Even if the B2B service you provide is not a physical product, keeping clients updated as much as possible on the status of your agreement can go a long way.

Quick Implementation and Customization

It now takes only a few weeks to implement a B2B eCommerce platform. This timeframe includes integration of other systems such as whatever ERP you use, followed by quick cycles of adding new functionality every 4 to 8 weeks.

You can also usually customize your site to be more product specific. If you need have a complicated product and need to emphasize product content, there are designs or templates that allow you to do so. Emerging commerce platforms also have more control than ever over elements of design and user experience. In other words, it's easier to quickly get your website to look and feel how you want it to without having a high level of expertise.

Focus on Global

In addition to their existing customer base, businesses are reaching out to international prospects. This involves offering their products in local currencies at prices that are suitable for the local market, using the preferred local payment methods, and ensuring that the entire customer experience complies with local regulations.

Companies that expand to a global market can scale more quickly because they are selling to an exponentially wider market. It's difficult to do, but more B2B businesses are taking a crack at it than ever before.

Omnichannel Marketing

Companies tend to engage potential customers on different platforms and across several channels. Such eCommerce sales trends generate more revenue as compared to multichannel marketing, according to the "The Case for Omnichannel B2B" report by Forrester.

Larger Economic Impacts

If we take a look into the future, we will see that B2B eCommerce will outsmart its B2C counterpart in terms of financial turnaround. A 2015 report by Frost & Sullivan informs us that the global B2B eCommerce market will reach $ 6.7 trillion by 2020. Only a couple of years left to see if this prediction comes true. But regardless, there is no doubt that B2B is having a larger economic impact than ever before.

B2B E-commerce Business Model

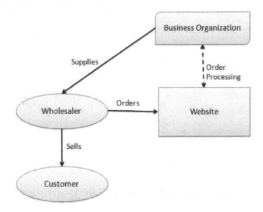

A website following the B2B business model sells its products to an intermediate buyer who then sells the products to the final customer. As an example, a wholesaler places an order from a company's website and after receiving the consignment, it sells the endproduct to the final customer who comes to buy the product at the wholesaler's retail outlet.

B2B identifies both the seller as well as the buyer as business entities. B2B covers a large number of applications, which enables business to form relationships with their distributors, re-sellers, suppliers, etc. Following are the leading items in B2B eCommerce:

- Electronics;
- Shipping and Warehousing;
- Motor Vehicles;
- Petrochemicals;
- Paper;
- Office products;
- Food;
- Agriculture.

Key Technologies

Following are the key technologies used in B2B e-commerce:

- Electronic Data Interchange (EDI): EDI is an inter-organizational exchange of business documents in a structured and machine processable format.
- Internet: Internet represents the World Wide Web or the network of networks connecting computers across the world.
- Intranet: Intranet represents a dedicated network of computers within a single organization.
- Extranet: Extranet represents a network where the outside business partners, suppliers, or customers can have a limited access to a portion of enterprise intranet/network.
- Back-End Information System Integration: Back-end information systems are database management systems used to manage the business data.

Architectural Models

Following are the architectural models in B2B e-commerce:

- Supplier Oriented marketplace: In this type of model, a common marketplace provided by supplier is used by both individual customers as well as business users. A supplier offers an e-stores for sales promotion.

- Buyer Oriented marketplace: In this type of model, buyer has his/her own market place or e-market. He invites suppliers to bid on product's catalog. A Buyer company opens a bidding site.

- Intermediary Oriented marketplace: In this type of model, an intermediary company runs a market place where business buyers and sellers can transact with each other.

Key Technologies of E-Commerce

Electronic Data Interchange

Electronic Data Interchange (EDI) is the computer-to-computer exchange of business documents in a standard electronic format between business partners.

By moving from a paper-based exchange of business document to one that is electronic, businesses enjoy major benefits such as reduced cost, increased processing speed, reduced errors and improved relationships with business partners.

Each term in the definition is significant:

- Computer-to-computer: EDI replaces postal mail, fax and email. While email is also an electronic approach, the documents exchanged via email must still be handled by people rather than computers. Having people involved slows down the processing of the documents and also introduces errors. Instead, EDI documents can flow straight through to the appropriate application on the receiver's computer (e.g., the Order Management System) and processing can begin immediately. A typical manual process looks like this, with lots of paper and people involvement:

- Business documents: These are any of the documents that are typically exchanged between businesses. The most common documents exchanged via EDI are purchase orders, invoices and advance ship notices. But there are many, many others such as bill of lading, customs documents, inventory documents, shipping status documents and payment documents.

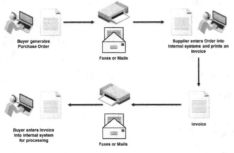

The EDI process looks like this — no paper, no people involved:

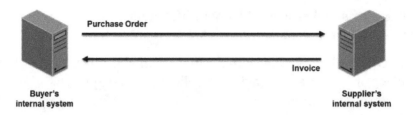

Buyer's internal system — Purchase Order → Invoice — Supplier's internal system

- Standard format: Because EDI documents must be processed by computers rather than humans, a standard format must be used so that the computer will be able to read and understand the documents. A standard format describes what each piece of information is and in what format (e.g., integer, decimal, mmddyy). Without a standard format, each company would send documents using its company-specific format and, much as an English-speaking person probably doesn't understand Japanese, the receiver's computer system doesn't understand the company-specific format of the sender's format:

  o There are several EDI standards in use today, including ANSI, EDIFACT, TRADACOMS and ebXML. And, for each standard there are many different versions, e.g., ANSI 5010 or EDIFACT version D12, Release A. When two businesses decide to exchange EDI documents, they must agree on the specific EDI standard and version.

  o Businesses typically use an EDI translator – either as in-house software or via an EDI service provider – to translate the EDI format so the data can be used by their internal applications and thus enable straight through processing of documents.

- Business partners: The exchange of EDI documents is typically between two different companies, referred to as business partners or trading partners. For example, Company A may buy goods from Company B. Company A sends orders to Company B. Company A and Company B are business partners.

EDI provides a technical basis for automated commercial "conversations" between two entities, either internal or external. The term EDI encompasses the entire electronic data interchange process, including the transmission, message flow, document format, and software used to interpret the documents. However, EDI standards describe the rigorous format of electronic documents, and the EDI standards were designed by the implementers, initially in the Automotive industry, to be independent of communication and software technologies. EDI can be transmitted using any methodology agreed to by the sender and recipient. This includes a variety of technologies, including modem (asynchronous and synchronous), FTP, e-mail, HTTP, AS1, AS2, AS4 etc. It is important to differentiate between the EDI documents and the methods for transmitting them. When they compared the synchronous protocol 2400 bit/s modems, CLEO devices, and value-added networksused to transmit EDI documents to transmitting via the Internet, some people equated the non-Internet technologies with EDI and predicted erroneously that EDI itself would be replaced along with the non-Internet technologies. These non-internet transmission methods are being replaced by Internet protocols such as FTP, HTTP, telnet, and e-mail, but the EDI documents themselves still remain.

As more trading partners use the Internet for transmission, standards have emerged. In 2002, the IETF published RFC 3335, offering a standardized, secure method of transferring EDI data via e-mail. On July 12, 2005, an IETF working group ratified RFC4130 for MIME-based HTTP EDIINT (a.k.a. AS2) transfers, and the IETF has prepared a similar RFC for FTP transfers (a.k.a. AS3). EDI via web services (a.k.a. AS4) has also been standardized by the OASIS standards body. While some EDI transmission has moved to these newer protocols, the providers of value-added networks remain active.

EDI documents generally contain the same information that would normally be found in a paper document used for the same organizational function. For example, an EDI 940 ship-from-warehouse order is used by a manufacturer to tell a warehouse to ship product to a retailer. It typically has a 'ship-to' address, a 'bill-to' address, and a list of product numbers (usually a UPC) and quantities. Another example is the set of messages between sellers and buyers, such as request for quotation (RFQ), bid in response to RFQ, purchase order, purchase order acknowledgement, shipping notice, receiving advice, invoice, and payment advice. However, EDI is not confined to just business data related to trade but encompasses all fields such as medicine (e.g., patient records and laboratory results), transport (e.g., container and modal information), engineering and construction, etc. In some cases, EDI will be used to create a new business information flow (that was not a paper flow before). This is the case in the Advanced Shipment Notification (ASN) which was designed to inform the receiver of a shipment, the goods to be received and how the goods are packaged.

Some major sets of EDI standards:

- The UN-recommended UN/EDIFACT is the only international standard and is predominant outside of North America.

- The US standard ANSI ASC X12 (X12) is predominant in North America.

- GS1 EDI set of standards developed the GS1 predominant in global supply chain.

- The TRADACOMS standard developed by the ANA (Article Number Association now known as GS1 UK) is predominant in the UK retail industry.

- The ODETTE standard used within the European automotive industry.

- The VDA standard used within the European automotive industry mainly in Germany.

- HL7, a semantic interoperability standard used for healthcare data.

- Edig@s (EDIGAS) is a standard dealing with commerce, transport (via pipeline or container) and storage of gas.

Many of these standards first appeared in the early to mid 1980s. The standards prescribe the formats, character sets, and data elements used in the exchange of business documents and forms. The complete X12 Document List includes all major business documents, including purchase orders and invoices.

The EDI standard prescribes mandatory and optional information for a particular document and gives the rules for the structure of the document. The standards are like building codes. Just as two kitchens can be built "to code" but look completely different, two EDI documents can follow the same standard and contain different sets of information. For example, a food company may indicate a product's expiration date while a clothing manufacturer would choose to send color and size information.

Specifications

Organizations that send or receive documents between each other are referred to as "trading partners" in EDI terminology. The trading partners agree on the specific information to be transmitted and how it should be used. This is done in human readable specifications (also called Message Implementation Guidelines). While the standards are analogous to building codes, the specifications are analogous to blue prints. (The specification may also be called a "mapping," but the term mapping is typically reserved for specific machine-readable instructions given to the translation software.) Larger trading "hubs" have existing Message Implementation Guidelines which mirror their business processes for processing EDI and they are usually unwilling to modify their EDI business practices to meet the needs of their trading partners. Often in a large company these EDI guidelines will be written to be generic enough to be used by different branches or divisions and therefore will contain information not needed for a particular business document exchange. For other large companies, they may create separate EDI guidelines for each branch/division.

Transmission

Trading partners are free to use any method for the transmission of documents. Furthermore, they can either interact directly, or through an intermediary.

Peer-to-peer

Trading partners can connect directly to each other. For example, an automotive manufacturer might maintain a modem-pool that all of its hundreds of suppliers are required to dial into to perform EDI. However, if a supplier does business with several manufacturers, it may need to acquire a different modem (or VPN device, etc.) and different software for each one.

Value-added Networks

To address the limitations in peer-to-peer adoption of EDI, VANs (value-added networks)were established. A VAN acts as a regional post office. It receives transactions, examines the 'from' and the 'to' information, and routes the transaction to the final recipient. VANs may provide a number of additional services, e.g. retransmitting documents, providing third party audit information, acting as a gateway for different transmission methods, and handling telecommunications support. Because of these and other services VANs provide, businesses frequently use a VAN even when both trading partners are using Internet-based protocols. Healthcare clearinghouses perform many of the same functions as a VAN, but have additional legal restrictions.

VANs may be operated by various entities:

- Telecommunication companies;

- Industry group consortia;

- A large company interacting with its suppliers/vendors.

Internet

As more organizations connected to the Internet, eventually most or all EDI was pushed onto it. Initially, this was through ad hoc conventions, such as unencrypted FTP of AS-CII text files to a certain folder on a certain host, permitted only from certain IP addresses. However, the IETF has published several informational documents describing ways to use standard Internet protocols for EDI.

As of 2002, Walmart have pushed the AS2 for EDI. Because of its significant presence in the global supply chain, AS2 have become a commonly adopted approach for EDI.

Interpreting Data

EDI translation software provides the interface between internal systems and the EDI format sent/received. For an "inbound" document the EDI solution will receive the file (either via a Value Added Network or directly using protocols such as FTP or AS2), take the received EDI file (commonly referred to as an "envelope"), validate that the trading partner who is sending the file is a valid trading partner, that the structure of the file meets the EDI standards, and that the individual fields of information conform to the agreed upon standards. Typically the translator will either create a file of either fixed length, variable length or XML tagged format or "print" the received EDI document (for non-integrated EDI environments). The next step is to convert/transform the file that the translator creates into a format that can be imported into a company's backend business system or ERP. This can be accomplished by using a custom program, an integrated proprietary "mapper" or an integrated standards based graphical "mapper," using a standard data transformation language such as XSLT. The final step is to import the transformed file (or database) into the company's back-end system.

For an "outbound" document the process for integrated EDI is to export a file (or read a database) from a company's information systems and transform the file to the appropriate format for the translator. The translation software will then "validate" the EDI file sent to ensure that it meets the standard agreed upon by the trading partners, convert the file into "EDI" format (adding the appropriate identifiers and control structures) and send the file to the trading partner (using the appropriate communications protocol).

Another critical component of any EDI translation software is a complete "audit" of all the steps to move business documents between trading partners. The audit ensures that any transaction (which in reality is a business document) can be tracked to ensure that they are not lost. In case of a retailer sending a Purchase Order to a supplier, if the Purchase Order is "lost" anywhere in the business process, the effect is devastating to both businesses. To the supplier, they do not fulfill the order as they have not received it thereby losing business and damaging the business relationship with their retail client. For the retailer, they have a stock outage and the effect is lost sales, reduced customer service and ultimately lower profits.

In EDI terminology "inbound" and "outbound" refer to the direction of transmission of an EDI document in relation to a particular system, not the direction of merchandise, money or other things represented by the document. For example, an EDI document that tells a warehouse to perform an outbound shipment is an inbound document in relation to the warehouse computer system. It is an outbound document in relation to the manufacturer or dealer that transmitted the document.

Advantages Over Paper Systems

EDI and other similar technologies save a company money by providing an alternative to, or replacing, information flows that require a great deal of human interaction and paper documents. Even when paper documents are maintained in parallel with EDI exchange, e.g. printed shipping manifests, electronic exchange and the use of data from that exchange reduces the handling costs of sorting, distributing, organizing, and searching paper documents. EDI and similar technologies allow a company to take advantage of the benefits of storing and manipulating data electronically without the cost of manual entry. Another advantage of EDI is the opportunity to reduce or eliminate manual data entry errors, such as shipping and billing errors, because EDI eliminates the need to rekey documents on the destination side. One very important advantage of EDI over paper documents is the speed in which the trading partner receives and incorporates the information into their system thus greatly reducing cycle times. For this reason, EDI can be an important component of just-in-time production systems.

According to the 2008 Aberdeen report "A Comparison of Supplier Enablement around the World", only 34% of purchase orders are transmitted electronically in North America. In EMEA, 36% of orders are transmitted electronically and in APAC, 41% of orders are transmitted electronically. They also report that the average paper requisition to order costs a company $37.45 in North America, $42.90 in EMEA and $23.90 in APAC. With an EDI requisition to order costs are reduced to $23.83 in North America, $34.05 in EMEA and $14.78 in APAC.

Barriers to Implementation

There are a few barriers to adopting electronic data interchange. One of the most significant barriers is the accompanying business process change. Existing business processes built around paper handling may not be suited for EDI and would require changes to accommodate automated processing of business documents. For example, a business may receive the bulk of their goods by 1 or 2 day shipping and all of their invoices by mail. The existing process may therefore assume that goods are typically received before the invoice. With EDI, the invoice will typically be sent when the goods ship and will therefore require a process that handles large numbers of invoices whose corresponding goods have not yet been received.

Another significant barrier is the cost in time and money in the initial set-up. The preliminary expenses and time that arise from the implementation, customization and training can be costly. It is important to select the correct level of integration to match the business requirement. For a business with relatively few transactions with EDI-based partners, it may make sense for businesses to implement inexpensive "rip and read" solutions, where the EDI format is printed out in human-readable form and people, rather than computers, respond to the transaction. Another alternative is outsourced EDI solutions provided by EDI "Service Bureaus". For other businesses, the implementation of an integrated EDI solution may be necessary as increases in trading volumes brought on by EDI force them to re-implement their order processing business processes.

The key hindrance to a successful implementation of EDI is the perception many businesses have of the nature of EDI. Many view EDI from the technical perspective that EDI is a data format; it would be more accurate to take the business view that EDI is a system for exchanging business documents with external entities, and integrating the data from those documents into the company's internal systems. Successful implementations of EDI take into account the effect externally generated information will have on their internal systems and validate the business information received. For example, allowing a supplier to update a retailer's Accounts Payable system without appropriate checks and balances would put the company at significant risk. Businesses new to the implementation of EDI must understand the underlying business process and apply proper judgment.

Internet, a system architecture that has revolutionized communications and methods of commerce by allowing various computer networks around the world to interconnect. Sometimes referred to as a "network of networks," the Internet emerged in the United States in the 1970s but did not become visible to the general public until the early 1990s. By 2015, approximately 3.2 billion people, or nearly half of the world's population, were estimated to have access to the Internet.

The Internet provides a capability so powerful and general that it can be used for almost any purpose that depends on information, and it is accessible by every individual who connects to one of its constituent networks. It supports human communication via electronic mail (e-mail), "chat rooms," newsgroups, and audio and video transmission and allows people to work collaboratively at many different locations. It supports access to digital information by many applications, including the World Wide Web. The Internet has proved to be a spawning ground for a large and growing number of "e-businesses" (including subsidiaries of traditional "brick-and-mortar" companies) that carry out most of their sales and services over the Internet. Many experts believe that the Internet will dramatically transform business as well as society.

For B2B marketers, wading into the Internet of Things will be essential, because the IOT is all about having a clearer window on customers and how they're using products. Read on for a deep dive into how the IOT can bring companies closer to their customers by helping identify when a product needs maintenance, how it can be improved, and how it can be used more efficiently.

Maintenance Alerts

General Electric is already using the Internet of Things in a variety of ways. For instance, sensors on GE's jet engines enable airlines (and GE) to monitor engine performance and when maintenance is necessary. "By using sensors to collect engine data, GE is able to perform short bursts of maintenance much earlier on, meaning that over an entire lifecycle the engine spends less time in repairs," according to this story in Computing magazine.

Insight into Product Usage

The IOT presents huge opportunities for B2B marketers to gain a deeper understanding of how their customers are using their products. As Indranil Mukherjee, an executive at SapientNitro, wrote in an opinion piece for an India Times blog, "The voice of the customer still rules but that voice is no longer enabled exclusively through surveys and call-centers. The IOT can tell the marketer about the customer's sentiments and needs (How does he like the product? When will he need a replacement?). This is fundamentally changing how products are going to be created, marketed, sold and serviced."

Using data generated by the products themselves, marketers and product designers can gain invaluable insight into how their products can be improved in the next iteration. In this blog post for Arc Advisory Group, Ralph Rio showed how Cummins uses the Internet of Things in the engines it manufactures. "The Cummins engines already have intelligence in the form of the engine control module (ECM) which has access to all the engine data," Rio wrote in an Arc Advisory Group newsletter. "By adding communications, it transfers data to IBM CloudOne with analytics. Now, product development has access to performance data that it uses to improve the engine's design. Configuration changes are sent to an engine to improve its operating performance and reliability."

Boosting Efficiency

Additionally, the Internet of Things can improve the efficiency of products. "By equipping street lights with sensors and connecting them to the network, cities can dim lights to save energy, only bringing them to full capacity when the sensors detect motion. This can reduce energy costs by 70 to 80 percent," John Chambers, chairman-CEO of Cisco, wrote in this blog post.

There's no ignoring the Internet of Things. It's already here, and it's only going to become more essential, particularly for B2B marketers who crave insight into their customers. By embracing the IOT and its potential, B2B marketers gain better insight into customers, provide customers with better products, and help deliver more efficient performance. And if that's the Internet of Things, it sounds like something you should never get sick of.

IOT Favorites

Here are some cool consumer Internet of Things products that show the possibilities of connected devices and that may inspire some ideas on how B2B marketers can leverage the IOT:

- Smart diapers

    Pixie Scientific has created disposable diapers that allows pediatricians and parents to analyze a child's health using sensors. Additionally, Kimberly-Clark has experimented with Huggies TweetPee, a diaper that would alert parents via Twitter that it was time for a change.

- Smart Scale

    The Withings' Smart Body Analyzer is a scale that sends information about your weight, body mass index, and heart rate to iOS and Android phones. The scale recognizes users and can be shared by a number of users.

- Tennis Racquet Sensor

    The description of this product is in Japanese, so I can't tell exactly what it does

– but it appears to analyze swing speed, ball speed, and ball spin. I do know what I'd like in a tennis racquet sensor: a device that can analyze the power of a stroke and calculate how often the ball is hitting the racquet's sweet spot.

B2B Move of the Week

Tracx, a maker of unified social media management technology for enterprises, named Amy Inlow as its CMO. Formerly a marketing executive at Experian, Inlow will oversee global branding, marketing, and communications at Tracx. "Amy's sheer breadth of technology marketing and analytics expertise, coupled with her passion for our industry, made her the ideal choice to serve as our CMO," said Eran Gilad, Tracx CEO.

B2B Resource of the Week

Embracing the Internet of Things can give B2B marketers deeper insight into their customers. Embracing full funnel marketing can help B2B marketers reach prospects and customers at every stage of the buying process.

The term Intranet refers to a corporate or private network of computers, that share part/parts of the organizations operations and information with employees. By using secure network connections and specific internet protocols. In certain situations, the term refers to only the most visible service, the organizations internal website. The same concept is used to build an intranet, using technology to run clients and servers on the same internet protocol suite. Common internet protocols as HTTP and FTP are commonly used. Often, there are attempts to use internet technologies to accommodate new interfaces to corporate "legacy" data and information systems.

Additionally, a Intranet can be understood as a "private" version of the organizations own internet. Or seen as a version of the internet confined to an organization.

Advantages of Intranet

- Work force productivity: Intranets can help public. and view information faster, while using applications relevant to their roles and responsibilities. Web browser interfaces such as Internet Explorer, Firefox and Google Chrome. Users can access data held in any database within the organization. Subject to security provisions, users can access the available data anytime, from anywhere within the company/organization. Increasing the employees ability to perform jobs faster, more efficient and accurately. Confident with secure information, constantly improving services provided to users.

- Time: Intranets allow organizations to make more information available to employees on a "pull" basis (i.e.. employees can link to relevant information at any time) rather than being deluged by large volumes of information. This comes in handy when spur of the moment meetings come up, needing the most current information available.

- Communication: Intranets can serve as powerful tools for communication within an organization. From a communication standpoint, Intranets are useful to communicate tactical initiatives that have global reach. The type of information to be conveyed is the purpose, the goal, e driving force, the results to date and whom to speak to for more information. By communicating this information on the intranet, all staff can access the initiative and stay current with the progress and tactical focus of the organization:

  - Web Publishing: Corporate knowledge is easily maintained and reached, using hypermedia and Web technologies. Some examples include: employee manuals, benefit documents, company policies and common training policies. Most of these types of files can be reached using common applications as Acrobat files, Flash files, and CGI applications. Allowing each business unit to update/input data on the document therefore, the most current information is always accessible. Available to all employees sharing the intranet within the organization.

  - Business Operations and Management: Intranets are also used as platforms for developing and deploying applications to support business operations and decisions throughout the enterprise.

  - Cost-Effective: Users can view information and data via web-browser rather than maintaining physical documents such as procedure manuals, internal phone lists and requisition forms.

  - Promote Common Corporate Culture: Every user is viewing the same information within the intranet.

  - Enhance Collaboration: With information easily accessible by all authorized users, teamwork is enabled.

  - Promote Common Corporate Culture: Every user is viewing the same information within the intranet.

  - Enhance Collaboration: With information easily accessible by all authorized users, teamwork is enabled.

Disadvantages of Intranet

- Inappropriate or incorrect information can be posted on an intranet, reducing credibility and effectiveness.

- In a developed and highly interactive intranet there is freedom to post abusive and possibly illegal materials. There are protocols put into place to ensure this freedom is not taken advantage of for corporate gain. Having these controls in place, meet the organizations legal and moral responsibilities.

- The need for expertise in the field to administer and develop intranet information within the organization.

- Security of the intranet can become an issue. Some users may post sensitive information which appears to another user. Furthermore, in an industry with high turnover the potential to acquire sensitive information for future gain at a competing company.

- With multiple users, information overload can occur, if not controlled well.

Extranet Applications

An extranet application is a software data application that provides limited access to your company's internal data by outside users such as customers and suppliers. The limited access typically includes the ability to order products and services, check order status, request customer service and much more.

A properly developed extranet application provides the supply chain connection needed with customers and suppliers to dramatically lessen routine and time consuming communications. Doing so frees up resources to concentrate on customer service and expansion as opposed to administrative office tasks such as data entry.

Just as intranets provide increased internal collaboration, extranets provide increased efficiencies between your company and its customers and suppliers. Developing and implementing an extranet application can provide you the competitive edge to stay ahead of the competition in the eyes of your customers and a better ability to negotiate prices with your suppliers.

Disadvantages

1. Extranets can be expensive to implement and maintain within an organization (e.g.: hardware, software, employee training costs) — if hosted internally instead of via an ASP.

2. Security of extranets can be a big concern when dealing with valuable information. System access needs to be carefully controlled to avoid sensitive information falling into the wrong hands.

3. Extranets can reduce personal contact (face-to-face meetings) with customers and business partners. This could cause a lack of connections made between people and a company, which hurts the business when it comes to loyalty of its business partners and customers.

E-commerce Business Models

Since eCommerce consists of doing business online or electronically, the business or revenue models are somewhat different than that of a "brick and mortar" business. Common eCommerce models are direct online sales, selling online advertising space, and online commissions.

Direct Online Sales Model

You can establish your website as your place of business and directly sell to those entering your "store" to make a purchase. Since delivery is often by mail, this is similar to customers buying from a mail order catalog. Software products, e-books, music and video files can be delivered to the customer through the downloading process. Amazon.com is a good example of a business using the direct sales model to gain revenue.

Online Advertising Space Model

Just as television and radio stations gain revenue from advertisements, related to the reach or number of viewers they have, so too can popular websites charge for the number of viewers seeing an ad. A better method is to count the number of viewers that click on an ad, taking them to the company's website.

Online Commission Model

Individuals and companies can also be established as affiliates, where they gain a commission for sales made through a company using the direct online sales model. Online companies such as eBay and PayPal charge a commission for their services. Google gains a commission for ads placed on others' websites.

Successful Ecommerce Business Models

Five different ways websites can generate revenue by Robert Samuelsen "There's no such thing as a free lunch!" While this simple economic aphorism seems to have been forgotten in the world of cyberspace, it holds true as much today as it ever has. First lets establish the fact that no site is free - every web site costs money. The web site is stored on a computer, uses web server software, accesses telecommunication resources, and must be maintained. Someone must pay for the computers, software, telecommunication charges, and time. The omnipresent cost either comes from your pocket or some benevolent benefactor.

Architectual Model

There are different types of e-marketplaces based on different business models or their method of operation - These are the following e-marketplace:

- Buyer-oriented e-marketplace: This marketplace is run by a body of buyers who want to establish an efficient purchasing environment. This helps the buyers to lower their administrative costs and get best prices from the suppliers. The suppliers can also use the buyer oriented e-marketplace to advertise their product to the set of relevant customers. An example of a buyer-oriented portal that links many suppliers to a few buyers is the Exostar.

- Supplier-oriented e-marketplace: This marketplace is operated by a large group of suppliers for establishing an efficient sales channel and increase their visibility and get leads from a large number of potential buyers. This type of Supplier-oriented e-marketplace are also called as supplier directory and are usually searchable by the product or the services being offered. The buyers can also access information about the suppliers, products or the region that they are not familiar with. Successful examples of this business model are (CCO) Cisco connection Online which operates Cisco's electronic marketplace.

- Vertical and horizontal e-marketplaces: Vertical e-marketplace provides online access to businesses vertically across every segment of a particular industry sector such as automotive, chemical, construction or textile. Buying or selling using Vertical e-marketplace helps increase the operating efficiency while decreasing the supply chain and inventories cost and procurement time. A horizontal e-marketplace on the contrary connects buyers and sellers across different industries or regions. It will allow the buyers to purchase indirect products such as office equipment or stationery.

- Independent e-marketplace: It is usually a business to business online platform operated by a third party and is open to buyers and sellers from a particular industry. You can register to these platforms and get access to classified ads, request for quotations and place bids on several products from your industry sector. Participation in these online auctions and exchanges mostly can be done through a minimal payment of the registration fee. Some popular examples of Independent e-marketplace are Alibaba.com, eBay.com etc.

Advantages of B2B E-commerce Business Model

- Market Predictability: Compared to the other business strategies, the B2B e-commerce business model has more market stability. B2B sectors grow gradually and can adapt to various complex market conditions. This helps to strengthen the online presence and business opportunities and get more potential clients and resellers.

- Better Sales: An improved supply chain management process along with a collaborative approach increase customer loyalty in the B2B e-commerce business model. This, in turn, leads to improved sales. It helps businesses to showcase product recommendations and unlock effective upselling and cross-selling opportunities.

- Lower Costs: Due to an effective supply chain management process, this online business model leads to lower costs for the businesses. In most cases, the work is done through automation that eradicates chances of errors and undue expenditure.

- Data Centric Process: One of the main advantages of the model is that it relies on effective and factual data to streamline the whole process. In this way, errors can be avoided and proper forecasts can be made. With an integrated data-driven approach, you can calculate detailed sales statistics.

Disadvantages of B2B E-commerce Business Model

Just like the other business models, the B2B e-commerce Business model has some flaws too, which are:

- Limited Market: Compared to the B2C model, this type of business has a limited market base as it deals with transactions between businesses. This makes it a bit of a risky venture for small and medium e-commerce businesses.

- Lengthy Decision: Here, the majority of the purchase decisions involve a lengthy process as there are two businesses involved. The process may involve dependence on multiple stakeholders and decision makers.

- Inverted Structure: Compared to the other models, consumers have more decision making power than sellers in the B2B business model. They may demand customizations, impose specifications and try to lower price rates.

Mobile Commerce

M-commerce is defined as 'the ability to purchase goods anywhere through a wireless Internet-enabled device. Primary mobile communication exists through web-enabled wireless phones.

It can also be defined as:

- "Providing E-commerce in a mobile context."

- "Using mobile technology to sell or buy items, access business information, conduct a transaction, perform supply chain or demand chain functions.

Mobile Commerce refers to wireless electronic commerce used for conducting commerce or business through a handy device like cellular phone or 1Personal Digital Assistant (PDA). It is also said that it is the next generation wireless E-commerce that needs no wire and plug-in devices. Mobile commerce is usually called as 'M-commerce' in which user can do any sort of transaction including buying and selling of goods, asking any services, transferring ownership or rights, transacting and trans-ferring money by accessing wireless internet service on the mobile handset itself. The next generation of commerce would most probably be mobile commerce or M-commerce. Presuming its wide potential reach, all major mobile handset manufacturing companies are making 2WAP (Wireless Application Protocol) enabled smartphones and providing the maximum wireless internet and web facilities covering personal, official and commerce requirement to pave the for way M-commerce that would later be very fruitful for them.

M-commerce has several major advantages over its fixed counterparts because of its specific inbuilt characteristics such as ubiquity, personalization, flexibility and dis-tribution. Mobile commerce promises exceptional business market potential, greater efficiency and higher fruitfulness. Thus it is not surprising that mobile commerce is emerging much faster than its fixed counterpart. M-commerce is more personalized than E-commerce and thus needs a gentle approach to appraise M-commerce applica-tions.

The difference between E-commerce and M-commerce is that E-commerce is limited to PC users with an Internet Connection. With M-commerce moving to an SMS plat-form among other things, M-commerce is open to almost the entire mobile population. An important barrier to M-commerce is the state of mobile networks today because there is a risk of transactions not maturing due to poor networks. For M-commerce an ecosystem between application developers, financial institutions, and mobile phone networks is required, for its effective utility. Simplicity is the key to proliferation of M-commerce coupled with the idea of developing trust with audiences.

Now a days the cell phone, on its own or in conjunction with an organizer is used for much more than simply making phone calls. It also acts as a flexible terminal for a huge range of applications. So the availability of information (weather forecasts, eco-nomic data, news), e-shopping, e-ticketing, e-banking and e-brokerage is greater than ever before, regardless of time or place. The WAP (Wireless Application Protocol) and 3WML (Wireless Markup Language) open standards mean the Internet's innovative solution strategies can now be applied to mobile telephony too.

Mobile Commerce (also known as M-commerce, M-commerce or U-commerce, owing to the ubiquitous nature of its services) is the ability to conduct commerce, using a mobile device e.g. a mobile phone (or cell phone), a PDA, a Smartphone while on the move, and other emerging mobile equipment, like dash top mobile devices. In an aca-demic definition it is characterized in the following terms.

M-commerce — The Concept

"Mobile Commerce is any transaction, involving the transfer of ownership or rights to use goods and services, which is initiated or completed by using mobile access to computer-mediated networks with the help of an electronic device." This definition provides for a differentiation of Mobile Commerce from other related fields such as Electronic Commerce, Electronic Business and Mobile Business. M-commerce is at a very early stage. It's about purchase and sale of goods and services through the mobile with the use of a financial institution. Purchase and sale of 4VAS content cannot be classified as M-commerce.

"M-commerce is the use of mobile devices to communicate, inform transact and entertain using text and data via a connection to public and private networks."

"The core of mobile E-commerce is the use of a terminal (telephone, PDA, PC device or custom terminal) and public mobile network (necessary but not sufficient) to access information and conduct transactions that result in the transfer of value in exchange for information, services or goods."

"Business-to-consumer transactions conducted from a mobile device."

"E-commerce over mobile devices."

"Mobile Commerce refers to any transaction with monetary value that is conducted via a mobile telecommunications network."

"The use of mobile handheld devices to communicate, interact via an always-on high-speed connection to the Internet."

"The use of wireless technologies to provide convenient personalized and location-based services to your customers, employees and partners."

MobileInfo.com definition is closer to that of Ovum. It defines M-commerce as "Any electronic transaction or information interaction conducted using a mobile device and mobile networks (wireless or switched public network) that leads to transfer of real or perceived value in exchange for information, services or goods.

Typical Examples of M-commerce are:

- Purchasing airline tickets;
- Purchasing movie tickets;
- Restaurant booking and reservation;
- Hotel booking and reservation.

"Mobile Commerce is any transaction, involving the transfer of ownership or rights to use goods and services, which is initiated or completed by using mobile access to computer-mediated networks with the help of an electronic device." This definition provides for a differentiation of Mobile Commerce from other related fields such as Electronic Commerce, Electronic Business and Mobile Business.

Different Areas that Come under M-commerce

(a) Travel and Ticketing: convenience is the key. Mobiles are and will reiterate their time saving devices.

(b) Movie Ticketing.

(c) Bill payments: making payments to utility and service companies.

(d) Merchant Transactions/Retail Transactions: Mobile and Internet transactions over the Internet is difficult as of now due to low speed of the Internet.

(e) Money Transfer: transfer from person to person through a financial intermediary.

The difference between E-commerce and M-commerce is that, E-commerce is limited to PC users with an internet connection. With M-commerce moving to an SMS platform among other things, M-commerce is open to almost the entire mobile population.

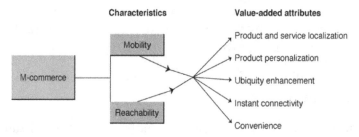

Characteristics of M-commerce

Mobile commerce is generally known as, any e-commerce done in a wireless environment, especially via the Internet:

- Can be done via the Internet, private communication lines, smart cards, etc.

- Creates opportunity to deliver new services to existing customers and to attract new ones.

M-Commerce — Customer's View

Mobile Commerce is explained from the customer's point of view as follows:

- The customer wants to access information, goods and services any time and in any place on his mobile device.

- He can use his mobile device to purchase tickets for events or public transport, pay for parking, download content and even order books and CDs.

- He should be offered appropriate payment methods. They can range from secure mobile micropayment to service subscriptions.

M-Commerce — Provider's View

Mobile Commerce is explained from the provider's point of view as follows:

- The future development of the mobile telecommunication sector is heading more and more towards value-added services. Analysts forecast that soon half of mobile operator's revenue will be earned through mobile commerce.

- Consequently operators as well as third party providers will focus on value-added services. To enable mobile services, providers with expertise on different sectors will have to cooperate.

- Innovative service scenarios will be needed that meet the customer's expectations and business models that satisfy all partners involved.

M-Commerce — Benefits

The benefits from Mobile Commerce Includes:

- Internet offerings are easier and more convenient to access.

- It offers considerable flexibility when conducting business.

- It offers intense customer orientation and high customer loyalty, and this is due to innovative service strategies.

- It offers lower transaction and personnel costs, which is due to the widespread automation.

Characteristics of Wireless Vs. Wired

- Ubiquity: The use of wireless device enables the user to receive information and conduct transactions anywhere, at anytime.

- Accessibility: Mobile device enables the user to be contacted at virtually any time and place. The user also has the choice to limit their accessibility to particular persons or times.

- Convenience: The portability of the wireless device and its functions from storing data to access to information or persons.

- Localization: The emergence of location-specific based applications will enable the user to receive relevant information on which to act.

- Instant Connectivity (2.5G): Instant connectivity or "always on" is becoming more prevalent with the emergence of 2.5 G networks, GPRS or EDGE. Users of 2.5 G services will benefit from easier and faster access to the Internet.

- Personalization: The combination of localization and personalization will create a new channel/business opportunity for reaching and attracting customers.

Personalization will take the form of customized information, meeting the users' preferences, followed by payment mechanisms that allow for personal information to be stored, eliminating the need to enter credit card information for each transaction.

- Time Sensitivity: Access to real-time information such as a stock quote that can be acted upon immediately or a sale at a local boutique.

- It reaches the destination server: And has to cover the same path again in reverse to complete the trip. There are many physical links (hops), wireless and wired line, between the end user's client application software and the information server. There are also several pieces of software involved, many of which featuring queuing (i.e., they are asynchronous).

- M-commerce in its true form is the ability to charge an amount of currency to a mobile phone either by applications like Mobilcash or Near Field Communications, the amount to be charged is actually taken from the Mobile device's account or preloaded 5RFID chip.

M-commerce and E-commerce refer to the field of marketing –buying, selling, distributing and servicing different products through commercial transactions on the internet with the use of specific devices or computers.

M-commerce stands for Mobile Commerce wherein commercial transactions are done using cellular or mobile phones that have access to the Internet. Before there was no M-commerce because phones with Internet capability were not yet available; however, when mobile phones with Internet capability were invented, marketing has expanded more. Not only are business transactions done outside and through the Internet, but also through mobile phones has sky rocketed. Today, many phones have access to the Internet. With the rise of such technology, M-commerce is becoming more popular.

E-commerce stands for Electronic Commerce wherein business transactions are done over the Internet. Usually transactions are done using a computer or a laptop. This has become very popular now because computers with Internet capability have become very accessible to people.

M-commerce is very portable because mobile phones are very easy to carry. You can do your business transactions anywhere you go as long as you can access the Internet on your phone. Unlike E-commerce, you have to do your transactions on the computer. Laptops are also portable but not as light as mobile phones. Then you still have to look for a place to do your transactions because it would be uncomfortable using your laptop anywhere or while you are standing.

M-commerce is usually charged through the caller's premium rates, charging the user's bill, or reducing the caller's credit, and also through mobile banking. E-commerce is charged through the use of swipe machines where you swipe your credit card. You can also transfer money through online banking and pay for products you have bought on the Internet using your credit card number.

M-commerce is available anywhere you go even if there is no Internet because the Internet is available in your mobile phone, while for E-commerce it is not available everywhere because not all places have an Internet connection.

In conclusion, M-commerce means doing business transactions on the Internet through the use of mobile devices, while E-commerce means doing business transactions on the Internet using computers or laptops.

Basis For Comparison	E-Commerce	M-Commerce
Meaning	Any kind of commercial transaction that is concluded, over the internet using electronic system is known as e-commerce.	M-commerce refers to the commercial activities which are transacted with the help of wireless computing devices such as cell phone or laptops.
Which device is used?	Computers and Laptops	Mobiles, tablets, PDA's, iPad etc.
Developed	In 1970's	In 1990's
What is it?	Superset	Subset
Ease of carrying device	No	Yes
Use of internet	Mandatory	Not mandatory
Reach	Narrow i.e. it is available only in those places where there is internet along with electricity.	Broad due to its portability.

References

- "B2C vs B2B Customers: How to Handle the Difference - OroCommerce". OroCommerce. 2016-11-24. Retrieved 2017-02-23

- B2B-beat-why-the-internet-of-things-is-crucial-for-b2b-marketers, marketing-solutions: business.linkedin.com, Retrieved 31 March 2018

- Forrester Research. "US B2B eCommerce To Reach $1.1 Trillion By 2020". blogs.forrester.com/. Andy Hoar. Retrieved 18 January 2016

- B2B-ecommerce-model-meaning-pros-cons: shiprocket.in, Retrieved 28 June 2018

- Global Mobile Commerce Forum. "Inaugral Plenary Conference". Christiane Morris. Retrieved 18 January 2016

- Difference-between-e-commerce-and-m-commerce: keydifferences.com, Retrieved 11 July 2018

Permissions

Index